Police Suicide

Prevention, Assessment and Intervention

THOMAS E. BAKER

43-08 162nd Street
Flushing, NY 11358
www.LooseleafLaw.com
800-647-5547

Baker, Thomas E., 1941-
Police suicide : prevention, assessment & intervention / Thomas E. Baker.
p. cm.
Includes bibliographical references and index.
ISBN 978-1-60885-062-4
1. Police--Suicidal behavior. 2. Police--Job stress. 3. Suicide--Prevention. 4. Police--Suicidal behavior--United States--Case studies. 5. Police--Job stress--United States--Case studies. 6. Suicide--United States--Prevention--Case studies. I. Title.
HV7936.S77B348 2013
363.201'9--dc23

2012032816

Cover by *Sans Serif,* Saline, Michigan

Table of Contents

Dedication

This book is for the men and women of law enforcement who risk their lives daily to protect us, and interventionists who try to save the officers at risk. In addition, let's not forget the unacknowledged law enforcement families who must endure the high-risk assignments. Most importantly, this book honors three police officers, and friends of the author, who committed suicide.

ACKNOWLEDGMENTS

I would like to thank Jane Piland-Baker. Her assistance in the area of graphic illustrations has made an immeasurable contribution to the text.

In addition, I would like to thank the staff at Looseleaf Law Publications, Inc., Mary Loughrey, Editorial Vice President; Maria Felten, Production Editor; and Michael Loughrey, President.

About the Author

Thomas E. Baker

Associate Professor

Thomas E. Baker is an associate professor of criminal justice and Lieutenant Colonel United States Army Reserve Military Police Corps (Ret.). In addition, Lt. Col. Baker has served as a police officer with Henrico County, Virginia and as an undercover/intelligence officer with the Organized Crime, Vice Intelligence Unit of the Montgomery County Police Department, Maryland.

Lt. Col. Baker's military assignments include: special agent, detachment commander, battalion level commander, and a Command Headquarters assignment with the United States Army Criminal Investigation Command. Additional assignments include: provost marshal, military police investigations, staff officer for Training and Doctrine Command, and instructor for the United States Army Command and General Staff College. He has earned over ten military and national police awards, including the Army Meritorious Service Medal.

Lt. Col. Baker is a graduate of the Basic Military Police Officer's Course, Advanced Infantry Officer's Course, Advanced Military Police Officer's Course, Criminal Investigation Course, Advanced Criminal Investigation Management Course, Psychological Operations Course, Field Grade Infantry Course, and the United States Army Command and General Staff College.

His academic degrees include: A. A. Law Enforcement, B.S. Social Welfare and M.S. Counseling from Virginia Commonwealth University; M.Ed. Sports Science, M.S. Health Education, East Stroudsburg University; CAGS Psychology and Counseling, Marywood University; and Advanced Study Education, Pennsylvania State University and Temple University.

He also served as Children's Supervisor in the Richmond Detention Center for Children and physical education teacher at the Diagnostic Center for Children. In addition, service includes Associate Professor at the community college and university levels. He taught Sociology, Social Problems, Criminology, and Introductory Criminal Analysis. His criminal justice courses include: Police Administration, Police Supervision, Public Safety Administration, Criminal Investigation, Organized Crime, and Police Criminalistics.

He is the author of seven books and over 170 publications, which have appeared in professional journals, peer reviewed articles, encyclopedias articles and has presented research at national meetings. Professor Baker is the author of ***Intelligence-Led Policing: Leadership, Strategies, and Tactics***, ***Effective Police Leadership: Moving Beyond Management***, and ***Positive Police Leadership: Problem-Solving Planning*** with Looseleaf Law Publications.

PREFACE

"A police officer dies in the line of duty every 57 hours. Contrastingly, a police officer commits suicide every 22 hours."

— The National P.O.L.I.C.E. Suicide Foundation

Researchers are beginning to analyze and address the police suicide enigma. The purpose of this book is to examine the need for improved research that focuses on related psychological components and successful prevention and intervention strategies. Primary discussions include: (1) police stress, (2) post-traumatic stress, (3) depression, and (4) police suicide.

Scope and Organization

Police Suicide: Prevention, Assessment & Intervention primarily serves the needs of readers interested in pursuing careers in counseling, social work, and law enforcement. This book targets multiple audiences, based on police suicide literature, and appropriate counseling practices as applied to crisis management strategies. In addition, the author seeks to serve the needs of academic criminal justice majors, law enforcement leaders, police officers, and personnel agency staff.

This book examines police suicidal behaviors and should prove helpful in developing suicide assessment and training programs. Refer to Figure P-1 for a list of selected topics.

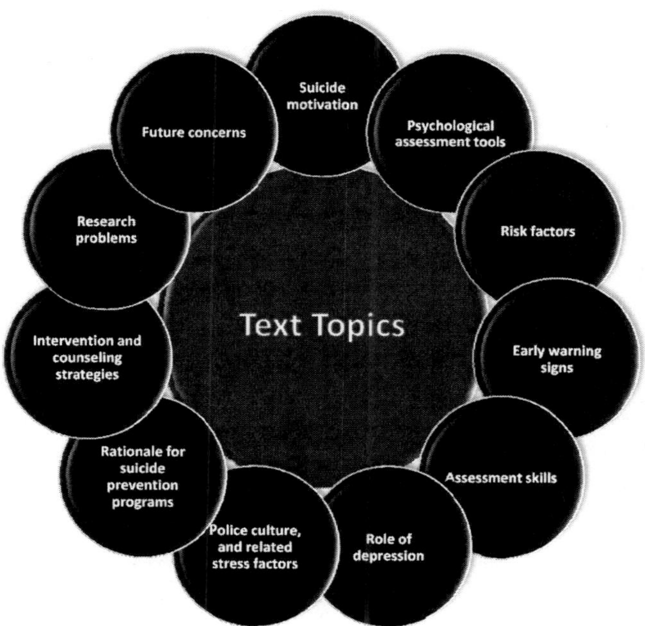

Figure P-1. Selected Text Topics

Police Suicide: Prevention, Assessment & Intervention Libraries would find this text an excellent resource book. Library acquisitions will elect to include this text in collections that strive to serve public needs. Moreover, community colleges, colleges, and universities might incorporate this book as a reader in their criminal justice program offerings and include the text as part of their literary collections.

Police Suicide: Prevention, Assessment & Intervention: The text includes many progressive educational practices, principles, and concepts. Graduate and undergraduate students interested in policing may benefit from the book's design. The themes serve as a reference and inform from teaching and learning perspectives. The emphasis is on police suicide prevention and intervention strategies.

Police Suicide: Prevention, Assessment & Intervention: Content and foundations serve as a resource document for federal, state, and local tribal law enforcement agencies.

Police Suicide: Prevention, Assessment & Intervention serves an expanding literature market for police practice and academia. The police suicide literature continues to evolve, and the associated research rapidly launches to address those requirements.

Police Suicide: Prevention, Assessment & Intervention will be of considerable interest to police organizations that are at a higher risk of experiencing disaster and traumatic stress. This text would be of value to law enforcement leaders and supervisory personnel. In addition, human resource personnel, health and safety professionals, mental health professionals, and consultants would find this text to be an excellent resource. The text will also be relevant to those researching traumatic stress, disaster stress, and emergency management as well as other protective services.

Educational Philosophy

Police Suicide: Prevention, Assessment & Intervention represents a reader-friendly format, which does not require prerequisite knowledge in the study of police suicide. The pursuit of knowledge is an honorable goal and that premise serves as the foundation for this book.

Police Suicide: Prevention, Assessment & Intervention emphasizes critical thinking, problem solving, and an active approach to learning. The philosophical and educational discourse is dynamic and action-oriented, incorporating critical thinking as the principal foundation. Critical thinking requires organizing information and applying concepts to new and unique situations. The educational philosophy of this book seeks to educate; readers ultimately appraise the police suicide literature and practice, think beyond mere facts, and reach out to expand the outer boundaries of the human mind.

Structure and Features

The purpose of this text is to support the reader with interesting analytical solutions to police suicide patterns. However, the author seeks a scholarly approach and attempts to dissect the content and analyze applied professional knowledge. In addition, case studies and graphics illustrate analytical applications.

The paragraphs and sentences are deliberately short and concise. The text addresses diverse learning styles; case illustrations and concrete examples clarify concepts and maintain reader interest. Crisis intervention strategies can be multifaceted; consequently, the text and illustrations enhance learner understanding and retention. Readability, clarity, and consistency of themes invite concept retention and enhance the learning process. The text strives for clarity in writing and excellent learning progressions.

Academic Content

This book incorporates an extensive variety of illustrative materials:

- There are considerable analytical concepts; therefore, numerous illustrations, models, charts, and tables supplement the text.
- Visual components assist in active explanation of text concepts.
- Subheadings and short paragraphs enhance transition, coherence, and clarity.
- Text includes case study analyses that illustrate the theories and concepts.
- The emphasis is on research methods and practical applications for law enforcement officers, counselors, and social service personnel.

PART I – POLICE SUICIDE FOUNDATIONS

Introduction – Prologue and Orientation:
Provides reader orientation and Basic Ten Focus Points

Chapter 1 - Introduction: Police Suicide:
Describes police suicide and discusses the associated risk factors.

Chapter 2 - Police Suicide: Risk Assessment:
Describes police suicide risk factors, psychological autopsy, and suicide typologies.

Chapter 3 - Police Subculture: The Social Climate:
Describes the subculture factors, work stressors, family stressors, and alcohol.

PART II – POLICE SUICIDE: STRESS ISSUES

Chapter 4 - Police Suicide: Stress Related Factors:
Describes the stress cycle, Post-traumatic Stress Disorder, and the DSM-IV diagnostic criteria and related research.

Chapter 5 - Suicide by Cop: Crisis Intervention Strategies:
Discusses the impact for the officer involved, family members, and witnesses. This chapter also addresses training and officer grieving issues.

PART III – POLICE GUIDEPOST BEHAVIORS

Chapter 6 – Police Leadership: Crisis Intervention Strategies:
Describes the suicide warning signs, intervention strategies, and the Question, Persuade, and Refer (QPR) Program.

Chapter 7 – Counseling Crisis Intervention Strategies:
Describes the role of the counselor and intervention, and identifies individual crisis counseling.

PART IV – RESEARCH FOUNDATIONS AND FUTURE IMPLICATIONS

Chapter 8 – Police Leadership: Abuse and Bullying:
Describes and explores some basic concepts regarding narcissistic leadership. It defines the cluster of warning signs of abuse, bullying, and relationship to perfectionism.

Chapter 9 - Police Suicide Prevention Programs:
Describes program development, educational goals, and Johari Window feedback.

Chapter 10 – Police Research Controversies:
Describes research obstacles and statistical limitations.

Chapter 11 – Proactive Leadership: Final Focus Points:
Describes the concluding focus points and proactive police leadership requirements, reexamines the ten basic themes outlined in the chapters, and applies the conceptual content.

Chapter 12: Epilogue: Future Implications:
Describes future implications for (1) police resilience, (2) entry level testing, (3) post-traumatic testing, (4) suicide testing, and (5) police training simulations.

Conclusion

The purpose of this book is to illustrate methods for dealing with police suicide. The primary goal is to provide a comprehensive conceptualization of traumatic stress and suicide processes as they apply to police officers. This text illustrates how agencies can provide a framework to guide research that supports positive prevention and intervention programming.

The author searches for a comprehensive and empirical resource to examine police suicide as a career path hazard. This text offers a practical resource for investigating issues of trauma and suicide. The intent is to draw upon empirical research to provide traumatic risk management programming. Secondary to that purpose is to provide a teaching resource for police officers, mental health professionals, and related support organizations.

PART I:
POLICE SUICIDE FOUNDATIONS

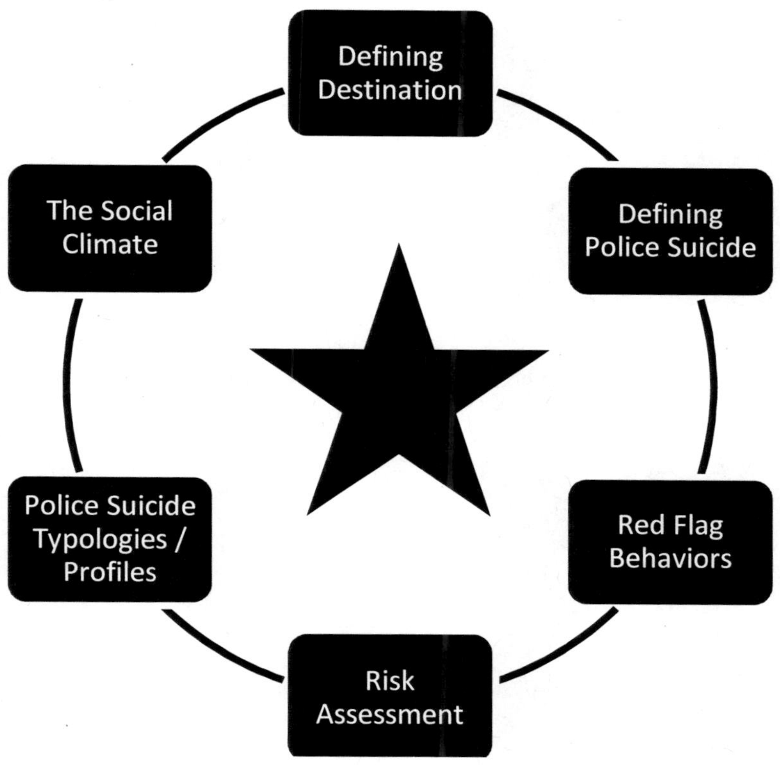

Leadership Foundations	Guidepost Behaviors
• **Police leadership and vision: Define the future forecasting and planning requirements**	• **Four steps in defining the police suicide problem:** (1) Where is the police agency is going? (2) How will the police agency get there? (3) How will the police agency know when it has arrived? (4) Where will the police agency go next?
• **Appraise the crisis incident management model**	• **Four components:** (1) the domain of police and crisis, (2) the paradigm of police work, (3) domestic domain, (4) crisis management strategies
• **List the police suicide red flags**	• Assess the literature on police suicide, risk behaviors and identify red flag behaviors: **(1) hopelessness, (2) helplessness, and (3) haplessness**
• **Research, train and evaluate police officers and leaders on the risk factors for police suicide**	• Define the basic strategies for trauma and suicide prevention.
• **Appraise the risk factors and psychological autopsy research findings.**	• **Suicide formula** = Suicidal Threats + Depression + Rage + Suicidal Fantasies + Alcohol and Drug Abuse + Domestic Violence + Accessibility to Weapon = Potential Suicide.
• **Appraise the literature on police culture.**	• Police leaders monitor critical incident stressors for acute stress disorders and monitor officers over committed to stressful assignments.

INTRODUCTION

PROLOGUE AND ORIENTATION

"Your vision will become clear only when you look inside your heart. Who looks outside, dreams. Who looks inside, awakens."

— Carl G. Jung

A 25-year-old female officer committed suicide with her service revolver; everyone was astonished. She was among the best and the brightest in her field. A middle-aged male officer with 20 years of service takes his own life for no apparent reason and is found slumped over in his police cruiser. A police chief commits suicide after an untarnished 30-year career in law enforcement.

Police suicide can devastate a law enforcement agency and community. The self-inflicted death of an officer is always a tragedy. The loss of just one life is a catastrophe in the police community, especially from suicide. In the aftermath, there is always astonishment and dismay.

Police officers have a special calling, or what the Greeks cited as daimon and the Romans as Genius. Psychologists refer to the awakening of the vision as a complete person, and the essential of what one exemplifies, one's life. This brings to mind an image of character and destiny. The role of police officer is difficult and a special calling.

Chapter Focus

The four steps used to define the problem of police suicide include:

1. Where is the police agency going?
2. How will the police agency get there?
3. How will the police agency know when they have arrived?
4. Where does the agency go next?

This chapter attempts to identify those planning goals, procedures, and objectives. The final articulation evolves through reading the chapter and the Conclusion.

Overview

Police work requires personal commitment and sacrificing personal safety to protect others from harm. Police officers think of the security of others before their own; the elevation of the community first, over personal interests, is a noble cause. In the end, police officers are not gods, but ordinary people doing an extraordinary mission. They have special gifts, but also their own fears, weaknesses, and breaking points. Many police officers survive; others do not awaken and are casualties of the calling.

Police officers live by a code that does not allow for mistakes, a standard impossible to reach. Police officers can find it difficult to adjust to the expectation of perfection. When the unidentified dark side ultimately prevails, the officer may fail to recognize the need for help. Assisting the officer with timely intervention and counseling may provide an awakening and the will to live.

Suicide has plagued us forever, a constant companion to the dark side of some of the brightest minds. Suicide lurks in the shadows and continues to outnumber homicides in the United States. Police suicides far exceed homicides committed by criminals. Some police officers give up on life and seek an exit. Many experience alcohol abuse, stress, and domestic strife, all a reaction to the job. How officers perceive and react to difficult psychological events has more impact than the actual experience of serving as a police officer.

Defining Destination

The concept of *vision* applies to law enforcement. Police executives, senior leaders, commanders, middle managers, and first-line supervisors need to look to the future. There is one core requirement for police leaders: critical thinking offers direction and provides a compass and map for reaching the desired destination. The key to establishing vision is strategic planning, training, and program development (Baker, 2005b).

Crisis Management Model

Crisis intervention planning strategies apply internally as well as externally to police agencies. Suicide intervention training would increase their effectiveness in the community and police leadership. The crisis response model is a practical structure to understand and analyze facets of police work that may require suicide intervention strategies. The model has four components: (1) the domain of people in crisis, (2) the paradigm of police work, (3) domestic domain, and (4) crisis management strategies.

The crisis response to potential police suicides requires immediate attention, planning, intervention, and policy development. The quest must persist for viable training and solutions, continue the research journey, and reduce the potential tragedy of police suicide. Moreover, we must remove the stigma that blocks police officers from seeking the help they so desperately need. Everyone must understand the basic steps in suicide prevention and provide the teamwork to elicit successful outcomes.

Crisis management methods include an eclectic range of intervention methods. Crisis management incorporates the total process of working through a crisis to a successful outcome. The process generally includes activities for the individual in crisis as well as various members of the officer's natural or institutional set of connections. Suicide intervention is an immediate response from police, mental health professionals, and others (Hoff and Adamowski, 1998).

One excellent example of the crisis intervention approach is the Living Works two-day Applied Suicide Intervention Skills Training (ASIST) program.

This program has been refined over the years using feedback from thousands of participants and active trainers. It recognizes that police officers who are first responders to people who need immediate cardiopulmonary resuscitation (CPR) can develop similar skills to prevent suicide (Eggert et al., 1997).

The ASIST program helps remove some of the mystique of suicide and provides training that builds wiliness and confidence in those who are gatekeepers. The empowerment from this suicide intervention program develops officers willing and able to intervene to prevent the immediate risk of suicide. In addition, many officers are willing to assume a leadership role in suicide prevention and may play a vital role in suicide prevention in their police organizations.

Police agencies scan the community; however, an internal search is necessary to avoid tragic consequences. Police culture needs to improve effective programming because of the emotional stress of police work. There is an urgent need to improve crisis management now and in the decades to come.

Important questions remain for analysis. Exploration of the police suicide enigma offers some of the answers while other parts remain a mystery. *The following ten suicide prevention and intervention strategies may maximize opportunities to save law enforcement officers' lives.*

Proactive Strategy 1 – Introduction to Police Suicide

Police leadership has many community problems; the tendency is to focus externally. The first step is defining the problem internally and assessing psychosocial factors. The second step involves suicide risk assessment, and the third step requires providing remedial intervention prevention programs. Police suicide intervention and prevention strategies require critical thinking and problem-solving skills. The identification of suicidal officers is a difficult priority and task.

Police leaders are resource managers and personnel are always the main priority. The execution of crisis management plans requires sensitivity and target specific responses. Police strategic planning offers the best pathway to effective decision making. This initially requires defining the suicide problem and includes examining risk factors.

I. Educational Goal: Appraise the elements of police suicide.

Behavioral Objectives:

a. Define police suicide.
b. List the red flag behaviors of suicide.
c. Distinguish the application of threat analysis strategies.
d. Identify the elements of police suicide by suspect.
e. Identify the elements of police indirect suicide.
f. Apply the basic definition of suicide to the Case Study Illustration.

Research Summary: Suicidal behavior is a purposeful act of desperation. Suicide is a decision-making process and problem-solving behavior principally aimed at improving a threatened self-image (Shneidman, 1996).

Proactive Strategy 2 – Police Suicide: Risk Assessment

Police leaders need to train their officers to recognize the red flag behaviors of suicide. The focus is on depression, which is central to preventing suicide, and poor police performance. Defining suicide means understanding the rationale for the red flag behaviors. Identifying the various suicide risks may assist in the intervention and prevention strategies. Identifying overt, passive, and unconscious forms of suicide may lead to early recognition. Psychological autopsies and typologies remain valuable tools of psychosocial analysis.

II. Educational Goal: Appraise the value of the psychological autopsy as a means to project risk factors for suicide.

Behavioral Objectives:

a. Describe the police profile or typology for suicide.
b. List the aggravating circumstances of police suicide.
c. Distinguish the risk factors for police suicide.
d. Identify the elements of depression.
e. Identify the elements of the police personality.
f. Apply the basic suicide risk factors to the Case Study Illustration.

Research Summary: The main risk factors include family history, previous attempts, lack of support, and psychiatric diagnosis (Klerman, 1987). Depression is a significant risk factor.

Proactive Strategy 3 – Police Subculture: Social Climate

Police subculture is described in the literature in a negative manner; however, there is a subculture in every occupational realm. Part of the subculture may have negative unintended consequences. There is corruption in every profession; however, an occupational subculture can provide positive outcomes, as well as unintended negative consequences. The police are in the spotlight, often caught in societal conflicts. Examining police organizations and their subculture from within ultimately means assessing elements of stress, alcohol abuse, and depression.

Policing needs a continuing employment assessment process for the negative unintended consequences. Protecting officers against internal stressors and improving the social network requires screening of the best police recruits. Improving the recruit mental health selection process and selecting in and selecting out police candidates will enhance the social climate and subculture.

III. Educational Goal: Appraise the role of police subculture as an occupational risk for suicide.

Behavioral Objectives:

a. Describe the highest levels of critical incidence stress.
b. List the red flag behaviors of police domestic violence.
c. Distinguish the alcohol abuse factor in cases of police suicides.
d. Describe the role of police subculture values as it relates to its possible link to suicide.
e. Identify the elements of addictive elements of the police subculture.
f. Apply the addictive (chemistry) of high-risk assignments to the Case Study Illustration.

Research Summary: Gilmartin (1986) defined the police cycles of stress as the "brotherhood of biochemistry." He suggested that physiological and social dependency on the excitement of police work has consequences. The officer must adapt to the excitement and dangerous lifestyle, and then shift into a kind of psychological depression in calm or normal cycles of living.

Proactive Strategy 4 – Police Suicide: Stress Factors

Police leaders concerned with social climate target unnecessary stressors as hazardous to their officers' emotional health. Police research on stress and the connection to police suicide continues to lack clarity. Police suicide intervention strategies are not ideal; additional research will offer further enlightenment.

Post-traumatic Stress Disorder (PTSD), Acute Stress Disorder, and depression require monitoring by police leaders. Commanders describe referral and assessment for PTSD is a normal response to abnormal crises. In addition, research needs to address resilience to stress and finding police recruits with those qualities. Supervisors encourage proactive reassignment after service in high profile and emotionally intensive critical incidents.

IV. Educational Goal: Appraise the role of police stress as an occupational risk for suicide.

Behavioral Objectives:

a. Describe Acute Stress Disorder.
b. List the elements of PTSD.
c. Distinguish police occupational stressors.
d. Describe Dr. Hans Selye's three basic types of stress.
e. Distinguish the fight or flight and exhaustion phases.
f. Apply the types of police stressors to the Case Study Illustration.

Research Summary: PTSD is as a major disruption in the lives of police officers. Reiser and Geiger (1984) cited that one of the causes of an adverse stress reaction or PTSD is the loss of control and feeling powerless. Trauma appears to result from the puncturing of the officer's prior illusion of control and invulnerability.

Proactive Strategy 5 – Suicide by Cop

Suicide by Cop (SbC) is a method of victim-precipitated homicide in which a suicidal person engages in a calculating, life-threatening, and criminal behavior to compel the police to use deadly force. The individual solicits his or her own suicidal death at the hands of an innocent police officer. The officer unwitting becomes the precipitator to a suicidal plan. In these SbC scenarios, the officer becomes the secondary victim.

SbC cases where the citizen provokes the officer into a fatal shooting require specific attention to support and referral. Cases of SbC and other critical incidents require immediate follow up and clinical assessment. The identification officers who exhibit high stress behaviors are a high priority, and early leadership warning responsibility is imperative.

V. Educational Goal: Appraise SbC occupational critical incident scenario.

Behavioral Objectives:

a. Define SbC.
b. List the elements of Shneidman's five clustered needs satisfied by suicide.
c. List the SbC major categories.
d. Describe the crisis management strategies.
e. Distinguish the elements of the group debriefing.
f. Apply the elements of SbC to the Case Study Illustration.

Research Summary: Lord (2001) indicated many SbC subjects began their own suicidal attempt, but rapidly reversed their actions and displaced the act to the responding officer(s). The combination of the SbC subject's past experience with the police and the police officer's prior interaction may play an important role in the suicidal outcome.

Proactive Strategy 6 – Leadership: Crisis Intervention Strategies

Excellent mentors provide support and protect their officers from adverse emotional consequences. Police leaders who are good mentors point out emotional obstacles to their officers. They encourage feedback, problem solving, and personal development. Trust and emotional support may be more important than information.

How can the police leader be an effective mentor? Police leaders who "take care of their officers" shape a positive social climate. Leaders who show concern for the emotional development of their officers provide the appropriate training, referral, and counseling follow-up procedures.

Police supervisor training must include how to recognize suicide warning signs. Training emphasizes directive leadership, telling the officer what the leader expects and requiring that the officer respond to directions. The supervisor or peer leader does something that directly interrupts the cycle of suicidal ideation. Peer programs are one way to remove the threat of coming forward and open the informal social network. Supervisors or peer leaders asking the right questions sets up the appropriate intervention and referral.

VI. Educational Goal: Appraise the role of leadership in police suicide intervention.

Behavioral Objectives:

a. Explain the Question, Persuade, and Referring (QPR) system.
b. List the elements of the suicidal warning signs.
c. Apply the situational leadership style.
d. Describe the appropriate questions for the police officer in a suicidal state of mind.
e. Distinguish the elements of leadership management programming.
f. Apply the principles of leadership intervention to the Case Study Illustration.

Research Summary: Violanti (1996) estimated 80% of suicide victims give clues or warning signs regarding their suicidal ideation.

Special Note: The officer may make covert statements similar to: "They don't need to worry about me anymore." Passive warning signs are more difficult to detect. Moreover, the denial factor may overlook serious statements made by police officers. The most recent research indicates an increase in stealth suicides.

Proactive Strategy 7 – Counseling: Crisis Intervention Strategies

Police leaders must apply the elements of liaison coordination to prevent police suicide. This requires cooperation from law enforcement, counselors, and personnel officers to develop timely policies and programs. Privacy and confidentiality rights are always the concern, but common areas of cooperation are necessary in this important endeavor.

Police leaders need to remove the stigma associated with seeking counseling and treatment. The critical incident exposure and psychological factors of traumatic stress justify the adoption of primary, secondary, and tertiary resources. The expenditures to prevent PTSD and suicide are minimal when compared with the consequences of the failure to act. Recent research indicates successful strategies in the area of cognitive behavioral therapy counseling and the use of related technology.

VII. Educational Goal: Appraise the role of counseling and crisis intervention strategies.

Behavioral Objectives:

a. Explain the obstacles to police officers regarding referrals to mental health professionals.
b. List the elements of primary, secondary, and tertiary resources for suicide prevention.
c. Identify the elements of crisis counseling.
d. Describe the basic forms of cognitive counseling therapy.
e. Distinguish the elements of peer leadership programming.
f. Apply the appropriate missing referral opportunities to the Case Study Illustration.

Research Summary: Cognitive therapy research indicates that suicidal persons benefit from treatment. Research by the National Institutes of Health (NIH), National Institute of Mental Health (NIMH) and the Centers for Disease Control and Prevention (CDC) targeted a form of cognitive counseling therapy that reduces repeat suicide attempts by 50%.

Proactive Strategy 8 – Police Leadership: Abuse and Bullying

The principle tool of narcissistic leadership is abuse and bullying, and the personality problem exists in many organizations; police agencies are no different. The author uses the term narcissistic leadership to identify those who engage in dysfunctional leadership behaviors that are self-serving and difficult to unravel. The narcissistic/bullying leader is part of the employment picture for public and private sectors.

The exploitation of the perfectionist personality by narcissistic leaders is the ideal opportunity to achieve glory through their work ethic. The perfectionist does not merely seek excellence, but absolute perfection. The standards are extremely high, and failure to meet those standards leads to feelings of inadequacy and suicide. This kind of perfectionist police officer is very vulnerable to critics and bullying and susceptible to intense self-doubt. There are other personalities open to exploitation, but the perfectionist is vulnerable to suicide according to the research.

Senior police leadership must develop policies and protocols to counter the effects of bullying. Eliminating abuse and bullying is noble and enhances morale and performance. The reduction of bullying builds a positive social climate and enhances the mental health of police officers. These improvements are beneficial for customer relationships and may contribute to better police community relationships.

VIII. Educational Goal: Appraise the role of bullying and its implications for police organizations.

Behavioral Objectives:

a. Define the potential role of bullying in police organizations.
b. Assess the research limitations concerning workplace bullying in police organizations.
c. Describe the National Institute for Occupational Safety and Health (NIOSH) finding on bullying.
d. Identify the basic bullying behaviors and methods.
e. Distinguish the basic forms of the perfectionism personality.
f. Select the appropriate perfectionism personality from the Case Study Illustration.

Research Summary: Lynch (2002) described the bullying research in police organizations as scarce. "The prevalence of workplace bullying remains unclear. However, the estimates are that approximately 25 to 50 percent of all employees in the general working population will experience bullying at some time during their working lives." There is preliminary research overseas or through Australasia to indicate the prevalence of workplace bullying among police personnel.

Proactive Strategy 9 – Police Suicide Prevention Programming

Leaders need feedback about the unknown factors of suicide, and the "Johari Window" suggests that denial is a two-way communication and feedback quandary. The Johari Window reveals insight into psychological and social domains. Police leaders and officers need access to the unknown; the solution to successful programs is the feedback process. Standing operating procedures (SOP) remain the starting point for a suicide prevention and intervention program. The good news is that most police agencies acknowledge the potential risk after years of denial. Open and forthright discussions concerning sensitive topics and research inspire endeavors to prevent future police suicides.

IX. Educational Goal: Appraise the need for prevention programming in police organizations.

Behavioral Objectives:

a. Define the elements of suicide risk assessment.
b. Distinguish the elements of the Johari Window.
c. Describe the components of the Critical Incident Stress Management (CSIM) program.

d. Identify the elements of the Critical Incident Stress Debriefing (CISD).
e. List the elements of the Family Support System (FSS).
f. Apply the elements of the Feelings, Input, and Tactics Model (FIT) to the Case Study Illustration.

Research Summary: Psychological insight and rapport requires candid leaders who establish trust and mutual respect. Excellent leadership suggests information exchanges, rather than one-way dialogs that do not involve feedback (Baker, 2009; Luft, 1970).

Proactive Strategy 10 – Police Research Controversies

Presently there is scarce research done on police suicide, and the paucity of data presents serious problems for the development of police intervention and prevention programs. The information available tends to be descriptive and statistically inadequate. The primary weakness of the research approach is not focusing on the role of police agencies and program evaluation. Most of the research does not reflect the role of the social environment, but addresses the role of the officer (Baker and Baker, 1995). Recently, the issue of inadequate research has become controversial.

Theoretical and applied research is necessary to create excellent prevention strategies such as (1) counseling programs, (2) alcohol abuse programs, (3) stress management programs, (4) recognizing the warning signs of suicide, (5) depression, (6) PTSD, (7) family stressors, (8) peer support systems, (9) monitoring police performance, and (10) leadership and supervision development. We must apply the elements of social scientific thinking to these issues to develop appropriate policies. Excellent theoretical research may lead to the solution of many applied problems (Baker and Baker, 1995).

X. Educational Goal: Appraise the need for additional research on police suicide.

Behavioral Objectives:

a. Describe the limitations of the present research data on police suicide.
b. Distinguish the present the statistical quandary regarding police research data.
c. Describe some of the symptoms of inadequate methods of research on police suicide.
d. Describe the most common police pre-employment psychological assessment.
e. Describe the purpose of psychological testing.
f. Appraise the military PTSD content in the Case Study Illustration.

Research Summary: The CDC estimates that Americans commit suicide at a rate of 12 per 100,000 residents and that suicide is the ninth leading cause of death in the United States. The most common measure of comparison is to statistically determine the number of suicides per 100,000 of the targeted populations.

Case Study Illustration

Joe was married with two children. He was quiet, even-tempered, and respected in the community and within the police department. He was a regular churchgoer. There were no indications that he suffered from any serious psychological difficulties. He had no history of alcohol abuse or depression. He had no history of marital difficulties due to extramarital affairs in the past. His marriage appeared stable to all observers.

Joe may have been unhappy about recently being passed over for promotion, but was engaged in broadening his work experience and acquiring further education to improve his chances for future promotion. He enjoyed generally good relationships with his colleagues. There were no obvious clues that he was at imminent risk for suicidal behavior.

Why would such an individual commit suicide? The clear precipitating event was an allegation of sexual assault made by a woman with whom he had a sexual encounter while on duty. The next evening, the woman went to Joe's home while he was at a class and, upon discovering that he was married, informed his wife of the incident.

The woman and his wife subsequently confronted Joe just before he was to report to work and he admitted to consensual sex, but denied sexual assault. He stated that he probably would lose his job because of the incident and so might as well not go to work, but de did report at approximately 11 p.m.

The alleged victim then called her lawyer, who advised her to call the police chief and the state police. The state police began an immediate investigation. At 4:45 a.m., while he was on patrol, the dispatcher requested Joe's return to the department...he responded that he would be there shortly. When he did not arrive, the dispatcher initiated another request ... Joe reiterated that he would be there shortly. He failed to respond to additional calls directly from the police chief and never arrived.

Eventually, located in his cruiser approximately 90 minutes later ... Joe shot himself with his service weapon. He was still in uniform but had removed his badge, nameplate, and gun belt and had put his last performance evaluation (which was good) on top of them.

Approximately six hours elapsed between the time that Joe was confronted by the two women and his suicide. During those six hours, he probably reached the conclusion that he was about to lose everything he considered most important. His marriage and family, his job, and his reputation were at stake. Although he had contact with several coworkers and even a family friend during those six hours, none of the people with whom he came into contact suspected that he might be suicidal.

In many cases of police suicide, the immediate precipitant is an event likely to lead to significant difficulties at work or at home. In this case, Joe was facing problems in both arenas. Joe's assessment that he would lose his job and family may have been accurate. Although the suicide may have ended Joe's psychological distress, it caused tremendous pain for his family and colleagues.

Source: This case study was adapted from JoeAnn Brewster and Alan Broadfoot (2001), Department of Justice publication.

Special Note: The authors make some interesting observations concerning the suicide's affect on police morale. The police leadership did not expect the almost immediate anger directed at the administration's decisions. The first category of criticism centered on the way the administration handled the brief investigation. The second category of criticism involved complaints about long-standing practices some officers felt contributed to Joe's death (Brewster and Broadfoot, 2001).

The authors suggest that three main lessons emerged: (1) departmental follow-up procedures after the suicide of an officer must be developed, (2) the leadership must understand the need for coping skills for the officers grieving response, and (3) prevention programming for preventing police suicide must be instituted (Brewster and Broadfoot, 2001).

The following chapters assist in understanding the risk factors of police suicide. A combination of internal and external risk factors played a significant role in the death of this officer. Some of the factors were organizational practices such as demotion or suspension and marital domestic problems were another factor (Friedman, 1968). Joe's immediate shame, irrational thinking, and sudden emotional depression made it difficult for police agencies to respond. There are many other risk factors to consider that enhance the understanding of police suicide prevention and intervention.

Conclusion

The ten basic strategies stated above provide a framework for the analysis and synthesis of the police suicide enigma. These ten strategies and themes from this book will provide the core foundation. Preventing police suicide requires a team approach that encourages appropriate training, early intervention, referral, and appropriate follow-up. Successful interventionists appreciate that police officers and their families have unique psychological needs that require appropriate acknowledgment and understanding. Breaking through denial is the most important first step to providing remedial assistance to officers and their families. Police agencies may save lives with further research, with innovative prevention and intervention programs, and proactive training.

Chapter 1

Introduction: Police Suicide

"That which we do not bring to consciousness appears in our lives as fate."

— Carl G. Jung

Police officer responding to a continuing investigation discovers a body of a woman. After stalking her for a prolonged period, a man sent her a bomb through the mail, intending to kill her. He planned to meet her in the afterlife. Videotaping his own suicide, he hyperventilated 24 times, and then pulled the trigger.

Source: This case study was adapted from Barry Perrou (2001), Department of Justice publication.

Police officers rarely experience this type of suicidal encounter. The more common event is with a weapon like a shotgun, with sleeping pills, or other imaginative forms of suicide.

How can police leaders and counselors implement appropriate suicide prevention and intervention programs? What common patterns emerge in police suicidal behaviors? This chapter defines police suicide and identifies the motivational patterns.

Chapter Focus

This chapter explores basic concepts regarding police suicide. It defines suicide and discusses red flag behaviors. In addition, the chapter endeavors to explain the role of the psychological autopsy and suicide typologies. The case study at the end is an illustration and application of the theory of suicide and an analysis of the causal social dynamics.

Overview

An officer's close relationship with a deadly weapon, which they eventually regard as their salvation, may eventually serve as their demise. Police officers understand that "eating your gun or weapon," equates to suicide in police jargon. A lethal weapon always waits nearby. Recognizing its lethality, police officers know that retreat from the world is only seconds away. The question ultimately remains: What kind of support system exists within the police department?

Does easy accessibility to a weapon and alcohol, combined with depression, make a lethal brew for possible police suicide? Could the primary contributing suicide factor be *depression*, the invisible police ride-along partner that occupies the same seat? Examining psychological risk factors makes early intervention and prevention possible.

Violanti (1995) reported that in 95% of police suicides in Buffalo, New York, investigators identified *guns* as the obvious cause and means of death. In addition, 94% of NYPD suicides involved an officer's personal weapon. The options are endless because police officers have experience and expertise; they investigate suicide calls and understand the lethal methods of suicide (Baker and Baker 1995).

Unfortunately, too many officers have taken advantage of the proximity and convenience of possessing a weapon. In the suicidal state of mind, and without proper support, law enforcement officers can find creative ways to take their own lives. The clues leading up to using the weapon may assist in preventing and unraveling the police suicide enigma.

Police Suicide: Methodology Issues

The search for answers concerning police suicide is elusive; however, they are attainable. Many issues remain unclear because research studies are scientifically vague and inconclusive. Researchers ask the wrong questions; much of the data are meaningless. For example, police suicide research should focus on prevention and intervention, not just the means of suicide (Baker, 1996; Baker and Baker, 1995).

Research suggests we do not have credible statistical data regarding police suicides. Suicide rates are enormously complicated and difficult to substantiate. Multiple statistical issues influence reliability and validity concerns regarding police suicide data. Police suicide literature has many associated reliability and validity research limitations. Resolving common universal methodological issues is required to improve scientific knowledge regarding police suicide rates, causes, and antecedents.

Defining Police Suicide

Suicide is an ancient societal problem; governments have imposed serious penalties in an effort to deter it. Generally, penalties included the denial of a proper funeral and penalizing the living heirs. The first recorded writing about suicide, , titled *The Dialogue of a Misanthrope with His Own Soul*, was written on Egyptian papyrus over 4000 years ago (Evans and Farberow, 1988). The secondary victims pay again, while governments and religions try to enforce the mores and taboos against suicide. The harsh legal, religious, and social penalties failed to stop the act of self-destruction over the centuries.

Generally, citizens regard suicide as a senseless act. However, in reality, the opposite is true; suicide represents a purposeful act of desperation. The struggle is twofold—within the suicidal mind and external forces believed beyond control. According to Bongar (1991), Maris et al. (1992) and Shneidman (1994, 1996), suicide is a problem-solving behavior principally aimed at improving a threatened self-image. Farberow (1980) suggested that suicide is a decision-making process, similar to those preceding any other major decision.

Based on the above-cited research, the definition of suicide is a purposeful, problem-solving behavior designed to seize control. The purpose is to restore power, control, and a sense of omnipotence. Police suicide represents a direct attack to eliminate one's threatened self-image and eradicate hopelessness and helplessness. The goal is to remove oneself from an untenable situation, take action, and stop psychological pain.

The insufferable self-hatred and shame is the crisis for which suicide is the solution, regardless of the consequences. One researcher suggested that sudden shame is the underlying mechanism in the acute onset of a suicidal crisis (Rangell, 1988). Suicide is the last resort in an effort to end intense and ongoing psychological pain. Shneidman (1995) described this pain eloquently in his own terminology: "psychache" is hurt, anguish, soreness, aching psychological pain in the psyche or mind. It is intrinsically psychological — pain of excessively felt shame, or guilt, or humiliation, or loneliness, or fear, or angst, or dread of growing old, or dying badly, or whatever. Suicide occurs when the psychache is deemed by that person to be unbearable."

While suicide is purposeful and may serve as problem solving or the only escape from an intolerable situation, it is also maladaptive. Suicide leaves multiple victims behind, even though the officer may feel he has a justifiable cause or excuse. When astute observers read the psychological clues, it is possible to respond to the behavioral suicidal signature risk factors.

Red Flag Behaviors: Police Suicide

The two prominent suicidal warning signs are hopelessness and helplessness. These two indicators are fundamental to appraising those in jeopardy (Schwartz and Schwartz, 1991). One key dilemma is that individuals who are predisposed to commit suicide choose not to use this kind of terminology. Police leaders and fellow officers must reason from their behaviors and passive statements. They must recognize the red flag behaviors to interpret the coded and passive statements. Refer to Figure 1-1 for a review of the red flag behaviors of suicide.

Red Flag Number One: Hopelessness

Officers who are experiencing high stress and feel hopeless are candidates for suicide. Police officers who verbalize this clue are in a high-risk category. They act when their lives offer no viable options; it is not a death wish. The final act of suicide may serve as a final exit, thus restoring control and offering the ultimate escape.

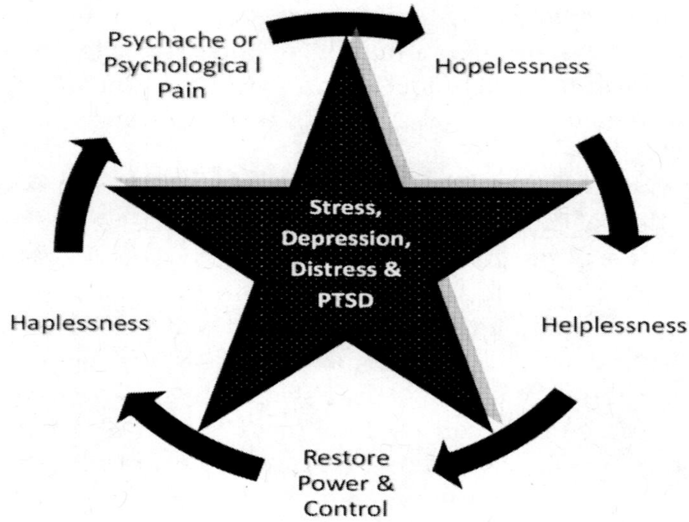

Figure 1-1. Police Officer Suicide Red Flags
(Adapted from Schneidman,1994 & 1996; Schwarts & Schwarts, 1991).

Red Flag Number Two: Helplessness

The officers may view themselves as helpless; therefore, feel that they cannot meaningfully alter their life situation. Moreover, officers who think and express helplessness are also in a high-risk category. The twin feelings of hopelessness and helplessness reinforce each other.

Red Flag Number Three: Haplessness

When hopelessness and helplessness prevail, there are no other possible solutions. The officer feels there is no way out of an impossible predicament, even though there is an obvious solution.

According to Allen (1986) suicide is not a disease or psychotic, self-directed violence; it is a problem-solving behavior. Some officers may create a delusion that suicide presents an opportunity that will restore feelings of former strength, courage, and mastery over the environment (Bonafacio, 1991). Both of the above citations represent powerful motivational factors to counter in cases of suicidal officers.

Police Suicide: Threat Analysis

Police officers focus on the external threat such as critical incidents like the killing of a police officer by criminals. Some officers scan their environment relentlessly for criminals and mentally ill persons. Many police officers consider the potential for assault as one of the most stressful aspects of police work. The statistical reality remains: police officers may fail to recognize suicide, depression, and alcoholism. The hazards in police work remain distorted; simply examining the death toll does not reveal the causes.

Brandl and Stroshine (2003) examined police injuries and death notes: "Assaults on officers—are relatively rare, even serious injuries and deaths. The overwhelming majority of incidents, regardless of the tasks, are not the result of assaults and, of course, do not result in deaths, but rather, most injury incidents are a result of accidents."

Traffic accidents kill more police officers than critical incident shootings. The bank robbery and shootout in California with automatic weapons stays in the forefront and typecasts LAPD models for police deaths. The Waco, Texas hostage scenario is an external threat, rather than internal, and the continuing threat of terrorism reinforces the notion of the external threat. Recent research reveals that the actual external dangers exist; however, they are overestimated by police officers and the public. "The concern for a fellow officer being injured or killed...reinforces the frequent perceived potential for crisis situations, even during a period of low crime" (Garcia et al., 2004).

Police officers are more at risk from their own self-inflicted behaviors. Those concerned about the welfare of police officers must learn how to protect them from themselves. This means addressing police suicide, depression, and alcoholism. Investigating police traffic accidents and the possible related field prevention and intervention strategies is also necessary. The lone gunman offers fewer statistical opportunities, and is open to considerable chance. Police training should emphasize the internal threat, not just the external one.

Police Suicide by Suspect

"Suicide by suspect" refers to a pattern of officers who intentionally place themselves in death wish and suicidal scenarios. The more overt cases of police suicide have considerable evidence, both physical and psychological. Many social indicators are present, especially depression and family history. The most prominent indicator of suicide is the presence of a discharged service weapon in the hand of the officer with cadaveric spasm, which is a rare event. Scientific evidence corroborates a self-inflected discharge of the weapon, and crime scene reconstruction places the weapon in the officer's hand. In the case of traditional police suicide cases, the psychological autopsy confirms the overt police suicide. Case closed and cleared as police suicide. Refer to Figure 1-2 for some of the more obvious indications of police suicide.

There are also undetectable suicides, when an officer simply remains passive and fails to take proper defensive actions. The investigating officer may have serious doubts, but be unable to prove his assumptions. The path of least resistance is to allow the officer to die a hero and close the case. The department, officer, and family benefit from the positive investigative outcome.

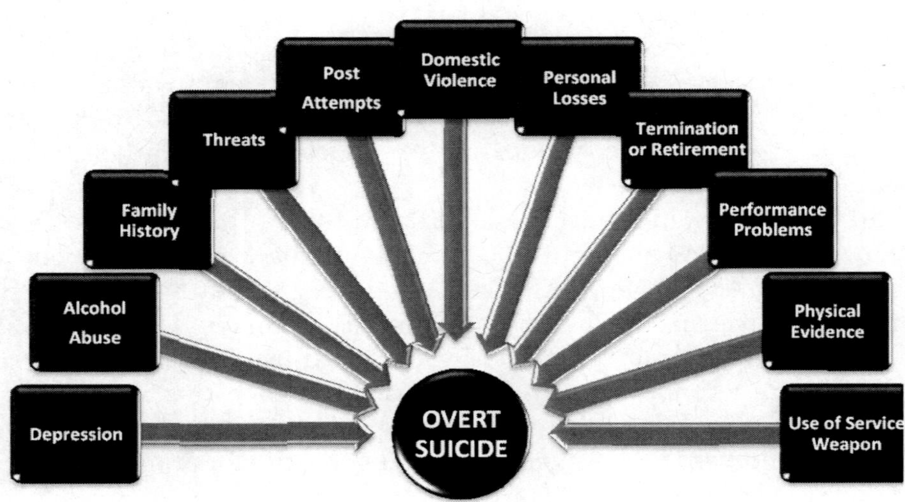

Figure 1-2. Methods of Suicide: Overt Suicide

"In suicide by suspect, the officer involved does not initiate victimization or make any furtive moves toward the criminal perpetrator. Instead, the officer is a passive participant in the incident allowing the perpetrator to complete an act of deadly violence ... Suicide by suspect is therefore specific to on-duty suicide, suicide by cop turned inside out in cases of suicide by suspect" (Violanti and Drylie, 2008). Refer to Figure 1-3 for less obvious passive conscious suicide clues.

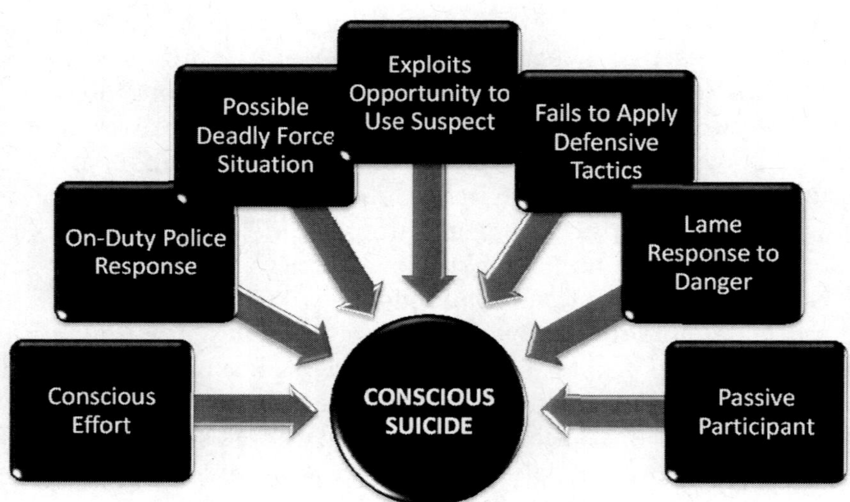

Figure 1-3. Methods of Police Suicide: PASSIVE/CONSCIOUS SUICIDE
(Adapted from Violanti & Drylie, 2008)

Police Indirect Suicide

The most understated cases involve an unconscious or indirect model as a means to commit suicide. These illusive cases are the most difficult to investigate. In cases of an indirect or subconscious wish to die, the officer is unaware of the intent to take his or her own life. These officers pursue danger on the edge of death and find comfort in the seduction of peril. The hidden agenda is to find criminals who present high-risk deadly scenarios; the officer is unconsciously moving toward his own death.

Carl G. Jung, the distinguished Swiss psychiatrist, noted that one important aspect of the psyche is the shadow. The shadow is the opposite of conscious self; however, it holds all of the unconscious negative energy and evil tendencies. People tend to deny the existence of their shadow; it exists hidden from others. The shadow or dark side might include greedy, dishonest, envious, or corrupt thoughts and behaviors. The goal is to confront the shadow and dark side to find self-enlightenment, and thus true understanding of oneself. "Unfortunately there can be no doubt that man is, on the whole, less good than he imagines himself or wants to be. Everyone carries a shadow, and unless it is embodied in the individual's conscious life, the blacker and denser it is" (Jung, 1975).

From the above citation, it is possible to conceptualize the unconscious mind operating in a self-defeating manner. The repression of the shadow fosters the denial process and provides the means for compartmentalizing suicide ideation. Thus sets the possibility of indirect suicide and living on the brink of danger, excitement, and self-destruction.

Shneidman (1968) investigated suicide among persons who appeared not to be consciously aware that their high-risk behaviors might bring about self-destruction. They either denied the possibility or were in a state of psychological denial. He describes a form of indirect or subintentional suicidal ideation:

"Subintentional suicide behaviors relate to those instances in which the individual plays an indirect, covert, partial, or unconscious role in their own demise. This concept of subintentioned demise is similar, in some ways, to Karl Menninger's concepts of chronic, focal, and organic suicides, except that Menninger's ideas have to do with self-defeating ways of continuing to live, whereas the notion of subintentioned cessation is a description of a way of stopping the process of living. Included in this subintentional category would be many patterns of mismanagement and brink of death actions, which result in cessation. In terms of the traditional classification of modes of death (natural, accident, suicide, and homicide), some instances of all four types can be subsumed under this category, depending on the particular details of each case" (Shneidman, 1968). Refer to Figure 1-4 for less obvious passive unconscious suicide clues.

Motivational factors are powerful incentives for suicide by suspect. The opportunity for the funeral of a hero provides honorable citations on the Wall of Fame. The life insurance survivors' benefits provide an additional financial incentive. Death in the line of duty is an incentive to glory, behaving with suicidal tombstone courage, and placing oneself in harm's way. The suicide by suspect or indirect method avoids the stigma associated with suicide. In addition, the officer's family would not feel shame from adverse publicity. Refer to the following case study for an example of an overt suicide; the officer is dealing with sudden guilt, shame, and suicidal ideation.

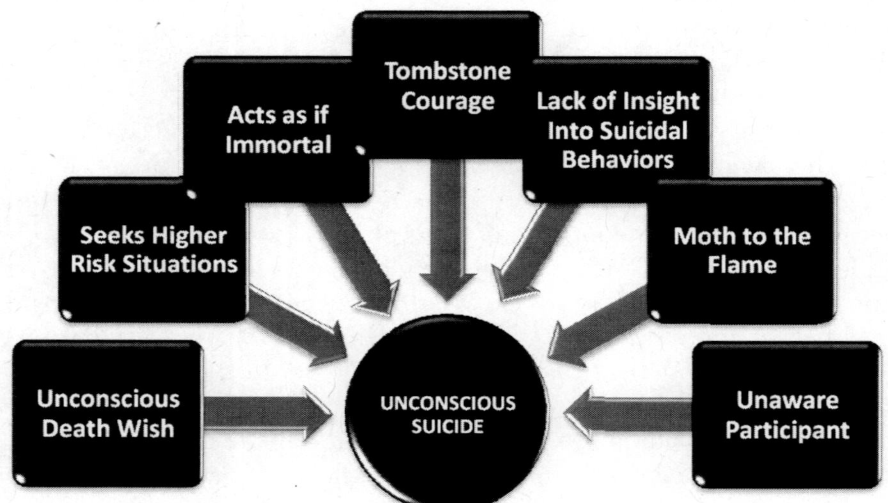

Figure 1-4. Methods of Suicide: Unconscious Suicide
(Adapted from Schneidman, 1968)

Case Study Illustration

Police officer Jack Smith serves in a large urban community that is notorious for its high crime rate. He always enjoyed taking challenging calls and continually pursued his sarcastic sense of humor, practical jokes, and pranks. He seemed happy and appeared well suited to his career in law enforcement. However, these observable behaviors concealed his masked self-loathing, depression, and alcohol abuse.

One midnight shift he and another officer played their usual quick draw game match. It was their way of greeting each other in the locker room, and served as a bonding ritual for their cowboy-like relationship. One officer made a complaint about the gunplay; it was just horseplay to his peers, not a prelude to a larger problem.

The following week, Smith discharged his off-duty weapon accidently in the continued gunplay scenario. The concealed backup semiautomatic was to be a humorous surprise for the other officer. However, one round was in the chamber and the weapon discharged, injuring the innocent officer who stood nearby getting dressed by his locker. The bullet ricocheted off the floor, and lodged near the officer's spine, causing prolonged hospitalization.

Officer Smith became withdrawn, defensive, and angry after the incident. He appeared gloomy and his uniform reflected his disheveled psychological climate. Smith's work ethic deteriorated and he deflected his calls to other officers on adjoining beats. His anger and rage over the smallest incident triggered an emotional outburst.

The shooting incident resulted in a suspension without pay. His downward spiral now out of control, Smith made nightly visitations to the hospital, crying and asking for forgiveness. This troubling sequence of events required an automatic referral for professional counseling. Earlier warning signs seemed more like bravado and police audacity. The gunplay was actually a rehearsal and lead- up activity for suicide. Interviews substantiated observations that Smith appeared preoccupied, distant, and nonresponsive after the incident.

Jack made dire predictions that he would die in the line of duty. He also verbalized subtle, seemingly innocent coded clues including repeated statements and declarations: "I won't embarrass my family anymore." Isolated and abandoned, with no intervention in place, Jack makes up his mind to end his mental pain and anguish.

Alone in his bedroom and alienated, Jack seeks refuge from his cycle of depression. Suicide seems his only alternative. He incessantly cleans his weapon after years of neglect and practices Russian roulette. Jack killed himself within two weeks of the incident, an off-duty chrome-plated .45 caliber automatic weapon found near his body. Officer Smith was steadfast in his problem-solving suicidal behavior because of embarrassment, humiliation, and extreme mental anguish.

Special Note: This case study illustrates Jack's sense of hopelessness, helplessness, and haplessness. In addition, his embarrassment, humiliation, and extreme mental anguish are apparent. According to the main theories in the field of suicidology from Allen (2004), Bongar (1991), Maris et al. (1992), Rangell (1988), and Shneidman (1987), law enforcement suicide is defined as a problem-solving behavior primarily aimed at improving a threatened self-image tarnished by sudden shame. Jack's driving motivation is insufferable self-hatred and shame, for which suicide is the solution. Suicide is the means to end the psychological pain or ache.

Focus Points

Suicide is purposeful behavior and a planned event. The goal may be to remove the officer from social stigma and humiliation. The outcome allows escape from disgrace and the opportunity to seize control. The elimination of psychological pain and suffering drives the officer to act on the suicidal ideation.

The officer may feel suicide is the ultimate solution to avoiding pain. The officer may even return to an optimistic point of view or sense of peace and freedom. The hopeful change in behavior is a destructive delusion, which masks its true intent. Family and friends may feel a sense of relief and allow their defenses to crumble. Counselors may even feel reprieve and comfort, but the end is near to everyone's shock and surprise.

Suicide by suspect cases are difficult to investigate; denial is a serious impediment to clearing these cases appropriately. These cases involve a conscious intent to commit police suicide by using a criminal suspect. However, the intent may not be obvious and it may be difficult to discern the unconscious underlying motivation to end the officer's life in the most difficult of cases.

In other suicide by suspect cases that are less difficult to investigate such as driving a police cruiser off a cliff, citizens are not involved. This traffic scenario requires in-depth accident reconstruction and may not lead to definitive results.

Discerning suicidal or courageous behaviors remains part of the enigma. What some may label as self-destructive, others may consider bravery. The need for excitement may be a means of alleviating depression, and the compulsive drive to run from the fear of death has a double-edged sword.

In some cases of suicide by suspect, the suicidal event may not involve planning, but is the indirect consequence of unconscious behavior. The overly heroic police officer may be seeking death and be in a psychological form of denial. These high profile and excitement craving behaviors may serve as a disguise for an indirect method of suicide.

Officers may deliberately position themselves to become the victim of a perpetrator suicide, an act designed to appear like a homicide. This phenomenon, known as suicide by suspect, identifies the behavioral pattern of officers who intentionally place themselves in a "death wish" or suicidal scenarios. The concept of indirect suicide remains an intriguing psychological concept that requires further investigation and empirical research.

Police supervisors and leaders need to monitor those officers who engage in negative risk-taking behaviors. While suicide by suspect is an insightful way of examining the range of immeasurable possibilities; empirical research data are not available. The creative means of police suicide by suspect remain underreported.

The key to prevention and intervention is proactive response to suicidal ideation. Train for the suicidal risk factors, and manage the exposure to serious and death. Identify the red flag behaviors of hopelessness, helplessness, and haplessness. Leaders should stay alert, identify the risk factors, and avoid denial of the possibility of suicide.

Conclusion

The search for answers to police suicide is elusive. In the suicidal state of mind, without proper support, officers envision many ways to take their own lives. The repertoire is endless because of concentrated training, experience, and expertise. Progressive police leadership provides the education and training necessary to understand how to recognize suicidal ideation, warning signs, and subtle clues. The dire predictions serve as red flag behaviors everyone should recognize and should result in appropriate remedial actions. Psychosocial assessment plays an important role in prevention and intervention strategies.

Chapter 2

Police Suicide: Risk Assessment

"One does not become enlightened by imagining the figures of light, but by making the darkness conscious."

— Carl G. Jung

Kenny was a 33-year old deputy sheriff with 5 years of service. His prior experience included service with the Naval Investigative Service. Kenny's career was going well until two events—the charge of excessive force and an agency vehicle accident. The excessive force investigation exonerated Kenny; however, the accident left him with lingering headaches.

Furthermore, he expressed resentment while appearing before the Citizen's Review Board. Referring to them as Monday morning quarterbacks...Kenny said, "I am afraid to do my job...I don't like being second-guessed."

Despite the unfortunate police department episodes, Kenny married for the first time. The couple purchased a new home and planned to have a family. When Kenny shot himself in the head, the shock was overwhelming. The location was a bench outside his hometown police department. Kenny's suicide note told his wife where to find him.

Source: This case study was adapted from James S. Herndon (2001), Department of Justice publication.

Suicidal people generally give active and passive warnings. On the surface, the suicidal officer may express confidence; however, there is a dark side not revealed to others. Suicidal officers may express passive comments that are disparate to the conscious self they present to others. Finding help allows suicidal officers to examine their dark side in therapy.

Providing assistance means that officers need to recognize the risk factors associated with suicide and depression. Police suicide training works in both directions; it protects both vulnerable citizens and police officers. This chapter outlines the signs of suicidal ideation and predisposition.

Chapter Focus

This chapter explores police suicide by defining aggravating risk circumstances. In addition, it endeavors to explain the role of the psychological autopsy, psychological risk factors, and depression. At the end of the chapter a case study illustrates the role of depression and underlying social dynamics.

Overview

Early research purported the notion that the personalities of police officers appear quite similar, if not the same. Stereotyping police officers leads to disingenuous impressions. Researchers portrayed police officers as having authoritarian, conservative, aggressive, cynical, and rigid personalities. However, research on police suicide has undergone a transformation. The influence of psychometrics, neurobiology, genetics, cognitive psychology, and other related sciences offers significant insight into the act of suicide. The psychological autopsy serves as the historical and scientific foundation for studying suicide.

Police Personality

Defining the police personality is an elusive task; researcher bias remains part of the dilemma. The tendency is to isolate negative police personality assumptions without examining all variables, constantly limiting the research. Personality is a cluster of enduring patterns of thoughts, feelings, and motivational predisposition. Personality behaviors emerge as an individual response to a variety of stimuli and environmental situations.

Law enforcement requires a certain degree of toughness to ensure personal safety and the preservation of both fellow officers and citizens. The ethos of bravery is important, but turning that persona off and reintegrating into society is challenging. Becoming part of one's family and community is the real test as it requires flexible personality adjustments and well-adjusted personality traits. Police officers are separate entities and they are participants in a subculture that has both positive and negative consequences for membership.

Gould (2000) suggested that the first deficiency is the tendency to treat each negative aspect of police personality as a separate entity rather than a multidimensional phenomenon. The second deficiency suggests poor research on the formation of police personality and phases of development. The third deficiency shows a failure to link measurable personality traits to discernable behavior as measured by performance evaluations.

Cynicism as it relates to policing can be problematic. Nevertheless, rather than an aspect of a police officer's personality, it is a coping mechanism employed to enable officers to deal with hostile and violent experiences. When viewed from this perspective, cynicism as a feature of policing can produce positive outcomes for police officers (Brown and Campbell, 1994; Lotz and Regoli, 1977). Furthermore, while characteristics such as cynicism and authoritarianism may not be desirable attributes for a police officer, they do have a function. Both cynicism and authoritarianism protect the officer at some level and are not necessarily the cause of stress outcomes for police (Carver et al., 1989; Davidson and Veno, 1980; Reiser and Geiger, 1984).

Carpenter and Raza (1987) noted that police applicants differ from other occupational groups in several important ways:

(1) Police applicants, as a group, when compared with other occupational groups, appear more psychologically healthy.
(2) Data revealed that police applicants as a group are less depressed and anxious and more assertive when making and maintaining social contacts.
(3) Police officers are a more homogenous group of people, which is probably due to sharing the personality characteristics that lead them to become police officers.

In another research study, two samples included 275 police applicants that took a battery of psychological tests. Lorr and Strack (1994) established that applicants seeking admission to police departments and training programs fell into one of three personality profiles. The largest group fell into a category considered normal and was described as a personality type for a "good or typical police officer." However, 27% fell into a category with relatively high levels of paranoia, schizophrenia, and psychasthenia. MMPI-I and MMPI-2 describe psychasthenia as a psychological disorder characterized by phobias, obsessions, compulsions, or excessive anxiety. This term is not a psychiatric diagnostic classification or term that is commonly used.

A third group fell in the mid-range of emotional adjustment, integrity, and intelligence; however, they scored lowest in interpersonal relations. While psychological testing is not perfect, it can serve as a general indicator. Conclusions regarding police personality appear controversial, and researchers have questions concerning the data reliability and validity.

Psychological screening protects individual applicants and the public from harm. Eliminating the psychologically unfit protects the police culture and supports a positive emotional climate. However, conclusions regarding police personality solicit controversial opinions by researchers who adopt different perspectives of human behavior.

Police Suicide: Psychological Autopsy

A study from the early 1930s revealed that 93 New York City officers killed themselves from 1934 to 1940. This study documented that *psychological problems* represented the most frequent reason for police suicide (Friedman, 1968). This research was conducted during the political reform era of Mayor LaGuardia, focused on individual officers, and applied the case study method. These early records provide the basis for suicide risk assessment, which eventually evolved into the "psychological autopsy." This analysis includes actual police department records and interviews with significant friends, co-workers, and family members.

Psychological autopsies offer the ability to examine past suicides from a retrospective approach. The information garnered assists in creating typology models for the assessment of suicidal persons. In addition, psychological profiles are useful in the preliminary investigation to assist in cases of accidental or suicidal outcomes. In some cases, the evidence is obvious, i.e., interviews, a suicide note, and other confirmatory evidence.

The investigator must prove death was self-induced and not the result of a homicide. The psychological autopsy may reveal a history of attempts. Statements to friends and relatives are classic clues used to verify the mechanism of death. Postmortem investigative procedures assist in understanding the psychological circumstances that contributed to the suicide.

Psychologists compile information and access information about behaviors, psychological states of mind, and motives of the deceased. Psychologists and criminal investigators ascertain if the deceased understood the consequences of his behavior or lethal intent. Major life disrupters may provide some clues, i.e., death of a d one or loss of employment. Investigating the final days spent by the deceased is particularly important and should include interviewing friends and family. The follow-up investigation consists of reviewing medical records, journals, and suicide notes (Shneidman, 2004).

Psychological autopsies provide comprehensive retrospective information about the victims of police suicide. This methodological design provides data on the risk factors associated with this behavior. Comparison groups and scientific procedures provide reliable and valid suicide results and improve selection procedures. Large cities are in the unique position to perform psychological autopsies and act as vanguard research venues for causes, typologies, and police suicide prevention and intervention programs.

Psychological autopsies are valuable tools for psychosocial analysis and discovering hidden psychological dangers in the field of law enforcement. Examination of officers' psychological autopsies and prior stressful assignments may provide underlying links to depression and suicide. Research on suicide and more data would prove helpful.

There are numerous qualitative studies; however, the need for empirical research continues. The need to explain police suicide causation and the social factors in law enforcement requires further analysis. Psychological autopsies are the primary way to examine critical behavioral precursors and risk factors, and are the best way to obtain retrospective data on the examination of completed suicides (Beskow et al., 1990; Robbins et al., 1959).

Psychological autopsies are the principle strategy used to defining the problem. These data form the basis for establishing the prevention and intervention of police suicide cases. The resulting analysis and synthesis assists in developing risk analysis, typologies, and protocols, which means extrapolating profiles from the psychological autopsies. Psychological autopsies serve as the basis for typologies or risk profiles that attempt to predict suicidal behaviors. Refer to Figure 2-1 for Police Suicide: Psychological Autopsy Measures.

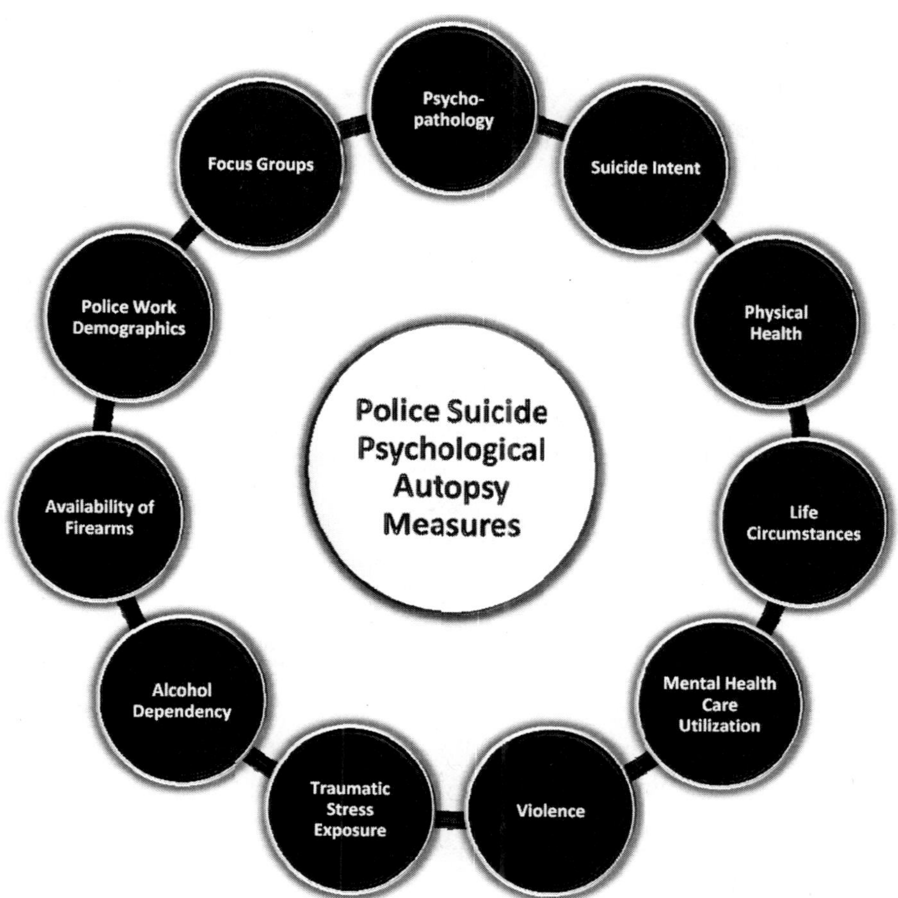

Figure 2-1. Police Suicide: Psychological Autopsy Measures
(Adapted from Breskow, et al., 1990; Robins, et al., 1959; & Schneidman, 1996)

Typologies/Profiles: Analysis

Goldfarb (2001) described the most immediate and salient factors leading to the police suicidal journey: "The suicidal officer is a 35-year-old white patrolman who is having severe relationship problems. He will likely experience performance problems, and some form of job disciplinary action. He is consuming a lot of alcohol, appears despondent, and is starting to isolate from his friends. Those around him notice that he is acting strangely, differently from his 'typical' behavior. He ends up killing himself with the most convenient and familiar tool: his service sidearm."

Several profile weaknesses remain; the main exception is the growing population of female officers in the ranks, minorities, and ethnic suicides. The danger exists that profiles could exclude those officers who might be in jeopardy. The profile might create an incorrect impression that would create a stereotype. Moreover, Pokorny (1983) noted that suicide high-risk group factors cannot deny an unworkable number of false positives.

Typologies or profiles are ideal types fraught with exceptions; however, they offer a starting point for the identification, intervention, and prevention of suicide. Many cumulative psychological issues develop over the course of a career and lifetime encounters. Research into the complex variables, individualization, and careful observation of the potentially suicidal officer offers the best recommendation for referral and treatment.

Police Suicide: Aggravating Risk Factors

Six aggravating circumstances may influence the officer's psychological climate. The following model attempts to identify key factors: (1) personality, (2) depression, (3) police culture, (4) work stressors, (5) family stressors, and (6) alcohol abuse. In some cases, multiple aggravating circumstances enhance suicidal ideation and can trigger an event. These aggravating circumstances serve as warning signs of a potentially significant suicidal episode. In others, there is no warning; the final act is an unexpected surprise, and a written explanation is absent.

Suicide is a planned activity; the preparation process is generally methodical. The suicidal police officer is experiencing multiple problems. Suicide is usually the result of a long-term, gradual, wearing away process that exhausts the officer's resources. The erosion of emotional coping skills results in the officer's inability to cope with stressful events. There is a long trail of evidence leading to the final act. Suicidal officers may even "practice" by holding a gun to their head or placing it in their mouth.

Detection is possible because suicidal officers may decrease their performance level over time before they are actually in crisis. Klerman (1987) identified 9 risk factors that correlated with a greater likelihood of suicide by a person over 30. The main risk factors include family history, previous attempts, lack of support, and psychiatric diagnosis. Review Figure 2-1 to examine the 11 risk factors. Refer to Figure 2-2 for an example of the six major risk factors as a flexible analysis model.

Figure 2-2. Police Suicide Model: Six Key Risk Factors

Comprehensive analysis includes a broad array of social/psychological resources. Important clinical assessments include suicidal ideation, frequency of suicidal thoughts, whether a plan exists, and plan specificity. In addition, biological issues and pathological disorders represent further significant areas for clinical analysis. Review Figure 2-3 to examine the 9 risk factors.

Developmental Life Stages

The first suicide alert system emerges from the officer's inner social circle, family, friends, and peers. When observers read subtle coded clues that may seem innocent at the time, lifesaving actions are possible. The second line of defense consists of first-line supervisors, or sergeants, and, finally, a third line that includes managers or lieutenants. The most important line of defense is proper intervention and referral to a professional counselor. When the first three defenses fail, the last will find it difficult to prevail.

Law enforcement officers move through critical stages of their careers that make them vulnerable to stress and suicide. Life stages and developmental skills acquired along the way can make a dramatic impact on a successful career transition or the journey to a premature death. The first five years of police service involve a stressful adjustment to career requirements, high profile scenarios, and violent episodes. Young officers experience difficult first responder calls to accidents, homicides, and suicides.

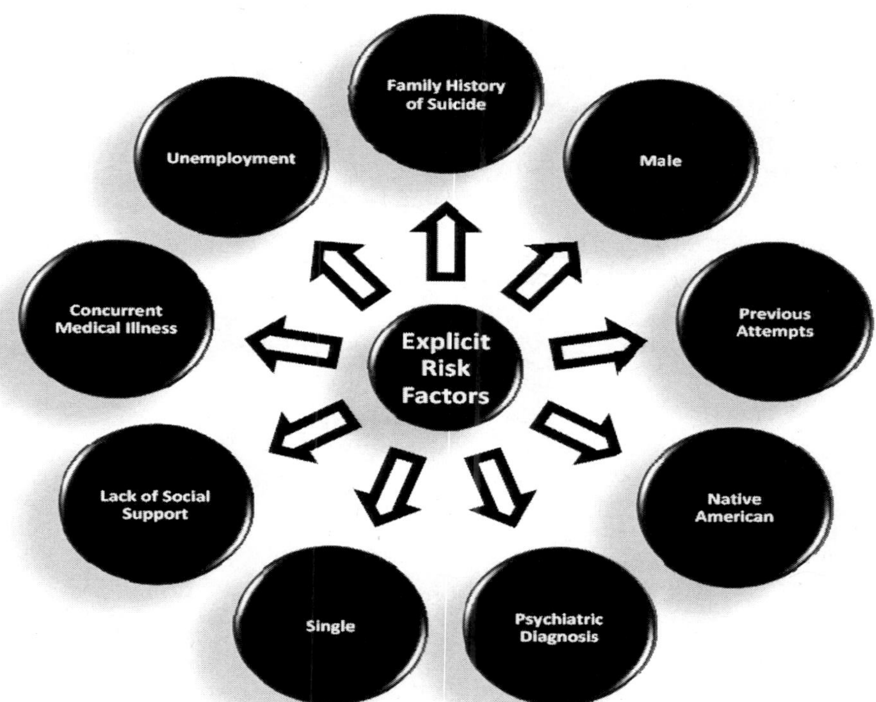

Figure 2-3. Nine Explicit Risk Factors: Correlate With A Greater Likelihood of A Suicide
(Adapted from Klerman, 1987)

A mid-life crisis or career adjustment may affect the need for appropriate transitions. Social and family breakdowns can lead to a downward spiraling of distrust, paranoia, and depression. Law enforcement agencies need to monitor these critical stages. Suicidal ideation, attempts, and completion of the act emerge rapidly at mid-life and during critical career stages. Generally, those who make successful career transitions will likely survive to retirement. Exceptions include officers who cannot make appropriate adjustments to being alone in retirement, and suffer severe or painful health concerns.

Police Suicide: Depression

When officers fail to perform at optimal capacity for several weeks, behaviors may be symptomatic of a clinical depressive episode. Clinicians agree that depression often plays a major role in suicide. While anyone can have an occasional gloomy day, people dealing with depression suffer from a deeper, long-term malaise.

Depression is a mood disorder that affects a person's overall "climate" rather than a temporary "weather condition." Significant depressive episodes last for at least two weeks. During this time, a person might experience changes in appetite or weight; altered sleep patterns and reduced psychomotor activity; reduced energy levels; feelings of worthlessness or guilt; difficulty thinking, concentrating, and making decisions; and recurrent thoughts of death or suicide. Behaviors such as exhibiting persistent anger, responding to events with angry outbursts, or blaming others over minor events are indicators of possible distress and depression (DSM IV-TR, 2000).

The U.S. Surgeon Generals' Office report (U.S. Public Health Service, 1999) identified *clinical depression* as the primary underlying cause for suicide. According to the report, *Action to Prevent Suicide*, countering clinical depression would serve as a major deterrent and primary suicide prevention strategy. Clinical depression affects the chemical balance of the brain. Major depression is the psychiatric diagnosis most commonly associated with suicidal risk. The lifetime risk associated with suicide in untreated patients is nearly 20%; about two-thirds of people who complete suicide are depressed at the time of death (American Association of Suicidology, 2001; Goalie and Hammen, 2002; Regier and Kaelber, 1995).

It appears that one of the dominant factors in police suicide is *depression*; many of the other factors are aggravating circumstances. Depressed police officers may experience problems associated with employment performance. One Canadian study revealed a serious drop in work performance six months prior to a suicide (Aussant, 1984).

Herndon (2001), in his article on psychological autopsies, described the model for depression. It examined the pre-suicidal behavioral patterns of officers who have committed suicide along with their pre-employment psychological profile. The following case study is illustrative of an officer who appears to have everything but feels that life is not worth living.

Case Study Illustration

Donald was a 41-year-old Caucasian man who had been a deputy sheriff for 11 years. His rank at time of death was corporal; however, he served in a civilian position due to emotional difficulties. Donald was twice married and divorced, had two children, and was involved with several girlfriends. He had a history of two previous suicide threats/ attempts. Diagnosed with depression, Donald took Prozac and Paxil as well as other antidepressants. Two psychiatrists, three psychologists, and four counselors made futile attempts to treat Donald who twice required hospitalization for inpatient psychiatric treatment.

Most noteworthy about Donald was his vanity and handsome appearance; women were immediately attracted to him. Nevertheless, he had apparent low self-esteem and feelings of worthlessness. Despite the fact that he had the looks of a male model, drove a corvette with license tag "Got It," and did not want for admirers; Donald was very unhappy toward the end of his life. After months of mood swings, highs, and lows, he disappeared one weekend. Nearly four months later his body was found in a secluded wooded ravine miles from home. He died from a single gunshot wound to the chest. Donald left several suicide notes, some mailed to loved ones and one on his computer at work. His death shocked and saddened most of the agency. Few believed he would really take his own life (Postscript to this case: The deputy's sister committed suicide in 1998 by standing in front of an Amtrak train).

Source: This case study was adapted from James S. Herndon (2001), Department of Justice publication.

Special Note: In spite of Donald's many gifts, he did not feel comfortable in his world. His behaviors clearly indicated many of the warning signs for suicide. The red flags of multiple divorces and separation from his children indicated a great deal of stress and loss in his life. The inability to sustain a long-term relationship leads to his loneliness and isolation. The diagnosis of depression and the use of Prozac and Paxil as well as other antidepressants were certainly red flags for potential suicide.

A family history for suicide is probably the key indicator. Denial from friends and members of the police department is the typical reaction. He had all of the red flag behaviors for suicide, but someone had to look for them. His "Got It" license plate was a cover-up for feelings of inadequacy, failed relationships, and depression.

Focus Points

The first suicide alert system emerges from the officer's inner social circle, family, friends, and peers. Identifiable risk factors serve as red flag behaviors. Life stages may predispose disillusionment, and a mid-life crisis can be a social factor. Critical stages and career disappointments can trigger suicidal ideation.

Personality, family, and work stressors may predispose certain police officers to suicide. Depression is a significant red flag in police suicides. Reading the signs of depression can alert others to this predisposition. Multiple high-risk factors should require supervisor follow-up and intervention.

When observers consider that police officers are armed and given broad discretionary powers over citizens, the absence of pre-employment psychological tests represents missed opportunities and incomplete hiring procedures. Excellent policing requires legislation that mandates entry level psychological testing and analysis by certified psychological testing experts.

Clinical depression is a significant red flag that results from chemical changes in the brain that regulate mood, energy, and sleep. The officer suffering from depression is not lazy, weak, or exhibiting a character disorder. Some physical symptoms include low energy, fatigue, and the inability to concentrate on complicated tasks.

The depressed officer no longer enjoys work or play. Sleep and rest cycles are constantly disrupted, leaving the lethargic officer incapable of successful participation in fitness programs.

What red flags suggest the potential for suicide? During the preliminary interview check the officer's body language, and look for sad facial expressions and flat mood. Statements that indicate mood can assess the feelings of the individual such as: (1) complaints of feeling down, (2) experiencing non-feeling or feeling anxious, and (3) complaints about bodily aches and pains may cover the officer's real feelings of suicide.

Typically, suicidal officers experience multiple problems and possible loss of significant others. Divorce and family alienation influences the suicide equation by adding fuel to emotional turmoil. It appears that one common factor associated with suicide is depression. Officers who are clinically depressed experience mixed emotions about committing suicide.

Conclusion

Suicidal feelings tend to be episodic; they come and go, often in cycles. The clinically depressed have fewer resources for averting a suicidal outcome. They are the most at-risk police officers who are the least likely to seek help and are the most artful at the "smoke and mirrors" deception games. Psychological issues and risk factors are important considerations; however, focusing on police culture and organizational structure may provide some important insights and answers.

Chapter 3

Police Subculture: The Social Climate

"If a way to the better there be, it lies in taking a full look at the worst."
— Thomas Hardy

Joe was a 33-year-old deputy sheriff with 4 years of service. After two years of service in uniform patrol, and two years in narcotics, his life was beginning to fall apart. Joe was on his way to establishing a solid career; however, he was neglecting his family. His marriage was floundering from the neglect. In addition, his two teenage daughters were beginning to show signs of conflict at home.

Then, the younger daughter committed suicide with her dad's backup weapon on the lawn of the neighborhood church. Joe was devastated. Understandably, his work suffered due to overwhelming grief and feelings of guilt.

Fellow deputies gave him widespread support and he sought counseling from the Employee Assistance Program (EAP). Nevertheless, at a low point on Saturday, he made statements to a coworker about joining his late daughter.

Special Note: Fearing for his safety, the sergeant referred him to the agency psychologist. Joe returned to light duty for a few weeks, and then gradually returned to patrol under close supportive supervision. Eventually, as the grief ran its course, noticeable improvements in his demeanor and motivation reemerged. Today, he is rebuilding his life and his career as a wiser deputy.
Source: This case study was adapted from James S. Herndon (2001), Department of Justice publication.

Chapter Focus

This chapter explores the role of police subculture and defines some of its culturally addictive qualities. It endeavors to analyze cultural constraints and work stressors. Examining the red flags of family and alcohol abuse is central to understanding its connection to police culture. The case study is an illustration of police values, subculture, and analysis of the underlying social dynamics.

Overview

The following chapter attempts to address police officers' cultural conflicts, and the complicated balancing act required to be successful. Many sociological researchers support the model that suggests that culture determines personality and behavior. Therefore, researchers must study the culture to understand police behavior. This model focuses on the cultural characteristics and not the personality. Some psychological theorists support the notion of individual personality and that people may differ in the culture. There are many ways to view behavior; however, those who suffer from mental health issues will find policing a difficult adjustment. Stressful policing assignments may aggravate an existing mental health condition.

Police culture influences behavior, and the socialization process is intense. The influence of police culture is not the only factor; genetics and personality are important variables. Inner-directed officers are less likely "to go along to get along." Many police officers will follow their own values and professional ethics.

Police culture does not have to be a negative socialization factor, which is contrary to some researchers' points of view. There are many positive aspects of police culture, although it has some social cliques or individuals that may offer specific negative connotations. Examining the worst of police culture is a starting point; the continuous cultural assessment prevents negative consequences.

The literature on police suicide emphasizes that police officers and their families endure unique social and psychological pressures, setting them apart from the general population. Police officers live in an environment that is structurally conducive to suicide, a conceivable option for relieving themselves from the grips of depression, loss, post-traumatic stress, domestic conflict, and so on. We must acknowledge and investigate the role police culture has in suicide prevention and intervention. The role of depression is the most significant factor in the interchange with other environmental considerations (Baker, 2008).

Death positions itself continuously in the path of a police officer and beckons at their heels. Consequently, police officers often become disillusioned, and many fall into despair. Unrecognized police cynicism, helplessness, and hopelessness may quickly spiral downward to suicide. Police officers move swiftly and without hesitation toward conditions others avoid. Policing does not allow flight, only the fight syndrome. Courting emotional disaster has its price tag and eventually demands payment (Baker, 2008).

Police Culture: Emotional Constraints

"Because of the police norms to refrain from displays of emotions, officers find few opportunities to deal directly with the pent-up feelings engendered by traumatic events. Police officers find themselves unable to reveal their feelings to other officers, much less discuss themselves, for fear of being viewed as inadequate or not having what it takes to be a solid, dependable police officer" (Pogrebin and Poole, 1991).

The expression of personal feelings is limited within police culture. In addition, organizations may discourage communication up the chain of command. The police profession instills conduct norms dictating that officers must remain calm and in control. They serve with an obligation to be on guard and keep their feelings "in check."

This lack of communication may interfere with early identification and prevention of suicide behaviors. Isolation from the main cycle of daily living and shift rotation serve as subtle components of the larger problem. Alienation accrues while police officers are asleep and others go about traditional daily routines.

Ultimately, constant psychological and physiological adaptations create stressful imbalances in homeostasis. The combination of family and work stressors can undermine the emotional stability of law enforcement officers. Restoring the rest cycle is therefore impossible; stress without rest stirs a caustic brew for even the best adjusted personality. Similarly, traumatic field encounters can become the precipitating event for a stressful, self-inflicted deadly encounter.

Police Suicide: Work Stressors

Violanti et al. (1996) and many other researchers identified stressful work conditions in police organizations as a major factor. The police environment generates high stress due to the nature of the work. It appears that stress-related alcohol dependency and the lack of exercise contribute additional stress to the social equation. Solutions for alleviating stressful factors may surface by examining the role of stress in the social network.

Sewell (1983) noted in his research that highest levels of critical incident stress experienced by male and female officers seemed to be involved with critical incidents such as the violent death of an officer in the line of duty (94.4%). At the same level of stress was the suicide of an officer who was a close friend (94.4%). The next highest level of stress was taking a life (87.2%) or shooting someone (83.6%) in the line of duty.

Special Note: Dismissal (83.8%) ranks as high as taking a life. Going through personal stressors like divorce or separation (74.1%) ranked more central. Responding to a scene involving the death of a child (73.8%) ranks as high as a personal family tragedy.

Violanti and Aron (1994) indicated that killing someone in the line of duty and the death of fellow police officer were at the top of the list of hierarchy of police stressors. Ten years later Garcia et al. (2004), discovered similar findings, and ranked their mean score results. They divided their results into three types of stressors: (1) occupational, (2) job related, and (3) external. Police officers cite death and injury as the most stressful part of law enforcement. Refer to Table 3-1 for a brief synopsis of the top stress factors in policing.

Norvell et al. (1993) cited that higher stress levels in female officers resulted from dissatisfaction with their coworkers. Overall, female officers did not have higher stress levels or lower job satisfaction than male officers. The male officers seemed to have more stress, more daily hassles, and greater emotional exhaustion than the female officers, and they had greater job dissatisfaction.

Table 3-1. Ranking the Top Four Police Stressors

The research on police stress spans decades. The studies indicated stressful police working conditions exist, but the causes, effects, or extent remains unclear (Gaines and Van Tubergen, 1989; Mallory and Mays, 1984; Terry, 1983), and there is a need to examine the causes or empirical relationships (Kappeler and Potter, 2005) between suicide stressors and how individual police departments deal with these stressors.

Police Suicide: Family Stressors

Research seems to focus on the officer and symptomatic behaviors, rather than the underlying causes that could offer remedial responses. The role of personal and family stressors may be the most significant factor in social network. There is a reluctance to scrutinize grieving family members because they are suffering, but the research on family dynamics is a contributing piece of the puzzle.

Studies estimate the incidence of domestic violence among police officers is higher than the general population. Other researchers found little correspondence between the personalities of law enforcement personnel and men who batter their female domestic partners. There appears little to suggest a predisposition of police officers toward domestic violence (Aamodt et al., 1998).

The family is the first line of defense against police suicide. Unfortunately, family members may not be able to respond because of fear, denial, and insufficient knowledge of the psychosocial dynamics of suicide. As suicidal depression spirals downward, poor communication and trust evaporate in the midst of despair. The police officer contemplating suicide is isolated and alone. Children playing and those who love the officer no longer stir life's emotions, and the will to survive is diminished.

Police officers do not live in a vacuum; police and family stressors overlap and remain connected. Some officers and family members are able to individuate and separate their personal lives from the rigors of police stress, but they never completely succeed. Police culture and the related stressors remain difficult to escape; their impact only mitigated. The stressors may actually coalesce and receive mutual reinforcement from each other, leaving no escape from the dynamic impact.

Some families are comprised of toxic qualities that magnify police stressors; others fan the flames that cultivate and maintain destructive forces. This is especially true when red flag behavior clues include: (1) jealousy, (2) controlling behaviors, (3) unrealistic expectations, and (4) blaming others. Numerous codes and domestic flashpoints can coalesce into suicidal catastrophe (Baker, 2005a).

Police officers work hard to protect their families; some retreat to a world of silence, which may enhance stressors. Financial issues enhance domestic strife and violence. This lack of communication may breed fear and suspicion. A spouse may become a stealth operative, scrutinizing an officer's every move, fueling suspicion, mistrust, and paranoia (Baker, 2005a).

Police officers frequently respond to domestic violence and abuse calls and are adept at reading domestic violence red flags. They develop code buster skills that allow them to assess abuse clues. Unfortunately, domestic arbitration skills may be absent in their personal lives.

Police officers may lack personal insight and engage in behaviors they seek to prevent. Officers and their spouses may attempt to establish dominance, power, and control. Initially, behaviors may include pushing, shoving, slapping, and serious assault, which are all designed to instill fear. The violence cycle escalates with interspersed apologies and emotional abuse. In addition, a spouse may become passive due to the fear of violence.

Occasionally, an officer, spouse, or partner may have an abusive personality and become an ingredient in the suicidal equation. The abusive personality demonstrates traits that point toward a strong potential for physical violence. Family climates that embrace rage and other aggravating factors set the stage for suicide tragedy.

Obsessive and compulsive behaviors increase rage, and the likelihood of homicide/suicide, especially when one partner leaves the relationship, is the final triggering event. Fantasies of homicide and suicide merge into a theme of consistent and persistent ideation. When the suicidal ideation is part of the equation in the midst of extreme stress, all threats are life-threatening.

When domestic and alcohol abuse are involved, action must be immediate. Multiple red flag behaviors warn that the officer is more likely to push domestic violence buttons for violence, homicide, or suicide. Alcohol abuse elevates the risk of lethality; depression may make the officer a candidate for homicide and suicide.

Police Suicide: Alcohol Abuse

White and Honig (2001) found that the use of alcohol (1) increases the feelings of depression, (2) increases impulsivity, (3) and is present in a large number of police suicides. Police "choir practice," the after-shift drinking party for venting war stories, serves as the conduit for self-medication. Many police officers have disdain for drugs, pills, and legitimate prescriptions; however, alcohol serves as a survival celebration of the last tour of duty.

White and Honig (2001) indicated that alcohol continues to serve as a coping strategy; however, it often initiates increased feelings of depression. Unfortunately, the after-shift choir practice and pseudo decompression is still practiced in many law enforcement agencies.

Emotional expression of suicidal ideation is problematic because of alcohol consumption and the bravado of the "choir boy practice sessions" after the swing shift. Many officers stay up to the early morning hours engaging in pseudotherapy, augmenting their previous stressful environment. Domestic problems become aggravated because of alcohol-related behaviors and the cycle of stress is never interrupted because of inadequate sleep. Officers return home to sleep until time to get ready for the next shift, missing family life (Baker, 2008).

Alcohol abuse is a primary factor in suicidal behavior (Lester, 1993; Schwartz and Schwartz, 1991). The suicide rate among police officers that abuse alcohol is high; however, officers commit suicide because of various personal problems (Lester, 1993). Lester suggested that work associated stress does not influence a police officer to commit suicide. His analysis of 92 police suicide cases revealed that alcohol abuse and personal problems appeared to be the main issues.

The relationship between the lengths of service socialization into police culture and alcohol consumption is an interesting hypothesis. Obst and Davey (2003) noted that police service has a significant impact on the drinking and socializing behavior of "recruits." They examined the social behavior of police officers before and after entering police service. They discovered the "amount of recreation time" spent with work/police officers rather than non-police officers increased significantly on entry into police service. In addition, they found drinking with fellow workers or police officers increased over time in service, while drinking with non-work friends and family decreased.

Police Subculture Values

Police culture has an unwritten motto: "We the brave, are not allowed any cracks in our armor." Suicidal behavior is unacceptable in the police vocabulary or professional lexicon. We take care of our own and do not need help; we are the helpers. Therefore, police officers may fail to see symptoms and miss opportunities for appropriate intervention.

Police officers must be strong, brave, and willing to engage danger. Many may have trouble expressing fears. Demonstrating emotion is not consistent with established officer role models. The expression of suicidal ideation is not encouraged or acknowledged because of the external dangers officers face in their daily work environment.

Therefore, there is difficulty in expressing suicidal thoughts or identifying the potential in others. The culture of law enforcement has its own code of conduct, which conceals signs of psychological distress. Police officers fear demonstrating weakness, or being soft and in need of assistance (Slovenko, 2002). Moreover, the denial factor may be operational in many cases.

Police values emphasize bravery and character as essential qualities of the subculture. Social acceptance and respect of the police rookie requires the demonstration of these qualities. These qualities are necessary attributes, and are important in the actual and perceived dangers in the field of law enforcement. The potential to become a victim of violence is always present.

The police officer must always demonstrate bravery to support other officers in harm's way. The failure to honor the code of bravery means the loss of respect and the death of a police career. The officer who fails to measure up will be socially isolated from peers in the face of extreme adversity.

Herbert (1998, p. 357) made the following assessment: "Officers thus encourage each other to summon the necessary bravery to handle potentially perilous calls. They also encourage each other to ensure the preservation of their own life and the lives of others...Roll calls regularly end with the admonishment 'stay safe out there.' Officers express satisfaction when a tour of duty ends without mishap."

Culturally-Addictive Qualities

Police work offers seductive and addictive qualities, triggering compulsive surges of survival hormones. Police officers vacillate from boredom to emotional tragedy. The addiction to the rush of running from emergency to emergency presents an exhilarating roller coaster ride. The long-term consequence of stress, without adequate rest cycles, has its consequences.

Gilmartin (1986) defined the police cycles of stress as the "brotherhood of biochemistry." He suggested that physiological and social dependency on the excitement of police work has consequences. The officer must adapt to the excitement and dangerous lifestyle and then shift into a kind of psychological depression in calm or normal cycles of living. The social response is to withdraw from relationships and detach from anything unrelated to police work. The hypnotic glare and allure of excitement excludes family and personal relationships to maintain a restricted policing focus. The following case study illustrates the need to demonstrate the ethos of bravery and the addictive power of alcohol chemistry.

Case Study Illustration

In this case study, Michael, a 26-year veteran police officer, had an evening ritual of alcohol consumption. When he was off duty, he would sit at home and drink until he passed out. When he was on duty, he would stop at a local bar every night after work.

On several occasions, state troopers stopped the officer for driving under the influence. In each instance, the officer displayed his badge and was extended professional courtesy. On one occasion, the trooper followed him home to ensure that he arrived safely.

The spouse admitted that she wished officers had arrested her husband for DUI and forced him into an alcohol treatment program. Perhaps he would still be alive today. Autopsy reports showed that the blood alcohol level was over the legal limit at the time of the officer's death. This raises the question as to whether or not the officer was consciously aware of his actions; perhaps, being intoxicated simply provided the courage needed to complete the suicidal act. Although alcoholism is a disease, like depression, it is possible to overcome with treatment programs.

Source: This case study was adapted from Teresa T. Tate (2001), Department of Justice publication.

Special Note: "Some officers would view drinking as nothing more than camaraderie, while others would view it as an understandable escape from the gruesome and horrendous events of a tough shift. It is a place to gather and forget all the pain that life has shown them. At what point does an officer go from social drinking to alcohol abuse? In addition, are some officers predisposed to become alcoholics? It is years of this behavior that finally take their toll on the officers" (Tate, 2001).

Alcohol abuse may serve as a form of self-medication in response to running on the chemistry of adrenaline and related stressors. Alcohol is a central nervous system depressant reducing the level of excitement after the shift. The call to "fellowship of chemistry" may also occur to maintain the culture and sense of social bonding. Additionally, drinking offers an escape from family related stressors. The gathering after the shift may take place in a tavern or in an open field after confiscating alcohol from juveniles.

Focus Points

Researchers continue to analyze the culture and social climate that accompanies police suicide. The social and cultural network that leads to the final act remains elusive and difficult to substantiate. Increased interest emerged throughout the 1980s when researchers started to define and acknowledge the problem. Original efforts produced little results regarding why and how to prevent police suicide in the United States.

The officer can never "back down," and those who demonstrate bravery become a legend in their own time. Every officer knows this basic value, and those who take great risks are the department's heroes. This can result in a form of tombstone courage in a subculture that demands cherished respect for bravery. The principle of fight rather than flight builds in a unique form of coping and bonding with danger and stress.

The role of police subculture needs additional research. The social dependency on the excitement of police work has consequences. The long-term consequence of stress, without adequate rest cycles, needs examination. Police officers find it difficult to express suicidal thoughts or identify the potential in others.

Police stress may vary considerably in jurisdictions; Hell's Kitchen in New York City and Mayberry USA offer different social milieus. Some perceptions of danger and violence may act as a considerable source of stress. The intermittent reinforcement of officer deaths by homicide is powerful incentive for concern.

The perceptions of violence and danger may be the significant factor for the accumulation of stressors. The disparity between the realities of the daily minor stressors and the combination of larger systemic fears of the culture may serve as reinforcement. Some perceptions are accurate; others may result because of fear and the culture.

The family dynamic is an important factor in police suicide. Police officers and their families endure unique social and psychological pressures, setting them apart from the general population. Police officers do not live in a vacuum; police and family stressors overlap and remain connected.

Alcohol abuse is a primary factor in suicidal behavior. The role of depression is the most significant factor in the interchange with other environmental considerations. Police officers are structurally predisposed to alcohol as a means of self-medication in a stressful cultural environment.

Identifying officers who engage in negative high-risk behaviors and who pursue harm's way may reduce their potential for disguised or unconscious accidental death or overt suicide. Their persistent heroic behaviors may act as a cover for conscious or unconscious self-destructive behavior.

Conclusion

Police culture is fraught with denial and is an important part of the solution. The identification of the family dynamic is the major assessment problem. The interplay of the culture, family, and alcohol abuse is very elusive and difficult to assess in police culture.

Alcohol abuse is the one factor that is relatively easy for supervisors to recognize. Excessive sick calls, lateness, and incompetence soon become obvious. The smell of consumed alcohol excreted by the human body serves as another telltale sign. However, police leaders may miss opportunities to address family abuse and further appropriate interventions. Moreover, alcohol, a central nervous depressant, compounds other social factors.

Part II
Police Suicide Stress Issues

Leadership Foundations	Guidepost Behaviors
• **Identify the critical incident trauma and exposure rate for police officers.**	• Leaders assess the sense of well being, mission performance and negative consequences as they relate to acute stress disorder and post traumatic stress disorder.
• **Identify symptoms of stress and their impact on police officers.**	• Leaders identify and examine unnecessary police stressors within their departments. The goal is to **eliminate** as many unnecessary and negative stressors as possible.
• **Develop a positive police culture and assess the stress levels of individual officers with regard to improving quality of life issues.**	• Collaboration with researchers and counselors on the **long-term consequences** of stress without adequate rest cycles is worthy of additional research.
• **Appraise the need to develop and improve intervention and prevention programs.**	• Directly connected to PTSD research and depression: **(1) personality, (2) high risk assignments, and (3) trauma exposure.**
• **Research and initiate a Crisis Incident Management Program for officers who have experienced trauma, deadly force shootings, and suicide by cop scenarios.**	• The program should **include intervention strategies, group debriefings and follow-up counseling** for the officers affected and their families.

CHAPTER 4

POLICE SUICIDE: STRESS RELATED FACTORS

"To win over your bad self is the grandest and foremost of victories."
— Plato

George was 45 years old and served as a deputy sheriff for approximately 2 years. He had prior police service with another agency, and most likely experienced prior cumulative stressors. However, this was a time of stress and his life crisis was out of control.

During this time, George was visiting a counselor for personal stress at home for several months. One evening the stress crisis peaked when his wife accused him of inappropriate sexual behaviors with their 13-year-old adopted daughter. Fearing the worst-case scenario, George departed the house and pulled out his service weapon in the yard.

His wife anticipated the potential suicide, and called the agency psychologist for help. George required emergency transportation to a psychiatric facility for evaluation and stabilization. Eventually, arrested on the charges for the sexual improprieties, convicted, and fired, his career in law enforcement was over. The suicide intervention was successful due to the law enforcement agency's program and the counselor's intervention.

Source: This case study was adapted from James S. Herndon (2001), Department of Justice publication.

Chapter Focus

This chapter explores some basic concepts concerning stress management. It defines stress management and discusses symptoms of stress. In addition, it endeavors to explain the role of the "fight or flight syndrome" and types of police stress. The case study is an illustration and application of traumatic stress factors: (1) General Adaptation Syndrome (GAS) theory (2) and the underlying social dynamics of stress.

Overview

Stress can overwhelm police officers in many subtle ways; it may emerge in little daily stressors or one traumatic event. Daily stressors unfold over the course of time, producing subtle traumas that are cumulative. The little unnecessary things may be infinitely more important; for example, daily internal organizational conflict can be quite serious. Let's not forget that stress is in the eye of the beholder.

Managing stress and coping with burnout remains a daily struggle for law enforcement officers. Shift rotation represents the core stressor in police work; every officer struggles with sleep and poor rest cycles. Changing one's sleep habits weekly or monthly impacts psyche and soma as the mind and body are inseparable. Stress and disruptive sleep cycles are an insidious combination that interrupts the rest cycle. Stress without a rest cycle puts police officers on a collision course for conflict.

The 911 response to a barking dog call or a family cat stuck high in a tree are perfect examples of those little things that become significant. Some officers respond occasionally with insider jokes about other similar citizen complaints. Some officers perceive those complaints as interfering with significant investigations of serious criminal offenses.

Ultimately, little events trigger a serious emotional reaction that results in citizen altercations and complaints. Little things become irksome stressful events that may initiate other related stressors in the law enforcement agency. Traumatic incidents in most police agencies are rare events; routine daily stressors likely trigger stressful reactions. If the officer perceives the event as stressful, then it *is* a stressful event.

The officer on the street may refer to feelings of stress as those "barking dog calls" are "getting on my nerves." The word stress has become the acceptable terminology for police officers and does not have loaded connotations. Terms like *anxiety*, *pathology*, and *mental disorders* are less acceptable to police officers. The historical factors of stress management are worthy of police review and helpful in assessing stress and potential burnout.

Identifying Police Stress Factors

The research on police stress is largely qualitative and usually highlights a participant observational approach. Carter (1994) constructed a useful common sense overview and seven-part typology for analyzing police stress. Review the seven categories of police stressors adapted in Table 4-1 in synopsis format for an overview of the police stressors cited in the existing literature.

Defining Stress

Hans Selye (1976), the leading researcher in the field of stress research, defined stress as "the non-specific response of the body to any demand made upon it." Stress occurs when there are demands on the person that tax or exceed his resources and ability to adjust to the demands. Basic types of stress include: (1) "distress" (harmful stress), (2) "hypostress" (too little stress), (3) "hyperstress" (too much stress), and (3) "eustress," (good stress) that is motivating or stimulating, rather than harmful. Refer to Figures 4-1a and 4-1b as illustrations of stress models.

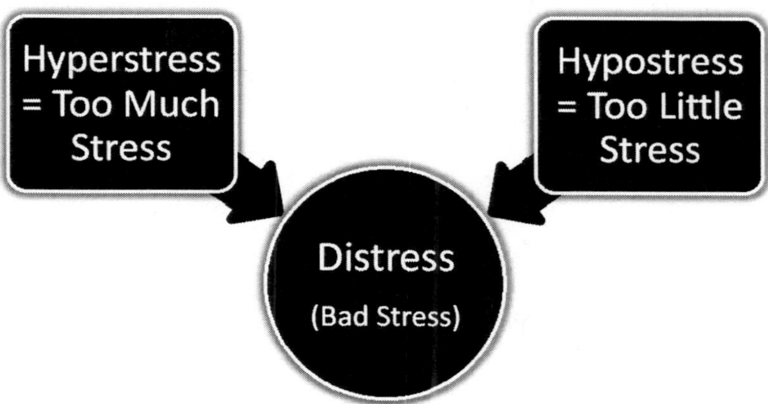

Figure 4-1a. Types of Stress (Dr. Hans Selye Model).

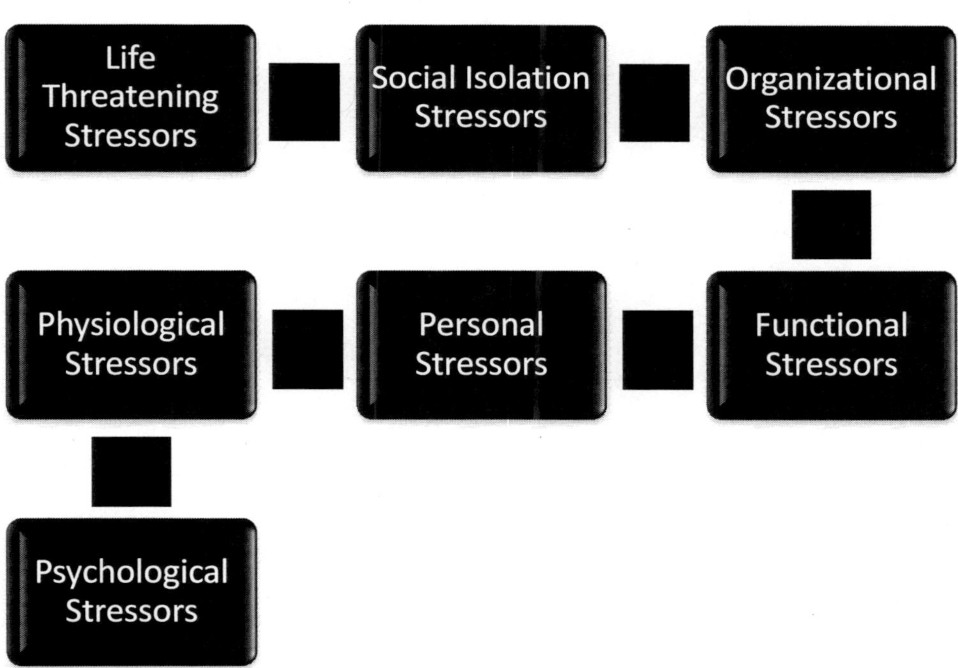

Figure 4-1b. Seven Categories of Police Stressors
(Adapted from Carter, 1994)

Police stress can be positive; for example, when finding lost children and returning them to their family. Those rare moments are typical eustress, and are rare moments of positive elation. Admittedly, positive stress does not usually overwhelm police officers; however, it still represents a form of stress. Positive stress in optimal levels maximizes interest in police work and challenges and inspires police officers.

Stress that does not threaten the officer may be pleasurable and exhilarating. Graduation from the police academy, surrounded by well-wishers, represents eustress. Pleasurable challenges in the police field are can serve as positive reinforcement. According to Selye, "The only complete freedom from stress is death" (Selye, 1976).

There are many definitions of stress. Cox (1978) offered this excellent definition: "Stress is defined as a perceptual phenomenon arising from a comparison between the demand on the person and their ability to cope. An imbalance in this mechanism, when coping is important, gives rise to the experience of stress, and stress response."

The definition from Cox represents an attempt at coping with the source of stress. "Coping is both psychological (involving cognitive and behavioral strategies) and physiological. If normal coping is ineffective, stress is prolonged and abnormal responses may occur. The occurrence of these, and prolonged exposure to stress per se, may give rise to functional and structural damage. The progress of these events is subject to great individual variation."

Symptoms of Police Distress

Police officers experience a life-threatening environment where real and perceived stressful events routinely occur. One of the most common stressors is working traffic on the highway. Highway accidents are the number one killer of police officers. The physiological reaction is automatically psychological and physical. The challenge becomes coping with the emotional traffic. Refer to the fight or flight syndrome in Table 4-2; it identifies the response symptoms.

The fight or flight response occurs when an officer experiences stress; however, police officers must choose the fight option. In most cases, the flight or retreat option is unavailable and unacceptable to them. Shaffer (1983) in Table 4-2 illustrates the fight or flight syndrome that corresponds to Selye's GAS. According to Selye's theory, this is the first stage of the "alarm reaction."

During the alarm stage of GAS, the officer recognizes the stressor and prepares for fight or flight by releasing hormones from the endocrine system. The officer experiences the physiological symptoms listed in Table 4-2 and must activate the appropriate coping fight strategy.

Table 4-2. Fight or Flight Response (Adapted from Selye's Stress Model)

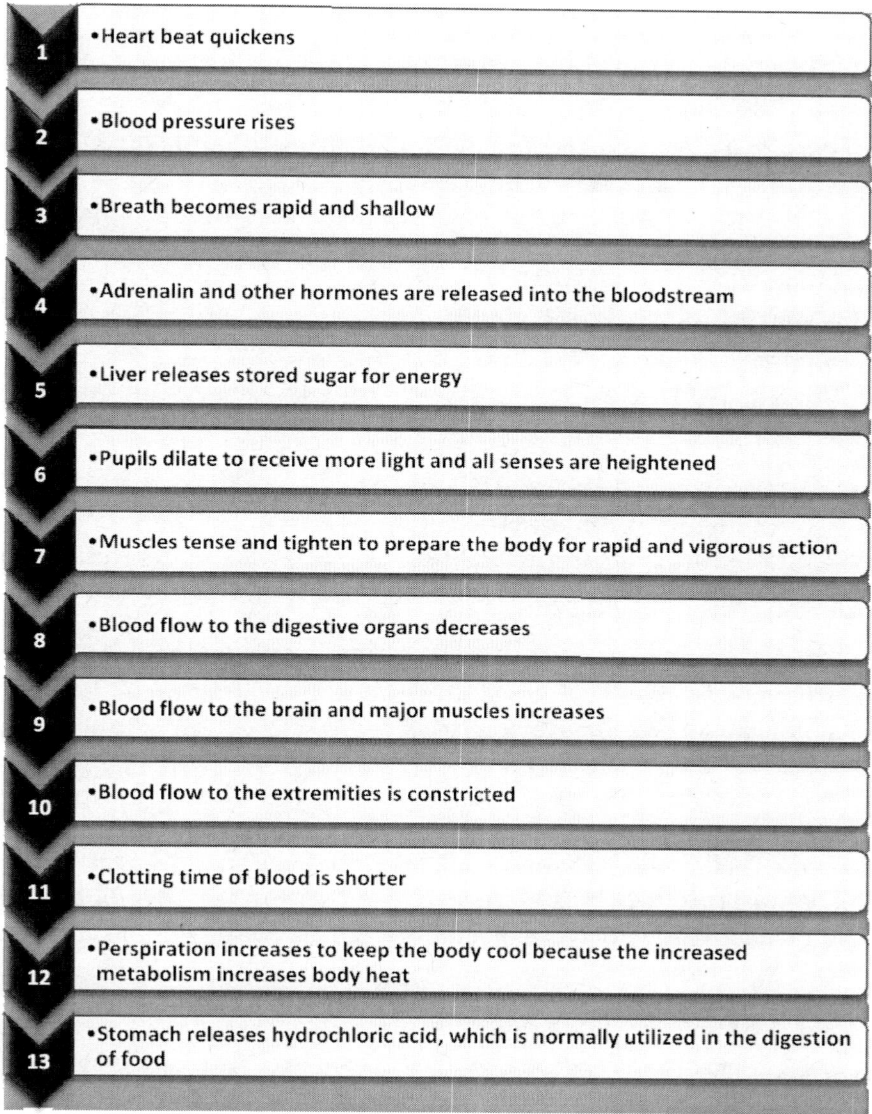

1	•Heart beat quickens
2	•Blood pressure rises
3	•Breath becomes rapid and shallow
4	•Adrenalin and other hormones are released into the bloodstream
5	•Liver releases stored sugar for energy
6	•Pupils dilate to receive more light and all senses are heightened
7	•Muscles tense and tighten to prepare the body for rapid and vigorous action
8	•Blood flow to the digestive organs decreases
9	•Blood flow to the brain and major muscles increases
10	•Blood flow to the extremities is constricted
11	•Clotting time of blood is shorter
12	•Perspiration increases to keep the body cool because the increased metabolism increases body heat
13	•Stomach releases hydrochloric acid, which is normally utilized in the digestion of food

In the second stage of the GAS cycle, the body repairs itself, unless the officer is still in the midst of the stressor(s). If the situation is ongoing, the officer's body remains in the alert stage. If there is no reprieve from the stressor(s), the officer's body moves into the third stage of GAS, the "exhaustion" stage. At this stage, it is possible to identify the symptoms of stress, if the observer knows how to read them.

According to Selye (1976), prolonged stress in the undesired exhaustion stage leads to serious consequences. The officer reaches a summit and is no longer capable of resistance. The hormonal defense breaks down, and many of the original emotional reactions re-emerge. The officer's alarm stage emotions intensify, and excessive hormonal secretions may result in severe physiological pathology or the "disease of adaptation."

The officer may experience ulcers, high blood pressure, and coronary heart disease. Continued exposure in the exhaustion stage may eventually lead to the officer's premature death.

At this stage, police officers may become depressed and consider suicide as a viable solution. Progression through the stages of stress is not without serious consequences. Interruption of the cycle requires knowledge and training in stress management strategies. Fight or flight is common to everyone. Police officers do not have a waiver; however, the signs and symptoms become noticeable under continuing stressful conditions.

The causes of police stress may be external, internal, or cognitive (the thoughts of the officer). These thoughts may include self or mental flashbacks of past incidents. The memories may be conscious or unconscious. External events have the potential for stress or trauma. The critical incident or police shooting has the potential for Post-Traumatic Stress Disorder (PTSD).

A stressor in an environment becomes apparent only when the officer views it as such and identifies it as one (Shaffer, 1983). This means that the officer's triggering of the stress reaction depends on cognition, the process by which the officer's mind comes to have knowledge of both the external world and his internal experience of thoughts and feelings. The officer's mind, in short, signals the body that a stressor is present and the alarm reaction follows. Refer to Figure 4-2 for an example of memories, events, thoughts, and streams of consciousness.

Life-threatening events are an extreme form of external stress for police officers or for anyone. Often etched in a person's memories, external events become internal flashbacks. Events and thoughts are not mutually exclusive. Flashbacks can occur when the officer least expects it. Although high-speed pursuits characterize routine experiences, these events have a cumulative effect.

If the officer continues to think about and have anxiety concerning life-threatening events, the emotional mechanism of recycling stress is served. The officer translates an external stressor into an internal stressor. This phenomenon may arise frequently, in particular while wearing the uniform. Thus, the officer, thinking about the event(s) or stressor(s), can experience the feelings of stress even in the absence of any real threat.

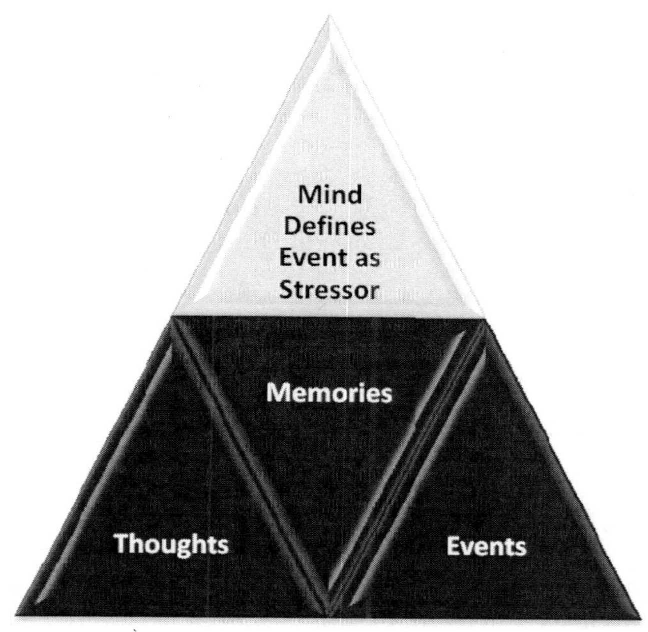

Figure 4-2. What Triggers Flight or Fight Response?

Police Critical Incident Stress

Police officers and first responders have high exposure to critical incidents, such as shootings, bombings, and accidents. The inventory is endless for violent crimes and numerous related police emergency calls. Critical incident trauma (CIT) may result because of the higher risk factor to crime, emergencies, and disaster incidents. During this time police officers are at amplified risk for assault, injury, or death (Federal Bureau of Investigation, 2007). Therefore, occupational induced trauma may have adjustment, mental health, well-being, and performance consequences.

Traumatic stress describes the emotional behavioral development, deviation, and pathology from an external event. A traumatic event affects the pathways within the brain, nervous system, and endocrine system. Powerful models explain the role of memory, post-traumatic stress, emotional modulation, concentration, and their affect on interpersonal behavior. Recently, therapies that access the frontal and lower brain center and right hemisphere functions have proven effective. These structures are ultimately involved in traumatic reactions (Lasiuk and Hegadoren, 2006).

Acute Stress Incidents

Acute Stress Disorder (ASD) is an immediate reaction of those exposed to traumatic stressors; for example, distressing automobile accidents, violent attacks, natural disasters, and other life-threatening events that impact oneself or others. This disorder may act as a precursor to PTSD, or it may be a temporary reaction with symptoms occurring near the time of the traumatic event.

According to the fourth edition of the Diagnostic and Statistical Manual of Mental Disorders (DSM-IV) published in 1994, ASD results in response to a traumatic stressor (e.g., a life-threatening event to oneself or others, and a sense of helplessness). Furthermore, ASD is an anxiety disorder as defined in the DSM-IV-TR (2000). Symptoms and diagnostic pathways of ASD are similar to those of PTSD and include re-experiencing the event, increased arousal, flashbacks, anxiety, and significant distress in social and/or occupational functioning. In addition, a diagnosis of ASD must also include dissociative responses.

The DSM-IV-TR describes the diagnostic pathway of ASD as changes in one's perceptions of the environment. The officer experiences a sense of numbing; everything is unreal, distorted, and sometimes "in a daze." This kind of emotional response would not signal escape, and disassociation, de-realization, and depersonalization adds to the officer's confused mental state. An officer who feels a sense of numbing, detachment, or absence of emotional responsiveness might have an unconscious death wish, and may be in an escape state of mind.

The five types of dissociative symptoms include: (1) a subjective sense of numbing, detachment, or an absence of emotional responsiveness; (2) a reduction in one's awareness of his surroundings (e.g., in a daze); (3) de-realization or a temporary feeling of sadness or low affect; (4) depersonalization or feeling detached from one's body or environment; and (5) dissociative amnesia (the inability to recall important aspects of the trauma). These dissociative features represent coping mechanisms for the adverse effect of the traumatic experience (DSM-IV-TR, 2000).

Another diagnostic requirement is that the disturbance in an ASD must last for two or more days and can persist for up to four weeks. Anything beyond this time factor is classified as PTSD. An example of a tool used to help diagnose ASD is the Acute Stress Disorder Scale, which is a 19-item self-report inventory based on the 1994 diagnostic criteria of DSM-IV.

Secondary Stress Trauma

Hidden daily traumas may emerge as collective vicarious stress, which is cumulative. Police officers may absorb trauma from the plight of others by experiencing the traumatic pain or events. This form of secondary stress trauma or compassion fatigue occurs during disasters when assisting victims. Palm et al. (2004) defined these symptoms of vicarious trauma as (1) intrusive imagery and thoughts; (2) avoidance and emotional numbing; (3) alcohol use problems similar to those experienced by direct trauma victims; and (4) changes in self-identity, world-view, spirituality, and general psychological functioning.

Primary Traumatic Stress (PTS) occurs when an officer is directly in harm's way and can lead to PTSD. Secondary traumatic stress affects those officers or helpers who assist the traumatized officer. These helpers may also include rescue and fire service supporters. Tertiary traumatic stress affects other supporters such as family and friends of those helpers who experience primary traumatic stress (Stamm, 1997). Some researchers describe the effects of "exposure to another's traumatic material by virtue of one's role as a helper with overlapping concepts of burnout, compassion fatigue, and vicarious trauma" (Figley, 1995).

Traumatic events can initiate post-traumatic psychosis or a psychotic episode in which the officer can no longer distinguish reality from unreality. In some cases, psychosis may be trauma induced in others as the result of a high incidence of childhood abuse. Some cases may be the result of an existing psychosis. In cases of ASD, the officer encounters a stress reaction immediately or soon after an event that may eventually lead to PTSD.

PTSD

PTSD is as a major disruption in the lives of police officers. Reiser and Geiger (1984) cited one of the causes of an adverse stress reaction or PTSD is the loss of control and feeling powerless. Trauma appears to result from the puncturing of the officer's prior illusion of control and invulnerability. Inherent in the authority role is the assumption of being in absolute charge of one's environment. According to Krystal and Neiderland (1968), the survivor syndrome includes: (1) depression, (2) inability to handle anger, (3) anxiety, (4) paranoia, and (5) sleep disturbance with recurrent nightmares.

Research suggests that police stress is the underlying foundation and causation for the basis of mortality statistics. The most logical link to police stress is the reaction to catastrophic events in the field, especially death related to police emergency scenarios. Facing multiple events in a brief time increases the dynamic effect of other stressors, and the baseline for committing police suicide may be simple related stressor(s) or event(s). On the other hand, PTSD may serve as the major foundation for police suicidal behavior. This is especially the case with major firefights or police shootings as well as other multiple high stress incidents.

According to Mullins (2001), "almost all police officers exposed to a critical incident or other traumatic event will develop Post-traumatic Stress Disorder (PTSD). Suicide incident rates among officers suffering PTSD are higher than rates for non-sufferers." His research proposed that the police suicide rate is primarily attributed to police officers' involvement in critical incidents, not a life crisis. The crisis is the catalyst; the mechanism of death is the reaction and PTSD disorder.

PTSD results from participating in or witnessing traumatic events. Generally, these events involve threatened or actual death, injury, or threat to the physical integrity of the officer or others. The officer's response may invoke intense fear, helplessness, or intense horror. The officer experiences flashbacks and intrusive, distressing recollections of the event(s). The re-living of the incidents includes hallucination episodes, and efforts to suppress the past events fail. Other major criteria include: (1) markedly diminished interest or participation in significant activities, (2) feelings of detachment or estrangement from others, (3) difficulty concentrating, (4) irritability or outbursts of anger, and (5) exaggerated startle response (DSM-IV-TR, 2000).

Officers who have taken the life of another human being experience considerable guilt, trauma, and remorse. Killing or unable to save the life of another is fraught with emotional content. Sworn to "protect and serve," this police motto serves as a substantial contradiction and ambivalence that is extremely difficult to reconcile. Suicide may serve as the means to flee from the stress, pain, and anguish of one single incident.

Police commitment to protecting life and the related belief system remains challenged to its foundation. Some might reason that the score must be made even; i.e., a life for a life. The PTSD flashbacks are full of guilt and remorse that need relief. This is especially the case if an innocent citizen, juvenile, or child dies in the crossfire.

The way to find an honorable solution is to sacrifice the officer's life and go down in a blaze of glory. One variation on the suicide theme is the officer who may deliberately position himself as the victim of "perpetrator suicide/homicide." This action avoids the stigma of suicide for those left behind, providing a hero's funeral and remembrance.

Generally, life insurance and "death in the line of duty" may serve as the incentive for behaving carelessly and placing oneself in harm's way. The officer reconciles the final obstacle; his family will receive assistance while he finds relief from PTSD and depression. The police cultural barriers and this subtle method of suicide may be the most difficult to identify and prevent.

Police peers may need additional instruction on PTSD; the emphasis is on how to interpret the officer's self-destructive behaviors. In many cases, significant others and family members may experience secondary related problems to PTSD (Mitchell, 1994; Ryan and Brewster, 1994). Family members require education on the effects of PTSD and negative behaviors that may influence friends and family. The following excellent case study by Seltzer et al. (2001) illustrates the cumulative effects of mutable stressors over time. The case study is a psychiatric autopsy modified to protect the individual identity and confidentiality.

Case Study Illustration

Arnold was a 36-year-old police officer who shot his pregnant girlfriend after a domestic dispute. A brief investigation was conducted and the case was ruled a homicide-suicide. The family of the slain girlfriend filed a wrongful death lawsuit alleging improper screening, hiring, and training of the officer.

Arnold was born in Chicago to a single mother. He spent most of his childhood in foster homes where he was subject to physical abuse. In addition, Arnold sought refuge with a neighbor, whom he considered his mother. His biological mother married his adoptive father when Arnold was 14 years old.

Arnold briefly belonged to a gang at age 13. He never had any legal problems as a minor. After completing high school, he entered the Air Force. Arnold served in the Security Police. He married during this time.

One year before he left the Air force he received an Article 15 for striking his wife. After arriving for work late multiple times, and punished twice more under Article 15, Arnold was demoted in rank to private E-1. Arnold received a general discharge in 1986 with the notation: "Discreditable involvement with military and civil authorities."

During his military career, Arnold fell from a helicopter on a training mission and was severely injured. He recovered but eventually ended up with a 30% service-connected disability from his injuries. After leaving the Air Force, he obtained employment as a federal police officer. We do not have access to his federal employment file, so it is uncertain how he passed the background investigation.

The Air Force personnel computer indicated an inaccuracy without authorization at some time to show his discharge as "Honorable." He served four years as a federal officer without any problems. During this time, he applied to be a police officer with the same department that eventually hired him. During the application process, the department did not initially hire him due to his service-connected injury.

His background files show that he lied about the circumstances of his discharge, claiming it was because of injuries and financial support to his ex-wife. He also presented a government computer printout showing his discharge as "Honorable." His psychological evaluation was normal and he passed a polygraph exam.

Two years later, he reapplied to be a police officer and then accepted the position. He completed the academy with high marks. His police files contain multiple commendations. There are also three reports of on-duty motor vehicle accidents the year prior to his death. That same year, Arnold was late to work multiple times and received disciplinary write-ups.

Other than incidents of tardiness, everyone who knew Arnold found him very friendly, professional, and ethical. He had a particular interest and specialized training in domestic violence issues. Why did an otherwise exemplary officer "snap" and kill his girlfriend, his unborn baby, and himself?

Source: This case study was adapted from Joel Seltzer, Robert Croxton, and Amy Bartholomew (2001) Department of Justice publication.

Special Note: Some researchers use the term psychiatric autopsy to document medical factors rather than psychological autopsy. PTSD is difficult to assess because of denial. There is reluctance on the part of police officers to admit the symptoms. There are no comments concerning a police PTSD episode in this case study.

The use of alcohol as a form of self-medication most likely was the reason for arriving late for work. The subject in this case study was the victim of child abuse by foster parents. He reported symptoms of PTSD due to his abandonment and abuse. His alcohol problem certainly was creating and recycling additional stressors in the area of employment.

The absence of Arnold's father and mother aggravated his sense of isolation and ability to manage stress. This police officer's poor impulse control, alcohol abuse, and girlfriend threatening abandonment set the stage for his violent episode. Arnold shot his girlfriend five times during an intense and emotionally charged domestic dispute. After killing her and the unborn child, the ultimate form child abuse ... Arnold could not live with dignity and self-respect. His dream of being a police officer and core values vanquished; he views self-destruction as a necessity (Seltzer et al., 2001). Shame and personal disgrace most likely played a role in his suicide.

Suicidal people are secretive, but there are clues to the careful observer. Murder-suicide cases generally include considerable domestic conflict and violence. Indications include the obsession mixed with jealousy, rage, and paranoia. The murder-suicidal offender has fantasies of the possible reunion or deliverance and salvation during episodes of a major depression. Alcohol or substance abuse can increase the possibility of murder-suicide when the social conditions are in the right sequence. Alcohol abuse leads to the release of inhibitions and self- restraint and serves as an additional source of depression. Cocaine and amphetamine use may increase impulsivity, volatility, paranoia, and grandiosity (Jacobs et al., 1999).

Pam (2001) noted "Sigmund Freud observed that suicide was murder turned inward. Similarly, depression and anger are two sides of the same coin, complicating the calculus of risk factors relating to lethality within police families or intimate relationships in which one or more of the parties are a law enforcement officer. Murder-suicide scenarios include other variables: batter typology, occupational stressors, psychiatric disorders, and personality and serotonin levels."

Focus Points

We may be acknowledging partial police stress generators and their relationship to police suicide. Perhaps the magnitude of the problem is greater than originally determined or less than estimated. However, in hindsight, pioneer studies represent a small percentage of the population and are not representative.

The role of police stress appears greater than other vocations on the surface, but the picture appears to lack research clarity. The link between stress and police suicide is unsubstantiated and needs additional research.

There is conflicting evidence regarding the role of stress and its impact on police suicide. How these statistics interconnect to stress and social networks remains empirically unproven. It is extremely difficult to distinguish physical heredity and psychological factors.

Critical incident events are traumatic and dangerous and take many forms. Natural or man-made disasters that require long hours and involve severe property damage and causalities can create secondary trauma. Traffic fatalities are common events for police officers adding to the stressful conditions in the field.

What can police leaders do to manage and alleviate stress in the lives of their police officers? They must assist in developing a positive police organization and culture. This means eliminating the unnecessary stressors and deciding what is essential to the mission(s). Recognizing the stress levels of individual officers is a necessary requirement for successful prevention and intervention.

PTSD is the major foundation for police suicidal behavior. The crisis is the catalyst; the mechanism of death is the reaction and PTSD disorder. PTSD results from participating or witnessing traumatic events. Significant others and family members may experience secondary related problems to PTSD. Training emphasizes that PTSD is a normal event, and officer do not need to suffer alone.

Extremely dedicated officers are at considerable risk. Analyze the workload of individual officers; identify who may be taking more hot calls. This is especially the case when officers consistently take stressful emergencies outside their assigned beats. They may be pursuing the action and excitement or avoiding the emotional stress.

Officers serving in high crime areas need to rotate to other assignments to avoid stressful reactions due to prolonged service and exposure. Some aggressive and perfectionist officers may respond to unusually high numbers of police service calls. Officer rest cycles are important. Expert supervisors mentor and monitor their officers, rotating shift assignments on a regular basis.

Specific assignments demand significant increases in psychological and hazardous police officer exposure. Does exposure to high rates of stress plus the officer's personality elevate opportunities for PTSD, depression, and suicide? This hypothesis is worth pursuing long-term, as well as screening for personalities who are not capable of sustaining a prolonged stressful lifestyle.

Multiple tours in high profile assignments including *narcotics*, *vice*, and *undercover* should not exceed two years. Research on low profile assignments and officer rest cycles from high profile assignments is worthy of examination. The rotation of these officers prevents burnout and other stress related consequences. In addition, other officers have the opportunity to gain experience.

Police leaders should rotate high-risk beat assignments that generate stressful calls for service. There is a tendency to leave these officers in place too long.

Conclusion

The police mission is important, but the personnel must have high priority. There is considerable effort in the training of police officers. The investment is both emotional and financial. The effort of assessing at-risk officers for stress related behaviors and PTSD represents a sound investment. Police officers deserve the effort; it will enhance their morale and safety. Identifying the causation of stress prevents personal and organizational burnout.

The dignity and healing of officers depends on the feedback, respect, and assistance extended to them by police leaders and peers. Trained peer leaders and supervisors are able to recognize the clues of PTSD. Taking care of basic human needs assists officers in starting the recovery process and prevents additional stress and harm.

CHAPTER 5

SUICIDE BY COP

"Suicide is a death which results directly or indirectly on the part of the suicidal person, who would have the expectation of the action resulting in their death."

— Emile Durkheim

"A 30-year-old woman noted a deputy sheriff on patrol and followed him in her car to the parking lot of a community hospital. When the officer exited his police vehicle to attend to an unrelated incident inside the hospital, the woman subsequently parked her vehicle two stalls down from his patrol vehicle. Later, when the deputy returned to enter his vehicle, the woman suddenly appeared beside her vehicle and stated to the deputy, 'I want to talk to you.' As the officer approached the woman, she suddenly went to the rear of her vehicle and produced a .357 magnum handgun. She then pointed the loaded gun at him. In response, the deputy immediately drew his firearm and fired a fatal single shot.

Later, upon checking the deceased woman's car, a note revealed her motivation: Please forgive me. My intention was never to hurt anyone. This was just a sad and sick ruse to get someone to shoot me. I'm so very sorry for pulling innocent people into this. I just didn't have the nerve to pull the trigger myself. P.S. My name is ... I live at ..."

Source: This case study illustration is from Richard B. Parent (2001), Department of Justice publication.

Suicide by cop (SbC) is a critical incident with overwhelming consequences for the police agency, officer, and family members. Trauma is the overt and latent outcome of the legacy. Even witnesses suffer the penalty. The hidden consequences of police trauma emerge, if someone takes the time to make some basic observations.

Chapter Focus

This chapter seeks to shed light on SbC. It defines SbC and discusses the theory, motivation, and patterns of SbC. In addition, the chapter endeavors to explain the impact of training and intervention programs. The case study is an illustration and application of the underlying social dynamics.

Overview

SbC as originally defined by Geberth (1993) states: "Incidents in which individuals, bent on self-destruction, engage in life-threatening and criminal behavior to force the police to kill them." It evolves when the suicidal person recruits an unknowing police officer to assist in a planned suicide. This person seeks to create a police proxy suicide where deadly force is the ultimate and final scenario. The officer believes that it is a self-defense or defense of a third deadly force situation.

The violator provokes his or her own killing as part of an impromptu or specified plan. Suicide by proxy scenarios are typically violent. The officer assists a citizen in his intended suicide and creates secondary psychological victims. The above-cited paragraph is a synthesis of the various definitions of SbC (Hutson et al., 1998; Wilson et al., 1998).

Other common terminology describing this kind of suicidal behavior includes victim-precipitated homicide and officer-assisted suicide. The officer-assisted homicide is not appropriate, because it infers criminal culpability and has negative connotations. The best terminology remains SbC or copicide. More recently, Violanti and Drylie (2008) coined the word copicide to describe SbC. The authors advocated and applied the term (victim-scripted behavior) as part of their copicide scenario.

Suicide by Cop Characteristics

SbC subjects, in a life-threatening state of mind, engage criminal behavior to force police into executing them. SbC is the better descriptive term, one the police prefer and the one most commonly used. Refer to Table 5-1 for the individual characteristics of someone who is planning an SbC scenario.

Table 5-1. Suicide by Cop Attributes
(Adapted from Wilson, et al., 1998)

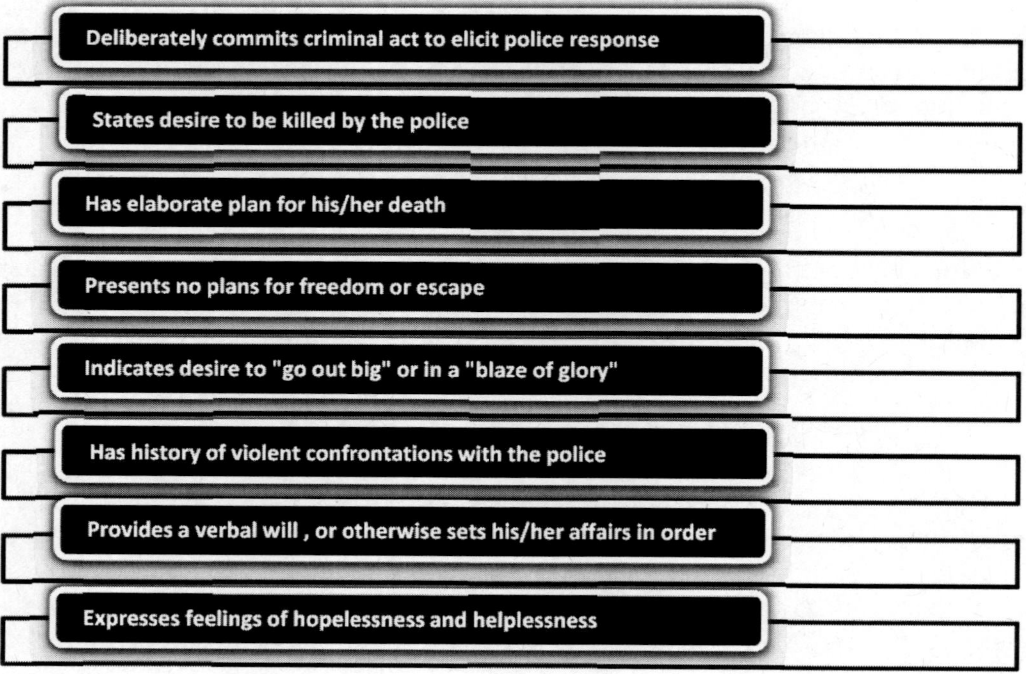

Deliberately commits criminal act to elicit police response

States desire to be killed by the police

Has elaborate plan for his/her death

Presents no plans for freedom or escape

Indicates desire to "go out big" or in a "blaze of glory"

Has history of violent confrontations with the police

Provides a verbal will , or otherwise sets his/her affairs in order

Expresses feelings of hopelessness and helplessness

Wilson et al. (1998) applied the term suicide by proxy, and identified several elements of the suicide by proxy scenario. In their case studies, they established the investigation must reveal a reasonable probability that the victim provoked the officer to shoot. The researchers excluded cases involving cocaine because this substance might confuse the ability to evaluate suicidal intent. However, other types of toxicology were acceptable.

Hutson et al. (1998) applied a rigorous standard: (1) evidence of suicidal intent, (2) evidence that individuals specifically wanted the police officer(s) to shoot them, (3) evidence that they possessed a lethal weapon or what appeared to be a lethal weapon, and (4) evidence they intentionally escalated the encounter and provoked the officer(s) to shoot them in self-defense or to protect other civilian(s).

This higher standard of proof is certainly difficult to establish in the investigative process. The case illustration in the beginning of this chapter easily matches these rigorous criteria; however, most cases require an intensive investigation. Psychological autopsy is one technique, but the follow-up investigation should produce additional information, statements, and evidence.

In summary, various patterns of SbC cases tend to be classified according to the following criteria: (1) the subject provoked the police to shoot them, (2) deliberate exposure to danger, (3) threatening police or bystanders, (4) a stand-off or barricade situation, and (5) the individual knowingly forces the police to attack while harming or threatening others.

Uniform Collection Issues

Pinnizotta et al. (2005) advocated a uniform definition of SbC. They defined SbC as ... "An act motivated in whole or in part by the offender's desire to commit suicide that results in a justifiable homicide by a law enforcement officer." They collectively analyzed research on the use of deadly force by law enforcement officers over the course of 15 years. The researchers recommended that attempted SbC incidents should be part of the research in an effort to ... "Better understand the magnitude of the suicide by cop phenomenon" (Pinnizotta et al, 2005, p.10). The definition is succinct and includes the basic essentials of an SbC shooting.

Additionally, Pinnizotta et al. (2005) recommended that SbC be part of the national uniform reporting system under the authority of the FBI Uniform Crime Reporting program. This high profile program would capture SbC cases and collect the data in a two-tiered investigative procedure. Identifying the 1990 expansion, they suggested a new category of SbC police use of deadly force.

The first tier in the investigative procedure involves a preliminary report submitted by the law enforcement officer at the scene. The purpose of this stage is to have the law enforcement officer at the scene make a determination as to the motive of the person killed by SbC. This would include statements made by the suicidal individual prior to the event, witnesses, and circumstances that indicate suicide as a motivating factor in the SbC shooting.

A second tier includes a follow-up investigation to the preliminary report. This report would serve as a classification of the incident by investigators with use of deadly force expertise. In addition, the supplementary report by an independent, objective investigator would examine new evidence unavailable during the preliminary investigation. The goal of the supplementary investigation is to establish whether or not the incident was an SbC shooting (Pinnizotta et al. 2005).

Theory, Motivation, and Patterns

As early as 1938, Dr. Karl Menninger, famous psychoanalyst and author, noted three elements of the suicidal person. His theoretical triad is an excellent analytical tool for appraising self-destructive and self-annihilistic or suicidal behavior. The three elements of the suicidal person include the wish to kill, the wish to be killed, and the wish to die. "Suicide is a death in which are combined in one person, the murderer and the murdered" (Menninger, 1938). Refer to figure 5-1 for the elements of Dr. Menninger's triad theory.

When these elements are elevated symmetrically, suicide is likely. When one of the elements is elevated out of balance, a homicidal or SbC reaction may occur. "In many suicides, it is apparent that one or more of these triad elements is stronger than the others. If the elements are elevated symmetrically, suicide is likely. This may explain the suicide by cop phenomenon, and identifies the wish to kill as being overwhelmed, by the wish to be killed, and the wish to die" (Menninger, 1938).

In addition, the theoretical construct may suggest the balancing of factors in favor of violence directed at the officer or other third persons before the person commits suicide. Menninger's theory may explain domestic violence killing of several family members followed by the suicide of the murderer. The suicidal triad may change in moments as the emotional climate surges out of control.

One of the nation's foremost experts discussed the five clusters of frustrated needs satisfied by suicide (Shneidman, 1996). These thwarted needs are "(1) thwarted love (such as the break-up of a desired relation); (2) frustrated control (when the individual feels that they cannot control their life, but can exert some control over their deaths); (3) avoidance of shame, defeat, or humiliation (perhaps after the loss of or inability to find or retain employment); (4) grief over ruptured relationships (e.g., fights with parents or partners); and (5) excessive rage, anger, or hostility."

Of these categories, individuals with the motive for suicide based upon 2, 3, or 5 might represent good candidates for SbC attempts (Oyster, 2001). The SbC subject attempts to regain control to reduce their defeat by "winning" a confrontation or to express their rage against an authority figure (Hutson et al., 1998). The subject's choice of suicide method represents a convergence of cultural and personal significance. A particular suicidal method may serve as a form of personal communication and meet social needs (Hendin, 1995).

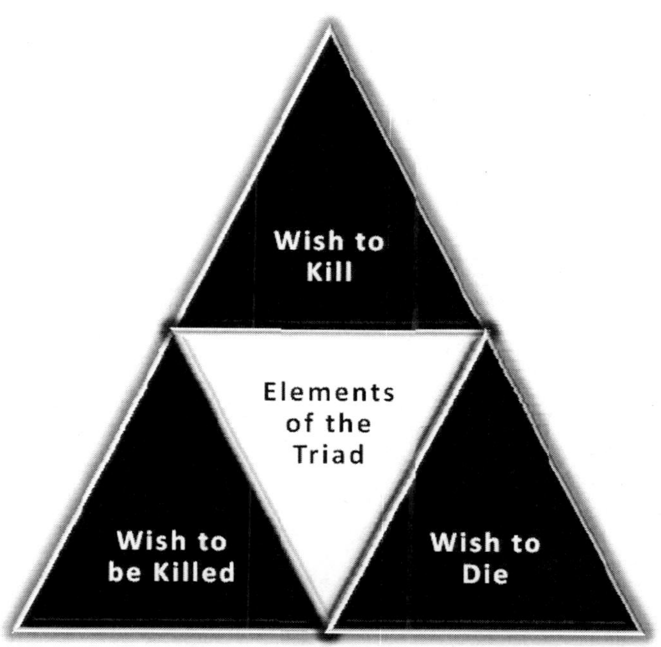

Figure 5-1. Karl Menninger's Self-Destructive & Self-Annihilating Persons
(Adapted from Menninger, 1938)

Hutson et al. (1998) cited typologies and cases developed from domestic violence, offenders confronting lengthy prison sentences, subjects with a history of alcohol or drug abuse, and individuals with psychiatric or suicidal behaviors. Homant et al. (2000) separated planned versus unplanned scenarios that led to the dangerousness of the incidents. The other distinction concerns emotionally disturbed persons versus normal criminal offenders. Dangerousness would serve as a primary factor in the negotiation or conflict resolution. The criminal population offers more opportunities for successful remedies than the emotionally disturbed population.

Homant and Kennedy (2001) provided excellent research in the major categories of SbC. Their review of 143 incidents of SbC revealed three major categories, and each of these categories contained two to four subtypes. Refer to figure 5-2 for an examination of the major SbC categories.

Research by Maris (1992) indicated that the primary reasons for those suicide completers were loss of a job, children, or spouse. The reason for nonfatal suicide attempts were mental illness, drug abuse, and interpersonal problems. In addition, 50% of the completed suicides did not have close friends. Social isolation increases the risk of suicide because of the need for social and human interaction. Moreover, this high-risk group had fewer opportunities for rescue by family and friends.

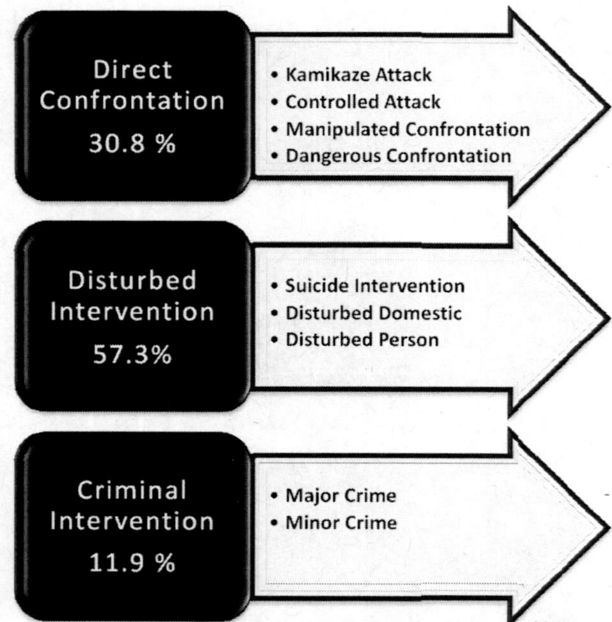

Figure 5-2. Major Categories of Suicide by Cop
(Adapted from Homant & Kennedy, 2001)

Lord (2001) research results indicated many SbC subjects began their own suicidal attempt, but rapidly reversed their actions and displaced the act to the responding officer(s). The combination of the SbC subject's past experience with the police, and the prior police interaction may play an important role in the suicidal outcome. The level of danger and perception of the officer can influence the response, if the prior offenses were minor. However, if the offenses were serious felonies and violence was a factor, the officer response may be different concerning the level of the use force. When events are unfolding rapidly without warning, the officer's opportunity for deadly force is the more likely response.

The perception of the officer heightens the arousal factor for the officer dealing with individuals with mental health problems. In addition, Lord found that SbC subjects with mental health problems frequently have schizophrenia or bipolar disorder. Monahan (1992) indicated in his research that persons who met the criteria for a diagnosis of schizophrenia, major depression, or mania/bipolar disorder were six times more likely to be violent than people without any diagnosis. Individuals with mental disorders are extremely difficult to negotiate with in many cases.

The following characteristics contribute to SbC attempts (Oyster, 2001), if there are clusters of frustrated needs satisfied by suicide (Shneidman, 1996): (1) frustrated control (when the individual feels that they cannot control their life, but can exert some control over their deaths); (2) avoidance of shame, defeat, or humiliation; and (3) excessive rage, anger, or hostility. Individuals who commit SbC do so to regain control, to reduce their defeat by "winning" a confrontation, or to express their rage against an authority figure (Hutson et al., 1998).

Grieving Officer Symptoms

This kind of shooting generates severe mixed emotional reactions. The officer(s) may feel guilt, betrayal, and sympathy for the deceased. Police officer grieving takes many forms. The grief concerns the victim, the loss of self-esteem, and the former sense of power and control over events. Doka (1989) acknowledged the concept of "disenfranchised grief," which entertains the notion that the reaction of the police officer to SbC or the victim precipitated death. Refer to Table 5-2 for examples of "disenfranchised grief." It includes the following manifestations.

Critical Incident Intervention

During any critical incident there is the opportunity for trauma, and the SbC incident is no exception. Police shootings of any kind invite trauma. Early definitions originating from the combat experience include shell shock, war neurosis, combat fatigue, combat stress reaction, and combat trauma. The officer involved in the SbC may experience a similar trauma response.

Therefore, police shootings, regardless of legal culpability, require a mental health intervention. The intervention should include the following components: (1) immediacy, (2) proximity, (3) expectancy, (4) brevity, and (5) accessibility (Allen, 2004; Lord, 2004; Monahan, 2001; Mullins, 2001). Intervention programs proceed through six distinct mental health stages. Refer to Table 5-3 for an illustration of the intervention components.

Table 5-2. Disenfranchised Grief (Adapted from Doka, 1989)

The *loss* is not recognized or acknowledged. Officer's peers or supervisors may not recognize incident as true incident of Loss. It is, however, very real to the officer

The *relationship* is not recognized. Relationship developed between the individual challenging officer and officer attempting to diffuse the situation.

The *griever* is not recognized. Grief officer experiences may not be recognized. Officer's actions may be thought of as a "normal" part of the duties and an essential part of protecting the officer's own life.

Death itself is disenfranchised (not recognized). Victim-precipitated homicide may be viewed as a suicide, its impact upon the officer may not be recognized or it may be devalued.

The *manner* in which individuals grieve may not be recognized. There may be culturally unacceptable actions, or there may be institutional patterns of grief. Demonstrating emotional vulnerability may not be an acceptable part of the invulnerable image that is desired.

(Table Adapted from Doka, 1989)

Table 5-3. Intervention Components (Adapted from Allen, 2004)

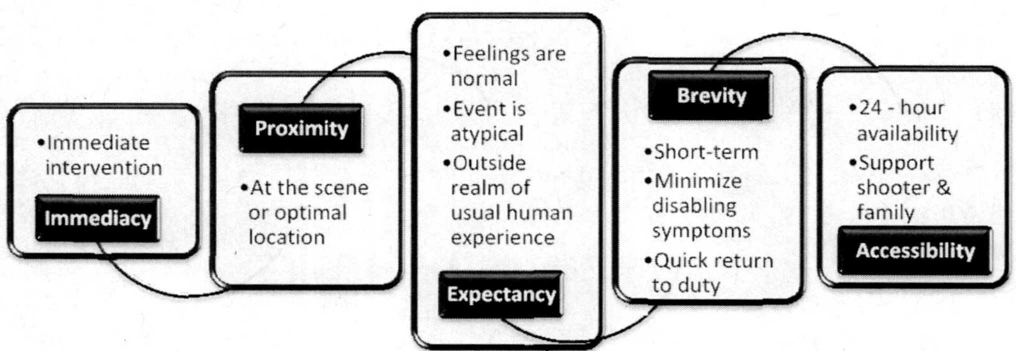

Group Debriefing

Group debriefings are most effective if several officers witness traumatic events like a police shooting. Incidents like SbC fall into that category as well other cataclysms, crises, and catastrophe emergency responses. Debriefing allows participants to vent their emotions, seek clarification, and emotionally bond.

Most important, it provides a confidential psycho-educational opportunity to explain the role of trauma. Group debriefing assists officers who are experiencing trauma in the recovery process. The optimal response takes place in less than first seventy-two hours. Early intervention is the optimal goal. Group debriefing should follow a general format (Allen, 2004; Lord, 2001; Mitchell, 1983). Refer to Table 5-4 for an examination of the various stages of the group debriefing process.

Post-trauma events from SbC incidents vary from officer to officer. Reactions range from minor, transient vegetative, to suicidal behavior. Immediate intervention offers the best opportunity for optimal response. Timing is of the utmost importance for an intervention to be successful. Some officers are not responsive to debriefing immediately after the event, and some will not benefit from it at all. SbC is a high-level critical incident for police officers. The goal is to facilitate the officer's sense of personal control and make the transition from hypercritical shooter to a competent and emotionally intact person (Allen, 2004).

Table 5-4. Four Stages of Group Debriefing
(Adapted from Allen, 2004; Lord, 2001; Mitchell, 1983)

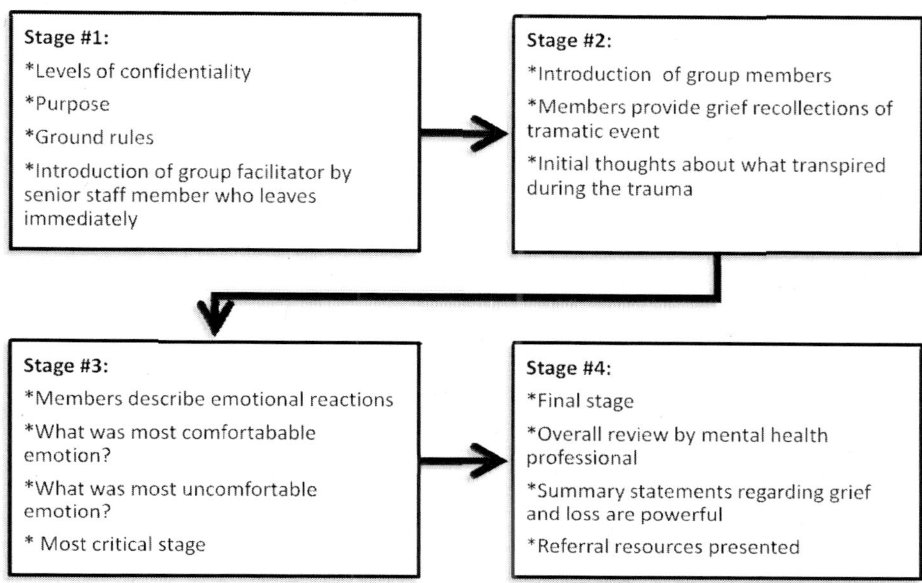

Crisis Intervention Management Strategies

SbC is an abnormal and critical event. Many of the protocols and training programs regarding SbC apply to PTSD intervention and treatment. Critical incidents similar to SbC require special leadership attention.

Generally, the most important internal work stressors do not receive the attention they deserve. Police leaders are reluctant to change management and leadership styles. Changes in police training could reduce the possibility of stress reactions to SbC critical incidents, and police administrators are starting to recognize that stress reduction is an important critical incident management strategy.

Keram and Farrell (2001) noted several training program requirements: (1) senior police administrators provide training programs and SbC incident-based protocols, (2) middle managers identify the SbC training needs for field officers and dispatchers, (3) the content of training programs includes information on the causes and effects of SbC incidents, and (4) the follow-up training units address training in tactical and post-event strategies.

Provide field training for police officers that educate the cause and effects of SbC, or suicide by proxy. The tactical training would emphasize pre-event and post-event operational strategies. The after-action response would deal with analysis and support for those officers involved in the debriefing.

The family part of the SbC conflict is a neglected area of responsibility. There is a tendency on the part of family members to close ranks and support the officer. They may be so concerned about the officer that they neglect their own emotional health. This eventually has family consequences, as the stress and tension continue to escalate. The family is subject to implosion, if the psychological and counseling issues remain unattended.

The police agency should support the officer in every way possible. The media release should portray the officer as a person who has his own feelings to deal with in the aftermath. Every attempt should be made to coordinate respectfully with the families.

Police coordination includes contact with mental health professionals that fulfills administrative, management responsibilities, or have expertise in dealing with suicides. This liaison involves collaboration, planning, and problem-solving strategies. The department's mental health counselors should participate and attend the SbC training sessions.

Routine procedures require performing post-incident psychological autopsies on the precipitators of the police-shooting incident. Data collection is an important first step toward building a local database. In addition, it allows appropriate incidents to be classified as SbC, or proxy suicide shootings. In the following case study Prial (2001) cited an excellent SbC case scenario and the consequences for the officer involved.

Case Study Illustration

A highway patrol officer traveling eastbound on a busy expressway at approximately 10:30 p.m. during a rain and snowstorm in the winter of 1997 noticed a green vehicle driving erratically at a high rate of speed.

When the officer pulled the car over, the driver exited and waved his arms around. The officer told the driver over the loudspeaker to return to his car, but the person was not responding to his commands. The driver pulled a silver revolver from his waistband and waved it in the air.

The officer commanded him to drop the gun, radioed a call to the dispatcher as a "man with a gun," and then took cover behind his marked patrol car while drawing his weapon. A second patrol officer noticed this situation from the service road, stopped, exited his car, and advanced toward the driver.

The second officer also commanded the driver to "drop the gun," whereupon the driver turned and advanced toward the second officer, pointing his gun at him. The second officer fired several shots, but the individual continued to advance toward him. The first officer fired two shots and the second officer fired three more until the driver fell to the ground. As the second officer approached the driver to check his pulse, he noticed the gun was a toy.

The follow-up investigation revealed the deceased was a 19-year-old white male who left eleven suicide notes at the scene: one was addressed "To the Officer who shot me!" He told his friends the previous evening, "Tomorrow I'm going to get pulled over, have a fake gun, and have the police kill me." Prior to puling him over, the police received calls concerning a green vehicle on the highway as a possible DWI and a man with a gun in the vehicle.

Imagine you are a police officer who has just been involved in a deadly force situation. An individual pointed a gun at you, necessitating that you shoot and kill the person holding the gun. You followed the correct training procedures and protocols. You call for backup and, upon its arrival, you are taken to the hospital for evaluation.

After a doctor's examination for ringing in the ears, you are escorted to your own precinct house for questioning by homicide detectives. Your heart is still racing, your blood pressure elevated, your hands are sweating, and you cannot seem to stop trembling. A thousand different thoughts are rushing through your mind at once. The investigators remove your service weapon as evidence for firearms identification examination.

Separated from your partner and others involved in the shooting, you are now interrogated by your own department's detectives. They are asking you to recount, in precise detail, the most terrifying moments of your life; when you came face to face with imminent death. You feel numb and unfocused. You wonder how this happened and more important, what will occur next.

Source: This case study was adapted from Elizabeth M. Prial (2001), Department of Justice publication, 2001.

Special Note: While this is the classic SbC case, many are more difficult to identify. Each officer reacts differently. Some officers have an immediate emotional response, while other officers have a delayed response of a year or more. The officer may begin to express doubts about the way he responded, and his own expertise. There is a need for acceptance by others and to repeat and vent their personal tragedy. The recurring pain and flashbacks may lead to PTSD.

Focus Points

In SbC cases, the offender recruits an unknowing police officer to assist in a planned suicide. Other common terminology for this kind of suicidal behavior includes victim-precipitated homicide, officer-assisted suicide, and copicide.

SbC initiators share a number of characteristics of persons who commit suicide alone. Once police officers arrive on the scene, SbC initiators may try to shift the responsibility for their own deaths to the police. Many of them have prior negative experiences with law enforcement and are suffering from anger, depression, and other mental disorders.

Everyone focuses on the investigation. They do not observe the sense of loss and psychological harm to the police officer. This is not just a routine event for the officer; the loss, grief, and harm are genuine.

Police leaders and peers may witness an SbC shooting, but not observe the consequences to the officer. The grieving officer may be lost in the shuffle of the paperwork. Leaders need to see, listen, observe, and open the door to facilitate communication and feedback.

SbC subjects are capable of changing direction from suicide to homicide quickly, killing or causing severe injury to the officer. When police officers under sudden attack have few options, deadly force becomes the reasonable course of action. The psychological aftermath of this type of incident may become very unreasonable, and the aftercare program should provide the support.

In some instances, the officer will be able to isolate and contain the SbC until assistance arrives. Trained hostage negotiators may resolve the incident without the use force. Time is generally on the side of the hostage negotiators; it allows them to reduce emotional conflict and start the communication process. In some instance persons will not submit to authority and take their own lives during the last minutes of the ordeal.

SbC is a high priority traumatic episode with the potential for serious consequences for an officer and family members. The involved critical incident officer may experience guilt and undergo a post-traumatic stress reaction.

Senior police administrators provide training programs and SbC incident-based protocols. Middle managers identify the SbC training needs for field officers and dispatchers. Leaders need to see, observe, and open the door to communication and feedback.

Conclusion

Suicides with weapons add to the stressful equation. At the top of the list are police shootings, in particular the death of an innocent person. In the case of SbC, the deception or trick multiplies additional anger directed inward. The secondary victim is wearing a police uniform, badge, and weapon.

PART III
POLICE GUIDE POST BEHAVIORS

Leadership Foundations	Guidepost Behaviors
• **Identify the leadership crisis intervention strategy requirements.**	• Leaders plan specific interventions using the appropriate questions and applying the **QPR** training program, which involves ***questioning, persuading and referring.***
• **Leaders identify obstacles that impede obtaining help, counseling assistance and treatment.**	• Leaders **assess the police culture and organization** for obstacles to receiving assistance for suicide, depression and post-traumatic stress disorder.
• **Police leaders identify the proper resources: primary, secondary and tertiary modes of assistance to police officers and civilian dispatchers.**	• Police leaders provide assistance concerning the **primary resources:** (1) police training and critical incident simulations. **Secondary resources** include: (1) crisis management programs and (2) debriefing support system. **Tertiary resources** include counseling support systems, cognitive therapy, and other treatment modalities.
• **Police leaders identify and coordinate resources for suicide intervention and treatment.**	• **Counselors provide treatment modalities:** (1) crisis counseling, (2) group therapy counseling, (3) cognitive behavioral therapy, (4) reality therapy and (5) various other high tech behavioral approaches.
• **Police leaders provide training for peer support program. This activity encourages access to intervention, counseling and treatment.**	• **Peer leadership objectives include:** (1) training peer support leaders, (2) quality instruction on focused listening skills, (3) focusing on what the officer is communicating and (4) building trust and rapport skills.

CHAPTER 6

POLICE LEADERSHIP: CRISIS INTERVENTION STRATEGIES

"Mentor: Someone whose hindsight can become your foresight."
— Unknown

John was a 38-year-old deputy sheriff who was having domestic difficulties with his wife. One evening an argument erupted over separation and divorce. During the dispute, Robert pulled his service revolver out, and sat down on the bed. His intent was clearly to commit suicide; his wife immediately requested assistance. His friends and fellow deputies responded, and a long intervention ensued.

The agency psychologist arrived at the scene and requested the Commander of the Crisis Negotiation Team to respond. The team members engaged the deputy in a long de-escalation and problem-solving sequence negotiations. After several hours, the crisis was over. John was now in a safe place and received the help he needed.

John was on light duty during his recovery and eventually recovered his former emotional stamina. John's optimism improved, he eventually remarried, and appears happy. John received a ten-year service award from his law enforcement agency.

Source: This case study was adapted from James S. Herndon (2001), Department of Justice publication.

Generally, police officers view a crisis as an external community matter. The focus is on the outside, not the inside. The enemy from within goes unnoticed; this is especially the case when denial is involved. Many officers do not know how to recognize the symptom of stress or suicidal ideation in themselves or others. Therefore, they may not be in a position to lead or mentor during an internal crisis. The above case study is an excellent example of the appropriate leadership response and proper deployment of resources.

Chapter Focus

This chapter explores basic concepts of leadership intervention strategies. It defines the cluster of warning signs and appropriate intervention questions. Moreover, it endeavors to explain the Question, Persuade, and Referring (QPR) Training Program, post-intervention supervision, and the role of peer support. The case study is an illustration and application of the underlying social dynamics.

Overview

Police supervisors require training to recognize suicidal warning signs. Formal suicide prevention training helps facilitate successful interventions. The police sergeant is in a unique position as a supervisor to demonstrate human relations and leadership skills necessary to take action.

Comprehensive training integrates suicide-warning signs as a component of the department's mental health program. Diminished performance and increased irritability may signal a major depressive episode. Persistent irritation, a tendency to respond to events with angry outbursts, and blaming others over minor events often indicate possible psychological distress.

The behavioral pattern is consistent and persistent over time, not a onetime incident. The officer is not having a bad day, but his overall climate concerns and alerts daily observers. About 75% of suicidal individuals give notice of their intentions (Grollman, 1988). The early warning signs must be recognized and treated as a serious form of communication. The officer may make covert statements similar to… " They don't need to worry about me anymore." Passive warning signs are more difficult to detect. Moreover, the denial factor may overlook serious statements made by police officers.

Depression Warning Signs

Observant law enforcement leaders recognize a cluster of warning signs that trigger intervention: (1) recent loss, (2) sadness, (3) frustration, (4) disappointment, (5) grief, (6) alienation, (7) depression, (8) loneliness, (9) physical pain, (10) mental anguish, and (11) mental illness. As mentioned previously, the strongest behavioral warning sign is an attempted suicide. Generally, the more recent the attempt the higher the risk factor for the officer.

Depression is a form of sadness and apprehension; feelings of worthlessness and guilt; withdrawal from others; and changes in patterns of sleep, appetite, and sexual desire. The most confusing part for leaders assessing depression in officers is that the symptoms may include lethargy or agitation. The most concerning part of depression is the dominant role it plays in suicide (DSM-IV-TR, 2000).

Supervisors should look for background histories that might include suicidal behavior, mental illness, chronic depression, multiple divorces, and alcoholism. Significant loss, drug abuse, and stress overload also contribute to the crisis. Older officers experiencing mounting medical concerns or facing impending retirement feel that they may become socially isolated and somehow incapacitated. Physical and social losses can generate the destructive feelings of hopelessness and helplessness (Schwartz and Schwartz, 1991).

Potentially suicidal officers may deliberately expose themselves to unnecessary danger, often recognized as bravery by other officers and even rewarded by the department. However, their unconscious intent may be to die "in the line of duty." High-risk behaviors may be quite purposeful and deadly.

Generally, the more recent the suicidal attempt, the higher the risk factor for the officer involved. Police leaders and supervisors need to assess significant distress or impairment in social and occupational performances during the conduct of police responsibilities. Follow-up interviews are helpful when the officer can be described as depressed, sad, hopeless, discouraged, or "down in the pits of despair."

During this interview, the supervisor should check the officer's body language, look for sad facial expressions, and be alert to a flat mood. The officer might complain of feeling down, not having any feelings at all, or being anxious. Complaints about bodily aches and pains are a cover-up for the officer's true feelings.

Supervisors should look for histories that include family suicidal behavior, mental illness, chronic depression, multiple divorces, and alcoholism. Look for the losses in the officer's life, drug abuse patterns, and stress overload (Schwartz and Schwartz, 1991). Intervention is possible if leaders take the time to notice and react to the telltale behaviors.

Specific Intervention Strategies

Most officers have mixed emotions about committing suicide, and suicidal feelings tend to be episodic, often coming and going in waves. Troubled officers want to be rescued, but do not want to ask for assistance or know what specific help to request. This state of confusion actually works to a supervisor's advantage because suicidal officers want a strong authority figure to direct their emotional traffic and make sense of the confusion. Therefore, supervisors should quickly assure suicidal officers that support and assistance is available (Baker and Baker, 1996).

The situational leadership style that applies here is one of directing and telling (Baker, 2005b; Hersey et al., 2008). Officers in a suicidal state of mind are open to suggestion and are likely to respond to direction. Supervisors must use their relationship and authority to tell officers what action they expect. Furthermore, supervisors should insist that officers respond to their directions.

The specific methods of intervention require preparation to avoid violence directed inward or outward at other employees. Without careful planning, officers confronted by supervisors could react unpredictably. Because their thought processes are garbled, they could strike out at coworkers, supervisors, or family members, resulting in a homicide followed by suicide. Even if that does not occur, a real danger of suicide exists at the point of intervention.

Timely identification of at-risk officers is the first step in a successful intervention program. What are some common behavioral patterns an interventionist might identify as potentially significant? Generally, a long trail of evidence typically leads to the final act, but there are cases that occur suddenly and are a total surprise.

Most suicidal individuals experience a suicidal episode only once in their lives (Grollman, 1988). It may last days, hours, minutes, or seconds. If you can stop them with appropriate intervention, they probably will not kill themselves in the future. Some of course will, but most will not if they can get past the crisis. Some officers see themselves as unable to alter their situations in a meaningful manner. When they reach this point, they often take action. Supervisors should listen carefully for expressions of these feelings.

The sergeant or lieutenant initiating the intervention process may save a life. Suicidal police officers act when their lives are devoid of hope. The officer charged with corruption and scandal probably feels rather hopeless in the face of that kind of adversity. The finality of the act of suicide may serve as a technique to restore control and reduce feelings of hopelessness.

A police officer is only of value to the living, not the dead. Officers cannot solve their suicidal problems alone. They need immediate intervention. Many of these officers spend a great deal of their time and emotional reserve helping others in tragic circumstances, but cannot seek help themselves.

Therefore, it is important that the supervisor quickly assure the suicidal officer that he or she is definitely capable of rendering support and assistance. The supervisor should do something that directly interrupts the cycle of suicidal ideation. Asking the right questions sets up the appropriate intervention and referral.

Appropriate Questions

An individual contemplating suicide is not in the position to make appropriate decisions. The officer is asking the supervisor to make decisions for them. To make these decisions, police managers and supervisors have to ask the basic questions. This is not a time or delegating ...it is the time for direction, support, and action! Do no leave the officer alone if he or she is having suicidal thoughts. Threats require appropriate action to solve the problem. Others may not have heard the officer's request for help. So it is up to supervisors to ask the right questions and take the appropriate actions.

You do not have to be a psychologist or counselor to help an officer contemplating suicide. The QPR system offers three bold steps to a realistic approach to police suicide intervention. The first step requires clarification of suicidal communications, the second step involves persuading the officer in crisis to accept help, and the third step refers the officer to the appropriate resource (LeBuffe, 2000). The QPR training course is available on the Internet for first crisis intervention responders.

Law enforcement agencies might consider QPR as a suicide gatekeeper program. The idea promotes the concept of being "your brother's keeper." Leaders and officers serve as observers of signs and symptoms of emotional distress (Ramos, 2008). This straightforward, easy-to-learn program prepares officers to work in a preventative mode rather than giving a reactive and late response. The QPR program seeks to avoid unnecessary stress and trauma and related feeling of distress. QPR is part of the new Badge of Life program (O'Hara, 2008).

Many leaders find it difficult to ask the basic suicide questions. Officers who indicate they are having suicidal thoughts need a caring response. Other people might not have heard their pleas for help. Supervisors should plan their intervention so that it leads to a professional referral.

Asking key suicide questions opens the door to helping the officer. The first question is: Are you thinking about hurting or killing yourself? How can I help you? is the subsequent follow-up question. Framing the questions in a straightforward manner is more likely to get a truthful answer. If you get an ambiguous answer, repeat the question in a compassionate manner; for example, "I really would like to help you get past these feelings." Suicidal officers may actually feel relieved that someone broaches the subject. Refer to Figure 6-1 for a general overview of the helping process.

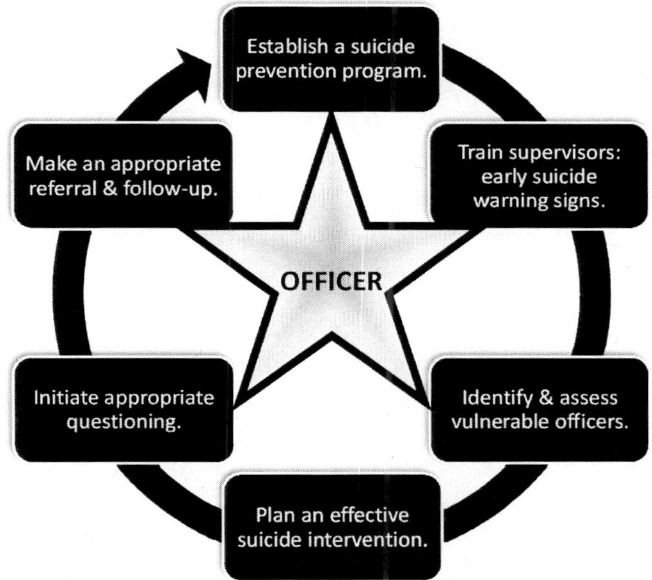

Figure 6-1. Suicide Intervention Strategies

Planned supervision and intervention should concentrate on the assessment of specific behaviors that lead to a professional referral. As a group, police officers and supervisors have often protected those experiencing depression. Do not accept the notion that you cannot confront the problem because of the officer's employment. Supervisors or peers are not being disloyal when they help an officer in distress.

Supervisors should refer officers to a certified mental health professional, even setting appointments and arranging for officers to appear. The department's responsibility does not end after the referral. Supervisors should monitor the situation to ensure that officers receive continued support and counseling.

The suicidal officer needs his leader's help and support. The proper referral and follow-up is essential to a successful outcome. Berent (1981) recommended follow-up aftercare postvention to prevent the return of morbid cognitions. This allows continued communication, observation, and opportunities to assess flat emotional affect and suicidal ideation. The follow-up process assists in developing mastery over complicated family and social relationships. The support allows officers the opportunity to return to employment; eliminate stressors; and reinforce creative problem-solving techniques.

Leadership Program Management

A team effort may save lives, and avoids squandering valuable human resources.

Police suicides can occur without warning, leaving family members very surprised. Perhaps the signs were subtle and family and friends did not identify the clues. The blame may shift to survivors, generally a spouse, and this compounds the trauma to family members. There is a tendency for survivors to become defensive, isolated, and distrustful of the police.

Police agencies need to provide accurate information and maintain a rapport with the family. Survivors need to feel they are still part of the police family because they need the emotional support. New York City Patrolman's Association Members Assistance Program (MAP), Manhattan Counseling, and Psychotherapy Associates initiated a training program with guidelines for the selection of peer support officers.

Insightful programming is the starting point; however, without trust and feedback suicide prevention programs will not reach the officers who need help. The Johari Window is a useful model for achieving the goals and objectives of excellent programming. Numerous programs are advocated, but the scientific assessment of those goals and objectives are rare events. There is the tendency to label a program successful when federal, state, and private funding may not continue otherwise.

Leadership: Mentoring Process

How can one be an effective leader and mentor? Police leaders who "take care of their officers," shape a positive social climate, lead from the front, and remain candid. Leaders who successfully show concern for the development and mental health of their officers mentor well. This means being an approachable leader who is willing to establish rapport and communicate with officers.

Approaching the officer in emotional turmoil requires tact and diplomacy, not force or intimidation. The objective is to gain voluntary compliance, understanding, and insight into the officer's point of view. This is not the time for imposing negativity, but providing a helpful presence and the right words. The nonverbal physical demeanor of the peer leader reflects concern for the officer. The verbal approach is that of reason and logic.

Expressing concern about the welfare of the officer is the first step. Thompson and Walker (2007) suggested three secrets to presenting options successfully: (1) present your option or options in a friendly and helpful voice, (2) be specific about the desired outcome, and (3) always present positive options. These three basic strategies may open the door to active listening and the helping process.

Peer Communication Link

Innovative peer programs and proactive training can provide a separate chain of thought that saves police officers lives. Peers are in the best position to see the two chains of thought interconnect, because they stand in the ideal intersection to direct emotional traffic. This can be done effectively if the peer officers understand the red flag behaviors of suicide.

Fear of losing the shield and service weapon presents an administrative block to receiving officer assistance. The communication from peers requires a reassuring approach, which encourages referral to counseling and therapy. The facts will flow logically after the officer has the opportunity to vent his emotions. The trained peer leader that recognizes the reaction to stress and trauma may facilitate the intervention process and provide an opening for communication and conflict resolution of the officer's anxiety.

The peer leader and officer must remain partners. A positive bond is essential to the recovery process. Training peer leaders to recognize the role of stress and officers who have experienced traumatic events is a police survival strategy. Police policy and protocols provide the guidance from police leaders; peer leaders deal directly with the human issues. The best of the peer leaders come from those who have been there and understand the emotional components of survival.

Police peer leaders are in the ideal position to identify other officers in emotional turmoil. The backup call is a strategic encounter for observing peers under stress. When an officer response to call for service is inappropriate—that is an alert red flag. Unfortunately, some peers rationalize that the officer is having a bad day, even when the pattern is obvious. Peer denial and personal friendship can delay the help that is desperately necessary to save a life.

Peer leaders are active listeners that intervene and manage conflict in a professional manner. What does active or focused listening mean? It means careful listening by leaders for the underlying as well as the obvious message. The first chain of thought for the peer leader is empathy and focused listening. The second chain of thought is trust and confidence on the part of the officer. The approximate interconnection of peer leader and police officer communication provides the necessary feedback to prevail in this lifesaving event.

The two most important outcomes of peer stress and suicide training are the ability to empathize, and establishing a rapport with police officers. The peer officer or helper recognizes the basic techniques of interviewing and acknowledges the unique needs of each officer. The peer helper is able to set the person at ease. His intervention with sufficient listening skills and nonthreatening body language will achieve interpersonal communication.

Peer Active Listening Strategies

Focus on what the officer is communicating. Avoid the interrogation or hostile approach, and acknowledge the stress and anxiety. Feedback is vital to listening because it ensures communication. One way of implementing feedback is for the peer leader to rephrase the officer's comments. Rephrasing allows the peer leader to validate the response. This technique may take time, but clarifies communication and enhances rapport.

Avoid sympathizing with the officer by attempting to feel like him or her, but empathize or understand the social dynamics of the situation. The former means the loss of objectivity, the latter develops the officer's point of view or position. Focused or active listening is the best means to prevent miscommunication.

Active listening includes postponing judgment until the "speaker" has many opportunities to express feelings and concerns. While this technique has some risks, both parties benefit with increased rapport and communication. Simply stated, you cannot listen if you are talking. Listening well requires concentration and, at times risk, but the payoffs are worth the outcome (Baker, 2005a).

Herndon's (2001) insightful article about law enforcement suicide has numerous case study illustrations. The following case study is an illustration of a positive intervention.

Case Study Illustration

David was a 34-year-old K-9 deputy who loved his job. A deputy for approximately nine years, he had struggled repeatedly with relationship difficulties. He needed to be in a relationship; his self-esteem suffered when he was not involved. One evening in February, David became despondent over the breakup of his most recent affair.

He called his bother (a deputy sheriff and supervisor with the same agency) and intimated that he felt so dejected that suicide seemed like the only way to end his misery. His brother immediately called for assistance from the agency psychologist. David in crisis sought immediate admittance to an inpatient facility under special arrangements. His treatment for situational depression started immediately.

David experienced excellent follow-up supervision in his treatment progress. His service included light duty with responsibilities at an absolute minimum. Few actually knew of his ordeal. In a few months, David appeared to be back to normal emotionally and he stated that the whole process was an important learning experience. The deputy is presently in a healthy interpersonal relationship, purchased a new home, and is planning marriage.

Source: This case was adapted from James S. Herndon (2001), Department of Justice publication.

Special Note: In this case, the respect and trust issues unfolded right from the beginning. His relationship with his brother was candid; the rank as supervisor may have played some role. The deputy's interpersonal skills in personal relationships were a triggering event, but the baseline depression remained the first priority. Once depression is treated, irritability, anger, and rage are less likely to interfere in personal relationships. Suicidal ideation symptoms and personal relationships can be controlled with the proper medication.

The lessons for police leaders and supervisors are obvious. Police officers will not communicate their worst fears to those they do not respect and trust. The threatening posture will only aggravate the situation. Denial of the potential for suicide only delays the needed help and assistance.

Focus Points

Police supervisors require training to recognize suicide warning signs, and comprehensive training integrates these signs. Passive warning signs are difficult to detect. Generally, the more recent the suicidal attempt, the higher the risk factor for the officer involved.

Look for the losses in the officer's life, drug abuse patterns, and stress overload.

Supervisors should listen carefully for expressions of suicidal feelings. The officer may act when his life is devoid of hope. Potentially suicidal officers may deliberately expose themselves to unnecessary danger.

Tell the officer what you expect and demand that the officer respond to your directions. Do something that directly interrupts the cycle of suicidal ideation. Asking the right questions sets up the appropriate intervention and referral.

Police officers experience a considerable amount of conflict on the job. The conflict is interpersonal, and their wants and needs are incompatible with others such as leaders, peers, and rules and regulations.

The stress generated from the daily events is multiplied by street-encountered stressful events, and there is little rest in the stress cycle.

Competitive relationships are common in police agencies and frequently cause stress at work and in family life as well as in other social settings.

Denial is a major survival strategy for police officers; it works in the short-term, but fails long-term. Police officers must believe they can survive and control the risks. The truth remains that police officers cannot control the risks. Denial of fear becomes a part of the police survival equation; you can become cynical, but not afraid.

Peer support leaders are essential to assisting officers in trouble, and are at the crossroads of the emotional traffic. Police officers that consider seeking help are more likely to reach out to someone they know and trust. They can serve as the conduit for coordination, trust, and referral to counseling and treatment. Peer support provides the critical link and lifeline for police officers to a variety of special programs and the police chaplain.

If the officer receives help, the individual may develop into a better officer. Seeking help is not the end of a career, but the start of improving an old career. Asking for help is not a sign of weakness, but one of strength. The overwhelming majority of suicidal officers do not want to die. The typical officer wants to be rescued, but does not want or know how to ask for assistance. Many are not certain how to address the plea for help and the officer does not know what he wants done. This state of confusion actually works to the advantage of the police leaders because the suicidal officer is looking for a strong authority figure to direct this emotional traffic.

Conclusion

When an officer pulls a weapon from its holster and threatens to use it to commit suicide, "the process" in is the advanced stages. Someone must break the silence of denial, take action, and stop the chain of events. An appropriate intervention is possible during a specific period, but denial plays a key role in the delay of assistance. Police officers must stop pretending that the problem of police suicide does not exist or that it will go away on its own (Baker and Baker, 1995).

CHAPTER 7

COUNSELING: CRISIS INTERVENTION STRATEGIES

"If thou are pained by any external thing, it is not this thing that disturbs thee, but thine own judgment about it. And it is in thy power to wipe out this judgment now."

— Marcus Aurelius

Robert was a 27-year-old deputy sheriff with approximately 2 years of service. Robert's relationship difficulties drove him to the point of threatening suicide with a knife. His girlfriend wanted out of the relationship. Robert became despondent. He put a kitchen knife to his neck; his girlfriend fled the apartment and called for help. The agency staff psychologist arrived to talk him out of taking his own life and personally transported him to a crisis center. Robert received support counseling and proper follow-up.

He responded appropriately. Robert eventually was able to heal his relationship difficulties, and improved his emotional strength to deal with life's disappointments. Unfortunately, he lost his position as deputy sheriff in the law enforcement agency for violating several policies; however, he survived to seek other employment.

Source: This case was adapted from James S. Herndon (2001) Department of Justice publication.

Counseling service referral is a controversial topic with police officers. Visiting a counselor is an emotional and sensitive issue. The referral process may cause additional turmoil, and the fear of a "rubber gun squad" assignment is another significant trauma. The loss of status among one's peers is a major deterrent to seeking counseling assistance. In the eyes of police officers, seeing a counselor means their self-esteem is under direct attack.

Chapter Focus

This chapter explores the role of crisis intervention strategies. Moreover, it defines several intervention techniques and discusses cognitive treatment modalities. The case study illustrates the need for counseling and cognitive therapy that includes: (1) appraising irrational thinking, (2) crisis counseling, and (3) the underlying psychological and social dynamics.

Overview

The biggest obstacle preventing police officers from seeking help for stress and suicidal ideation is the fear that personal disclosure will damage their careers. Police officers fear their association with counselors and psychiatrists (Janik and Kravitz, 1994). The notion of peers knowing about their time "in treatment" creates professional and personal difficulties for officers. The principal challenge for the counselor and mental health official is the lack of acceptance encountered while attempting to evaluate officers at risk.

Mental health attitudes change and constantly require addressing by police organizations due to the high levels of trauma exposure. The high cost of traumatic exposure requires a shifting emphasis to primary prevention. Research needs to address ways to increase resiliency to trauma, promoting successful adjustment, and counteracting negative consequences (Amaranto et al., 2003). This requires an assessment of police culture and a change in philosophy to include the utilization of primary, secondary, and tertiary resources. Refer to Figure 7-1 for an example of police prevention resourcing.

Critical incident simulation offers one promising primary prevention strategy. Arnetz et al. (2009) achieved positive results in their controlled study of trauma resilience training. They concluded that "our imagery and skills training intervention provides incremental utility above police training as usual in enhancing performance and attenuating stress responses in police during critical incident simulations. The critical incident simulation was a potent and realistic paradigm for inducing occupational stress and testing effects of our intervention. Therefore, our trauma resilience training intervention for police should transport readily to implementation in the field of police work."

The treatments for PTSD and marginal exposure include secondary prevention interventions such as critical incident stress debriefings. The purpose is to allow officers to express and discuss their reaction immediately after exposure to a critical incident. Moreover, the post-incident debriefing is supported by many police agencies.

However, debriefing and psychological interventions have limited research-randomized designs in the literature. Limited reviews and published papers suggested the inadequate effectiveness of these interventions (Feldner et al., 2007). Coordination and cooperation between police officials and researchers is necessary.

Figure 7-1. Primary, Secondary and Tertiary Resources
(Adapted from Amaranto, et al., 2003)

Tertiary treatment modalities for PTSD such as cognitive processing therapy are empirically supported in the literature. Unfortunately, the police, for the reasons stated previously, under utilize these tertiary approaches to intervention. The benefits for police agencies, officers, and their families require acknowledgment by leaders. The stigma and labels are inappropriate for those who seek help.

Crisis Counseling

Crisis counseling refers to a short duration, even just one session, which is similar to short-term psychotherapy. The effectiveness of crisis counseling has considerable support, especially if the focus is on a particular situation or problem. For a general review and discussion concerning short-term psychotherapy and its effectiveness, refer to the research of Crits-Cristoph and Barber (1991). For a discussion of techniques for integrating behavioral counseling techniques for disaster survivors refer to the research of Stricker and Gold (1993).

The goal of crisis counseling and short-term psychotherapy is to focus on a specific problem and restore the officer's functioning in a few short sessions. Therapeutic techniques include supportive listening, normalization of reaction to a critical incident event, and cognitive-behavioral coping skills. In addition, crisis counseling may include on-the-spot relaxation training.

Group Therapy Approaches

Group counseling and therapy seeks to bring together those affected by a common need. Along with debriefings, it worked well during the September 11, 2001, attack on the World Trade Center buildings (Galea et al., 2002; Malekoff, 2001). Group dynamics and the related therapy works best for critical incidents where officers experience similar trauma. Group therapy is one of the possible treatment modalities; however, it may be less successful with suicidal police officers. There may be some resistance to this approach because of the open forum. Trust and privacy issues can create a fearful climate.

Rational Emotive Behavior Therapy

Dr. Albert Ellis pioneered and founded Rational Emotive Behavior Therapy (REBT) during the 1950s. Cognitive Behavior Therapy and other similar forms of therapy followed (Ellis, 1998). This form of therapy differs in that it differentiates between healthy behaviors, negative emotions, and unhealthy negative emotions. For example, healthy negative emotions are sorrow, regrets, and frustration. Unhealthy negative emotions include panic, depression, rage, feelings of worthlessness, and self-pity (Ellis, 1998). The latter are particularly dysfunctional, especially for police officers.

ABC Theory of Emotion

Cognitive behavior therapy emerges from several prominent theories that have wide acceptance. Ellis (1998) advocated REBT, which targets irrational, demanding, and excessive perfectionist belief patterns. For example, one self-defeating pattern is to expect that everyone will love you. Perfectionist behaviors can produce disturbing mood patterns. The therapist seeks to assist the client to substitute more rational and less demanding thoughts.

Ellis' REBT made a significant contribution to irrational thinking. His theory relates to contemporary effective interventions. The ABC theory of emotions concerns people in general, but has potential for police oriented stressful events and suicide interventions. In many cases, the hopelessness, helplessness, and haplessness of the officer are irrational thinking. Therefore, the counselor must disrupt the irrational thinking and communicate illogical consequences. The objective is to provide temporary insight that permits the appropriate treatment.

Ellis' theory unfolds in a direct manner: "A" is the activating event or critical shooting event, "B" represents the belief system (Thou shall not kill), and "C" represents the consequence(s). His theory proposes, that A does not cause C, but irrational beliefs (IBs) cause C. Thus, the activating event does not cause the consequence(s). The officer's irrational belief system is about the activating event that causes the consequences. It is not necessarily the event, but the officer's personal perception and reaction to the event. Refer to Figure 7-2 for an analysis of the ABC theory of REBT.

An officer experiencing extreme stress after a police shooting in an ongoing bank robbery may be recycling the stress over several months. The officer has choices about labeling the experience. If he decides to label the experience as extremely negative and his fault, the trauma will be a haunting occurrence. The negativity will transfer to the officer's social and family life. The stress cycle will most likely repeat until the exhaustion stage or possibly suicide.

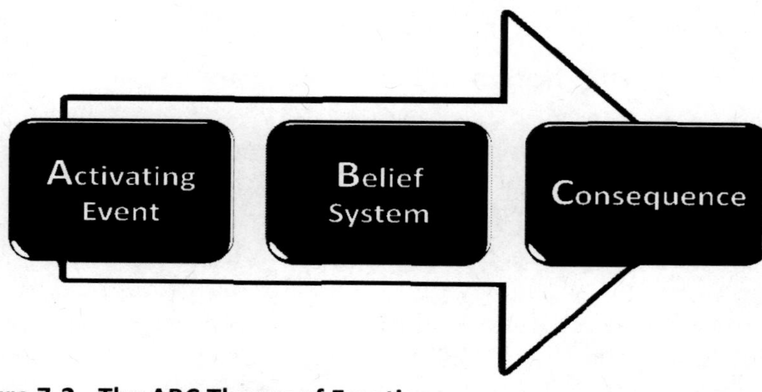

Figure 7-2. The ABC Theory of Emotion
(Adapted from Ellis, 1998)

The shooting was a justifiable action on the part of the officer, the activating event. The officer's irrational belief is "If only I could have done something differently." The officer's belief system, the B in Ellis' theory of emotions, consists of a series of dysfunctional irrational beliefs. These irrational beliefs result in inaccurate interpretations of events or situations that cause stressful consequences.

The counselor's first attempt is to present the evidence that offsets the officer's irrational beliefs. Everyone in the police department may have assumed the officer acted rationally, but the officer focuses on the shooting and the irrational thought of assumed responsibility. The counselor understands that no matter how justified the use of force, the officer may experience trauma. At this point, the therapist introduces logical methods of disputing the officer's irrational beliefs. The other therapeutic approach involves using empirical methods of disputing irrational beliefs.

Irrational beliefs may persist even though the bank robber fired his weapon, initiated the shooting, and jeopardized the lives of innocent bystanders. Heroic accolades will not persuade the officer because of personal irrational beliefs and guilt. The after-action briefing should alleviate some guilt. However, there are situations where follow-up and counseling referral is required.

Counselors assist police officers with insight observations that allow the officer to recognize that help is available. In most cases, police officers considering suicide are harboring irrational beliefs. The evaluation of the individual officer's stressors involves a belief system. The belief that suicide is the only option is irrational and may involve tunnel vision.

The appraisal of stressor(s) requires assessing the accumulation of the officer's past traumatic experiences. If the officer operates with partial information or an irrational belief system, they are applying irrational thought processes. Counselors may be able to point out the faulty logic and improve the officer's point of view. Cognitive awakening is possible when the officer establishes insight.

Cognitive Therapy

Aaron T. Beck, the founder of cognitive therapy, provides a practical method for navigating the emotional and belief systems. His research, which is internationally acknowledged, provides guidance for counselors and clinicians. His cognitive therapy approach effectively helps people change dysfunctional thinking and behavioral patterns. Cognitive therapy and medication remain primary treatment modalities for those who have depression and suicidal ideation.

Behavior therapy regards emotional disturbances as accidental conditioning that accrued previously in the officer's life. According to behavior therapy theory, the officer cannot modify these conditioned reflexes simply by knowing about them and using willpower. The elimination of the behaviors in most cases requires the application of "counter-conditioning" by a qualified behavioral therapist (Beck, 1976).

Questions concerning cognitive behavioral counseling validity are always relevant issues. Cognitive phenomena are observable by the officer through introspection. The empirically validated studies of cognitive behavioral counseling offer a realistic way to counter self-defeating notions. A series of systemic studies seems to support the tenants and efficacy of cognitive behavioral counseling.

Beck (1976) offered a form of cognitive therapy that seeks to eliminate illogical thinking processes and help the client recognize negative thoughts. The therapy introduces the concept of biased interpretations and errors in logic. For example, over generalization represents illogical thinking, such as the belief that if something was harmful once, it will always happen in the same repeated manner. Clients must realize that isolated errors or mistakes do not predict failure every time. Emphasis on logic and guidance over time assists the client in accepting that they have over generalized the fear and trauma.

Cognitive Behavioral Therapy

Recent studies have demonstrated that cognitive therapy, also described as cognitive behavioral therapy (CBT), decreases the risk for suicide attempts by 50%. For example, Brown et al. (2005) found that over an 18-month follow-up, only 24% of subjects in the cognitive therapy group attempted suicide compared to 42% of subjects given other services in the community. However, many of the cognitive therapy studies have methodological issues that need addressing.

Cognitive therapy research indicates that suicidal oriented persons can benefit from the treatment. Research by the NIH's National Institute of Mental Health (NIMH) and the CDC targeted cognitive therapy and found that it reduces repeat suicide attempts by 50%. Brown and Beck (2005) evaluated a form of cognitive therapy that prevents suicide. Their positive results indicated that cognitive therapy: (1) proved better at lifting depression, (2) reduced feelings of hopelessness, and (3) the series of sessions reduced the likelihood that high-risk previous suicide attempters will make a subsequent attempt.

Reality Therapy Approach

Dr. William Glasser advocated the Reality Therapy approach, which is "a therapy that leads all patients toward reality, toward grappling successfully with tangible and intangible aspects of the real world, might accurately be called a therapy toward reality, or simply Reality Therapy" (Glasser, 1975). He suggested that, in their unsuccessful efforts to meet and fulfill their needs, people engage in a variety of unrelated behaviors and dysfunctional symptoms. The therapist assists clients in accepting reality and provides support. The basic concept is that clients will be successful when they give up denying the world around them. They must face reality, and the therapist provides the underlying coping skills for acceptance.

Clients must learn to fulfill their own needs, and not deny there is a realistic framework for making those decisions. Glasser (1975) suggested: "Millions drink to blot out the inadequacy they feel, but that need not exist if they could learn to be different; and far too many people choose suicide rather than face the reality that they could solve their problems by more responsible behavior."

Glasser (1998) believed that certain human universal principles guide the client's decision-making process. He noted some common sense principles: we need people in our lives; at least one person who cares for us and we care for them. The more caring people in our lives the better, especially when the relationships are reciprocal. "Psychiatry must be concerned with two basic psychological needs: the need to love and be loved and the need to feel that we are worthwhile to ourselves and to others. Helping clients fulfill these two needs is the basis of Reality Therapy."

Reality therapists might provide insight by asking the question: What are you doing to promote your isolation and depression? Glasser (1998) noted that personal insight is important; people must be in touch with reality and fulfill their own needs within the world. "Responsibility, a concept basic to Reality Therapy, is here defined as the ability to fulfill one's needs, and to do so in a way that does not deprive others of the ability to fulfill their needs" Glasser (1975).

In many cases of suicide the officer is alone and isolated. This is the time of their life when they need social interaction, but they are pushing others away who might help them through the crisis. Suicidal officers have their own agenda, and they are trying to meet their dysfunctional needs at the expense of others. These officers are not accepting reality, and are in a state of denial when it comes to the real world and depression.

Glasser (1975) warned that depressed clients should not be the recipients of sympathy; it emphasizes their feelings of worthlessness and adds to their condition of depression. The goal of the therapist is to teach the tenants of responsibility and acceptance of reality. The suicidal officer is trying to meet his needs in an irrational manner and not facing reality. These officers need to find a new pattern of perception and behavior.

Behavioral Therapy Technology

Police officers, emergency responders, and citizens confronted with a critical incident may encounter severe emotional reactions. Treating severe trauma like PTSD requires more than short-term counseling. PTSD counseling requires an extended intervention that follows a ten-week program. This form of ten-session behavioral therapy is quite comprehensive, even though the duration is not as long as traditional psychotherapy. The therapy involves traditional techniques: (1) psycho-education and (2) relaxation therapy in the initial stages. The closing sessions include: (1) Imaginal Exposure (mentally reliving the traumatic experience) and (2) Invo Exposure (directly exposing one's self to situations that the officer has been avoiding since the trauma). Invo therapy protocol has an effective case history in treating PTSD (Freeman et al., 1990).

Vivo Exposure Therapy

Vivo exposure therapy combines both cognitive psychology and behavioral therapy. The client focuses on the stimuli or event for 30 to 45 minutes, or until the discomfort level decreases approximately 50%. During this form of exposure, the therapist requests that the client overtly face the situation associated with the trauma. The Vivo Exposure objective requires officers to confront the feared situation in a realistic, but safe environment. For example, Vivo therapy relates to the traumatic event. It might include the location, clothing, and weapon at the scene of the episode.

Virtual Reality Exposure

Virtual Reality Exposure/Virtual Reality Graded Exposure (VRE/VRGE) demonstrates promise in the treatment of PTSD. A computer-generated environment in lieu of self-generating images offers a therapeutic environment in which to release emotional pain. The computer's powerful generated sights and sounds allow graded exposure, leaving the client with a sense of control. Virtual images allow the client to play an active role in the therapy as well as offer a monitoring capability.

Rothbaum (2001) described VRE and its effectiveness while working with clinically assessed PTSD Vietnam veterans. The veterans wore headgear with a display screen and stereo head phones with visual and audio cues from the war zone. The former soldier reentered the battlefield environment – the sights and sounds of the helicopters over the virtual jungle relived in a safe zone. During the treatment, soldiers were able to diminish anxiety-provoking cues in a gradual and controlled manner. Soldiers have shown encouraging results with a significant reduction from the baseline measurements established at the beginning of VRE therapy. Specifically, the soldiers reduced symptoms associated with traumatic experiences after six months of treatment.

Research Issues: Counseling

Crisis counseling involves a variety of strategies that may involve both short- and long-term psychotherapy. The various approaches have individual applications for those who need assistance. Some of the current research seems promising in the treatment of PTSD and cognitive therapy; however, a number of scientific results have methodological flaws in this area.

The criticisms of cognitive therapy and PTSD research stem from internal validity issues regarding attention to standardization of treatment and outcome measures. In addition, researchers need to follow-up on individuals dropping out of clinical trials and improve the handling of missing data. Moreover, attention to conflict of interest, assessor independence, and the length of follow-up assure the appropriate reliability and validity of the data (Foa and Meadows, 1997; Harvey et al., 2003).

The following case illustration is an example of an officer who did not receive the proper counseling support. This incident took place prior to recent research. Some officers still elude the support system. In many of the smaller police agencies, which are the most typical in the United States, the officer with emotional difficulties does not receive the proper referral and assistance.

Case Study Illustration

It was one of those warm summer evenings, officers working the midnight shift started to assemble. The night started with reading the daily offense bulletins. Most of the conversation centered on a local high school basketball star, making local news, and one of those pleasant summer evenings that turned deadly.

Ted was one of the best officers, known for his friendliness and aggressive patrol strategies. He left headquarters early to arrive on his beat, a departure from his normal routine. One concerned officer noticed his departure, and followed him for safety and back-up procedures.

In less than two minutes, Ted picked up his radio, and called 239, his former rookie partner for backup support. He whispers, "It looks like a burglary going down, the safe is missing from the window."

Arriving directly behind Ted, the first responding officer fired one shot at the fleeing felony suspect; the burglar fell over bleeding profusely. Ted approached the burglar, a well-known criminal, and asked, "Why didn't you stop?"

The ambulance arrived in minutes, the burglar yelling and cursing, "I didn't think you would really shoot me." He stopped his screaming suddenly and slumped over. He was dead! Ted said, "He deserved it for not stopping," but his right shooting hand started shaking.

His former probationary partner knew something was terribly wrong, but he simply did not know what to say or do. His only reply was, "Are you alright Ted?" They passed several times, after shift change. Ted did not acknowledge his old partner's cheerful greetings.

Ted built a wall around himself, and no one could get in and hurt him. The inability to express feelings to yourself and others is a barrier to social interaction. Police officers may not want to connect in relationships because friends and family might see their pain.

Ted started to miss his shift assignments and withdrew from everyone on the job. He was pale, sullen, and shaken to the core. Recently divorced, he resigned from the police department and disappeared.

In those days, peer counseling or referrals to a police psychologist did not exist. There was little assistance or professional help. How many officers have suffered alone without any support over the years? Ted might have received some relief from his pain if the events had occurred today. His depression was one important indicator for potential suicide.

Special Note: Police officers are vulnerable to critical incident stress reactions and PTSD not only because of their environment, but because they stifle emotions. This case study is a classic example of an officer's need to be in emotional control. Control can extend to other areas of the officer's life, even family.

Ted lived in a world of perpetrators and victims where denial of personal emotions was accepted. He was the classic example of the perfectionist and irrational thinking. He had to be perfect and catching criminals was his obsession. When he killed one, he was not perfect.

He was in need of peer leadership, assessment, and counseling intervention. He was an excellent candidate for PTSD. Shooting a fleeing felon, under the law and police regulations of the time was legal. However, his perception of the shooting may have been the opposite. It is not the event, but the officer's perception of the event that often works as a catalyst. There was zero to offer Ted in the area of peer support and departmental programs. Everyone knew there was something wrong, but no one knew how to fix the problem.

Focus Points

The officer who must surrender his service revolver receives the final blow. The officer will eventually return to full duty and removing the officer's weapon requires tact and cooperation. If the police leader or counselor allows the officer to keep their weapon, they had better be right. Taking the weapon scenario is a lose/lose situation, and the decision requires balancing the interest of the public and the officer, with the former a first priority.

The literature consistently cites that police officers have career reasons for resisting professional counseling and treatment. Police organizations and culture offers many barriers to seeking help, which further adds to the isolation. These barriers include trust and the related fear of losing professional status.

An affirmative message and plan communicates the idea that ..."We care about our officers." Effective police leadership coordinates successful programming. Leadership emphasizes that stress disorders are normal reactions to critical incidents and field crises. A Critical Incident Stress Crisis Management Program (CISM) remains the starting point. The related Peer Support Program (PSP) is an integral part of an outreach method of communication.

Conclusion

Police leaders assist in meeting the needs for officers that need help for stress related disorders, mental health issues, and suicidal ideation. This is a team effort that requires CISM resources and financial support to overcome the obstacles to the proper assistance. Police research identifies the barriers in police organizations and seeks positive intervention strategies. The core obstacle to treatment is respecting the privacy of the officer. Confidentially and trust hold the door open to outside agency referrals.

PART IV
RESEARCH FOUNDATIONS AND FUTURE IMPLICATIONS

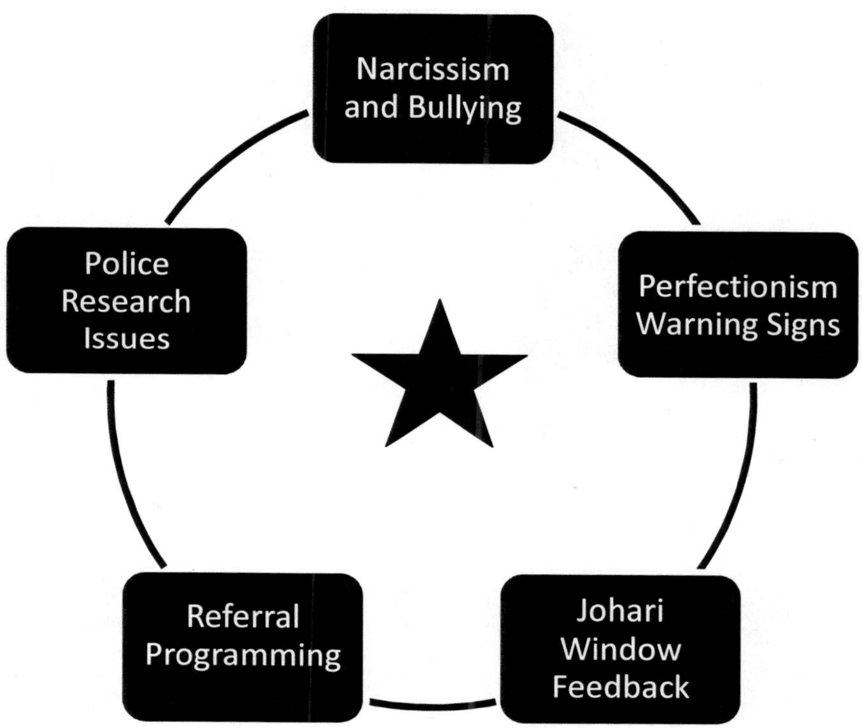

Leadership Foundations	Guidepost Behaviors
• **Police leaders take the initiative in researching abusive and bullying behaviors within police organizations.**	• Research in the area of bullying abuse inside police organizations is **almost non-existent** on the national level. While there has been some research on the international level, the United States is **late** in addressing these vital issues. The connection between bullying and abuse, post-traumatic stress disorder and depression remain **worthy of expert research**. In addition, links to suicide and the perfectionist personality **merit** thoughtful and deliberate police research.
• **Identify the suicide risk assessment process that is appropriate for the police population.**	• The **risk assessment process** includes the following: (1) identify the **health problem**, (2) identify the **risk factors**, (3) examine the elements of **elevated exposure**, (4) modify the **work process**, (5) reduce exposure to the **hazard**, (6) introduce **protective factors** and (7) treat the **series of exposures** and (8) **monitor and assessment.**
• **Initiate the Critical Incident Stress Management Plan (CISM). In addition, monitor and research effectiveness of CISM program.**	• The main goal is to identify **crisis symptoms** in traumatized victims. In addition, develop pre-crisis preparation, defusing, counseling services, critical incident debriefings, and implement the seven-phase process.
• **Researchers resolve the statistical quandary: The primary obstacle to gaining the best actionable research for the intervention and prevention of police suicide.**	• **Research data improvement** requires appropriate collection methods, analysis, and synthesize of empirical research. The statistical measurement problems concerning police suicide are improving, but more needs to be accomplished.
• **Police managers assess the ten leadership strategies that are essential to the intervention and prevention of police suicide.**	• Suitable research might **resolve many enigma issues**. Effective evaluation helps redirect the leadership and research process. It answers three critical questions: (1) Is the research valid and reliable? (2) Has the agency arrived? (3) Where does the police agency go next?

CHAPTER 8

POLICE LEADERSHIP: ABUSE AND BULLYING

"Bullies are always cowards at heart, and may be credited with a pretty safe instinct in scenting their prey."

— Anna Julia Cooper

Lieutenant Smart believed he was talented and destined for higher purpose and command. He always sought the limelight and media attention, all opportunities to glean the credit he needed to advance his career. His every motivational move ingratiates himself with the power structure, especially the chief of police. The lieutenant appeared aggressive and highly motivated to succeed at everything to advance his career and grandiose agenda.

Eventually, promoted to captain after less than ten years of service; his record of accomplishment for success was always short-term. Typically, the programs he took credit for were the result of the efforts of other officers. He was always present to take the accolades and publicity. If officers conceded to his every desire, they became loyal soldiers in advancing his career.

The lieutenant frightens others into submission through bullying and other unethical tactics. The temper tantrum was his basic strategy, a means to control and apply power tactics. If that failed to achieve his objective, the abuse and bullying strategies escalated to public embarrassment, threatening letters, or cyberbullying.

The captain's career ended when he failed to respond tactically to a police officer bleeding to death after a shooting in a domestic violence case. He was more concerned about advancing career aspirations. The captain failed to develop his tactical proficiency skills and failed to respond to the emergency and save the officer's life. His failure to respond appropriately because of fears concerning career consequences had the opposite effect. The disrespect that this command failure generated rallied every officer in the department; the morale problem that followed required his resignation. Captain Smart's narcissism, bullying, or intimidating behaviors led to long-term effects and failure.

Chapter Focus

This chapter explores basic concepts of the authoritarian narcissism style of leadership. It defines the cluster of warning signs of abuse and bullying. In addition, this chapter may assist police leaders and officers in recognizing psychological abuse and bullying behaviors. The narcissism leadership enigma is solvable when a pattern emerges and parts of the puzzle fit together.

Overview

Empirical evidence for the negative outcomes for narcissism is abundant in the private sector. Narcissist leaders thrive on controlling others, and they prefer the covert ambush approach to eliminating those who stand in their way. Ironically, the paradox is that narcissism-oriented leaders may contribute to the destruction of the social climate of police agencies. If gone unnoticed, this form of defective leadership creates havoc, costly resignations, early retirements, and high personnel turnover. The financial loss to local governments may erode their financial base and hinder efficient police services.

This kind of personality is insensitive to the feelings of others, but extremely sensitive to negative comments about themselves. They have a low frustration tolerance and are prone to public displays of anger. The narcissism leadership style demonstrates tyrannical behaviors and calculated temper tantrums to instill fear, power, and control. Relentless, controlling behaviors of the authoritarian personality have a higher survival rate in police or military organizations. These status seekers see others as puppets for manipulation for their domineering, public humiliation, and extremely controlling behaviors.

Private Sector: Leadership Research

Private sector research indicates success in business is not dependent on narcissism, but on those who are humble. Twenge and Campbell (2009) advocated the CEO profile of a humble leader, not the charismatic, ultra-confident personality you would expect. They did not advocate individuals who possess narcissism personality traits, but endorsed cooperative, low-conflict leaders who seek cooperation. Successful CEOs were team players who downplayed their role and gave credit to others. The best corporate leaders do not engage in narcissism, nor are they particularly self-confident (Collins, 2001; Hambrick and Chatterjee, 2008).

Their research indicated companies that had CEOs with huge egos eventually contributed to the demise or mediocrity of their companies. Moreover, the performance of narcissism-oriented CEOs was volatile, vacillating between successful projects. When they did fail, it was a disaster. The humble leaders produced steady performance and fewer business risks. In addition, the narcissistic leaders were unpopular with employees and created conflict. This research has considerable implications for police leadership and the related stressors these types of leaders create (Collins, 2001; Hambrick and Chatterjee, 2008).

Narcissism Leadership Issues

Excellent leaders have a primary responsibility to achieve the highest standard of conduct. The narcissism leadership style denies the basic principle of leadership: selfless service to others. This type of leader engages in selfish service and blind ambition to achieve power over others. When narcissists engage in poor leadership and their hidden agenda remains unnoticed, it adds mystique. Armed with bullying research and information, police executives can assess the symptoms of abusive/narcissist leadership behaviors. The analysis of pathological and authoritarian leadership helps provide appropriate prevention, interventions, and remedial referrals.

The narcissist is self-absorbed and is therefore, unable to empathize with other people. This defect leads to power and control games. There is a pre-occupation with promoting self in the pursuit of power, glory, and status. The narcissist's sense of entitlement and poor empathy skills allow them to do whatever they desire regardless of the cost. Goleman (2006) found that those individuals who lack the ability to empathize with others may treat them as objects, rather than human beings.

Narcissist leaders seek to accomplish personal goals to impress those who are in the best position to advance their career. They impose the highest standards on others to achieve their goals. Moreover, they feel the need to appear perfect and others must assist in that endeavor. This kind of leader engages in demeaning and bullying behaviors to fulfill career needs. Narcissists are perfectionists and want their way no matter the personal cost to others. These leaders are detached, demanding, and cannot offer a genuine apology. They are compulsive and overly consumed with minute details.

Law enforcement agencies are not unique when it comes to abusive and bullying leadership; it exists in many organizations, i.e., business, education, and the military. Narcissist leaders work for their own benefit, not for the police agencies or communities they serve. A narcissist leader who engages in abusive and bullying behaviors may come from every rank in police agencies from police officer to the chief of police, and can be male or female. In a competitive promotional system, power and greed generate considerable peer conflict and professional jealousy.

The narcissist prevails because of the organization's inability to recognize the psychological behaviors that contribute to abuse and bullying. In addition, police officers have pride and are likely to engage in denial when encountering abusive and bullying behavior. These inappropriate behaviors are embarrassing due to the painful nature of the acts. Even competent and confident officers respond to the fear factor and develop a go-along to get along attitude. Bullying behaviors are difficult to recognize and police officers are less likely to recognize the related personal and family consequences.

Research on the authoritarian personality best describes the foundation for abusive and bullying behaviors. Authoritarian personalities are conservative, aggressive, cynical, and rigid. Their view of the world is rigid and they see issues as black and white (Adorno, 1950). They are submissive to their superiors; however, will not tolerate anyone who does not submit to their authority. Absolute obedience to their established criteria and authoritarian rule is the basic requirement for acceptance. Those who remain noncompliant become unrelenting targets for elimination.

Twenge and Campbell (2009) stated, "Narcissists are aggressive exactly because they love themselves so much and believe that their needs take precedence. They lack empathy for other people's pain and often lash out when they feel they aren't getting the respect they deserve—and they feel they deserve a lot, because they are, of course, better than everyone else. Consider the mass murderers of history, such as Hitler, Pol Pot, Saddam Hussein, or Stalin. Do they strike you as people with low self-esteem? No, they were so confident in themselves and their beliefs that they killed millions of people. Their narcissism allowed them to disregard the most basic rights of others." The authors also commented that narcissism included anti-social personality disorder as well as related psychopathic behaviors.

This kind of leader is extremely obsessive, compulsive, and applies fear tactics as the primary weapon. The basic goal is to gain abusive power and control over fellow officer(s). Narcissistic leaders generally begin the relationship professing praise and enthusiasm. The abuse cycle emerges when the officer has insight into the poor character and motivation of the narcissist leader. Narcissistic Personality Disorder (NPD) appears in the Diagnostic and Statistical Manual of Mental Disorders and may offer more dire consequences, especially when anti-social personality disorder occurs as a multiple diagnosis.

Narcissist leaders are quite charming initially; especially if they feel that the officer(s) can meet their needs or promote their career. If charming other officers fails to work, the next attempt will be coercion and intimation. If both attempts fail, then targeting the threat for elimination follows. In many instances, overt or implied threats concerning the officer's career are part of the abuse. Other officers may fear becoming a target on the narcissist leader's hit list and fail to assist the targeted officer.

The first objective of the narcissist/bullying leader is to isolate the officer. They weave a web around their subordinate and seek to eliminate all influential relationships. They target and destroy friendships and finally isolate the officer so that he is alone. The officer soon has no social support or way out of the web. The primary objective is to force the officer to leave the organization. When another officer assists a targeted officer or confronts the narcissist leader, he becomes enraged and defines the next target.

The higher the police rank, the more easily the narcissist/bullying leader operates in the cloak of formal authority. Leaders have a position of trust and therefore are above suspicion. However, the narcissist leader does not accept responsibility for his own behaviors; he blames others for his own inappropriate and impulsive behaviors. The narcissist leader's friendly chameleon qualities blend well into the command element, defining a subordinate officer as the problem. The friendly mask is a disguise that is removed when the narcissistic leader has the targeted officer alone.

If challenged, the narcissist/bully escalates the punishment. The subordinate has the inferior position and is less likely to have credibility by members of the power structure. It may take many complaints to identify maladaptive leadership. Unfortunately, many officers remain silent, and numerous grievances are necessary before the problem is corrected. The real source of the destructive energy is the narcissist leader's power and control issues.

Bullying narcissist leaders believe that "blind ambition" will drive them to the pinnacle of power and abusive behaviors will ultimately gain superiority and dominance. Their behaviors may change in adulthood from physical bullying to emotional bullying; those who did not have the physical stature tend to remain in the latter covert style. This is the preferred mode, because it invites less attention and an unwelcome reaction from others.

Abusive and Bullying Behaviors

Researchers and legal scholars in the United States are currently focusing on bullying behaviors in the private and public sectors. California and other states are developing new laws to cope with the problem. Police agencies that do not address abuse, bullying, and the hostile work environment will face civil litigation as employees increasingly acknowledge the legal and psychological implications of this behavior. Police abuse and bullying can have a ripple effect throughout the organization.

The CDC and NIOSH define bullying as the repeated intimidation, slandering, social isolation, or humiliation by one person against another. This maladaptive and dysfunctional behavior has serious consequences for the social climate of police organizations. There is a professional need to research the bullying narcissist personality and assess the damage it incurs to organizations. Refer to Table 8-1 for the typical bullying behaviors and Table 8-2 for bullying actions and methods.

Research on bullying is rather limited at this stage of development in the United States; however, Scandinavia, the UK, and Canada have collected wide-ranging data. NIOSH conducted two preliminary studies in 2003 and 2004. According to the first preliminary NIOSH study, 24.5% of 516 private and public organizations reported some form of bullying.

A consensus on what constitutes bullying behavior is still in the preliminary stages of development. NIOSH determined that 14.7% of bullying behavior involved a supervisor; however, because of their leadership position and insulation, there may be some reluctance to report bullying.

Table 8-1. Bullying Behaviors

(Adapted from the National Institute of Mental Health and the Workplace Bullying Institute)

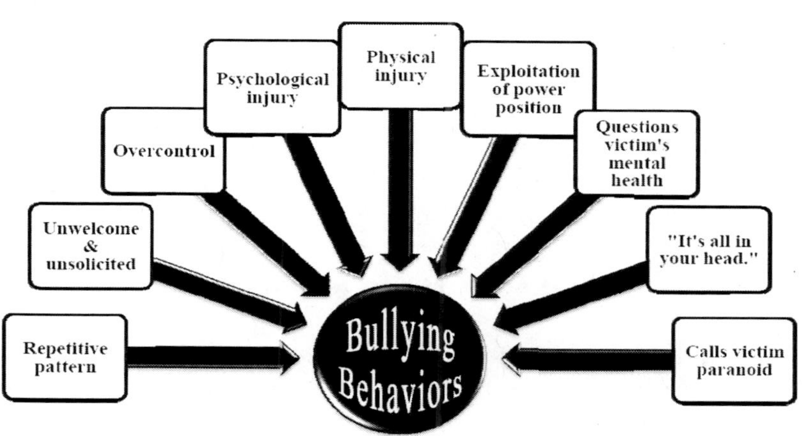

Table 8-2. Specific Bullying Actions and Behaviors

(Adapted from the National Institute of Mental Health and the Workplace Bullying Institute)

Intent to harm	Name calling	Verbal abuse	Undermining reputation
Threatening statements	Discrediting reputation	Intimidating conduct	Ostracizing and isolating
Work interference	Undermines legitimate department interests	Micromanaging	Belittling opinions
Spreading malicious gossip	Sarcastic remarks	Taking credit for another's success	Inappropriate glaring

Lynch (2002) described research on bullying behaviors in police organizations as scarce. "The prevalence of workplace bullying remains unclear. However, the estimates are that approximately 25 to 50 percent of all employees in the general working population will experience bullying at some time during their working lives. There is some preliminary research overseas or through Australia to indicate the prevalence of workplace bullying among police personnel. However, the few studies available indicate that police organizations may experience workplace bullying. The effects of workplace bullying on targets of this behavior are considerable. They include psychological and physical consequences such as anxiety, sleeplessness, depression, self-destructive behaviors, post-traumatic stress disorder, panic attacks, headaches, hypertension, and exhaustion."

Police officers experience emotional stress when conflict persists in police organizations. When bullying and abuse exist, it leads to serious conflict and negative interaction with others. When conflict and stress become part of the culture, it has consequences for police officers and the communities they serve. Eliminating unnecessary abuse and bullying in the leadership climate has positive consequences. Zero tolerance for abuse and bullying builds a positive leadership climate and police culture. Reducing abuse and bullying in police organizations might assist in preventing depression and police suicide.

Police Suicide: Perfectionism

The narcissist leader exploits various personalities in different ways. The perfectionist personality helps reflect a positive image for the benefit of police commanders and may serve as the source for creative ideas and extraordinary work accomplishments. The narcissist leader can steal credit from the perfectionist's supreme efforts. There can be a subtle interplay of social dynamics between these personalities. The recycling of a considerable amount stress has serious consequences throughout the organization and a potential for tragic consequences.

The role of perfectionist personalities in police organizations may generate excessive hyper-stress that can sequence the pathway to depression and suicide. The narcissist leader easily exploits officers who have personalities predisposed to perfectionism. This kind of defective leadership manipulates police officers to further their careers. They get others to take the risks and absorb stress to enhance their image. The other perfectionism subtype, similar to the narcissistic leader, may impose his difficult or unreasonable standards, and when others fail to comply, there are consequences. The following paragraphs describe the role of perfectionism in police suicide.

One theme connected to these related issues is the psychological concept of *perfectionism* and the *police personality*. Clearly, law enforcement officers confront brutality, violent behavior, and death at an elevated rate compared to other occupations. Life can never be perfect, especially for police officers. Refer to Figure 8-1 for an analysis of the personality characteristics of perfectionism.

Figure 8-1. Striving to be Flawless/Perfectionism Personality
(Adapted from Blatt, et al., 1999; Slorsar, 2001)

Perfectionist thinking leads to considerable stress, and the fear of failure leads to obsessive and compulsive behaviors. The reverse may also be true. Obsessive-compulsive disorder can lead to perfectionist thinking. In some cases, the fear of failure may have the opposite effect and produce stress related behaviors such as procrastination, failure to complete projects, and self-recrimination. Perfectionism and self-criticism are counterproductive to establishing interpersonal relationships (Blatt et al., 1999).

Police officers with elevated perfectionism qualities are in demand for high profile and stressful assignments. They can get the job done under adverse circumstances, but over time, this may have adverse consequences for the officers and their families. These officers have a tendency to take on multiple diverse goals with extreme deadlines. Self-imposed unrealistic demands can lead to a sense of failure, shame, and suicidal ideation when substantial itineraries of designated goals are not accomplished. Leaders and supervisors need to monitor "star performers" for mission impossible assignments and stress burnout.

Police suicides of the most successful and talented officers may be due to their personality and the pursuit of perfectionism. This significant personality and character style, rather than individual stressors, may play a dominant role in law enforcement suicides. In addition, perfectionism is an important multidimensional construct that has negative social consequences (Slosar, 2001). Perfectionism might lead to stardom; however, it also serves as a possible predictor of suicide. The stars may implode under the weight of their own irrational thoughts and perfectionism.

One can conclude that the perfectionist officer experiences high levels of inferiority in spite of great accomplishments. Their strong need for excessive achievement is overcompensation for feelings of inferiority. They are never content or happy over the long-term, even though basking in the glory of the present. The intense competition results in serious consequences for others as well as the officer. Ultimately, depression and suicide may follow because of disappointment over minor frustrations.

Slosar (2001) cited that perfectionism consists of three basic subtypes. These subtypes are associated with suicidal ideation and present a moderate link between stressors. This research advocated the importance of *perfectionism*, rather than *stress*, as a crucial predictor in law enforcement suicide. One excellent assessment tool used to identify and measure perfectionism is the Multidimensional Perfectionism Scale (MPS) by Hewitt and Flett (1991).

Perfectionism subtypes include: (1) self-oriented perfectionism, (2) other-oriented perfectionism, and (3) socially prescribed perfectionism (Hewitt et al., 1994). Hewitt and Flett (1991) described self-oriented perfectionism as "an active striving to be flawless." This type of officer imposes excessively high standards mixed with self-scrutiny and continuous self-criticism. The result is an officer who cannot accept his personally perceived inadequacies or failures. When this occurs, depression and suicidal ideation prevails. Refer to Figure 8-2 for an example of the three subtypes of perfectionism.

The other perfectionism subtype has the same projected multidimensional personality and character criteria. These individuals produce significant amounts of stress for others in their law enforcement agency. This is especially the case if the officer serves in a supervisory or command position. When they impose their difficult or unreasonable standards and others fail to comply, there are consequences. The behaviors may include poor performance ratings, blaming, and hostility toward others. The criticism of significant others' behaviors and tantrums is likely to lead to personal and domestic strife.

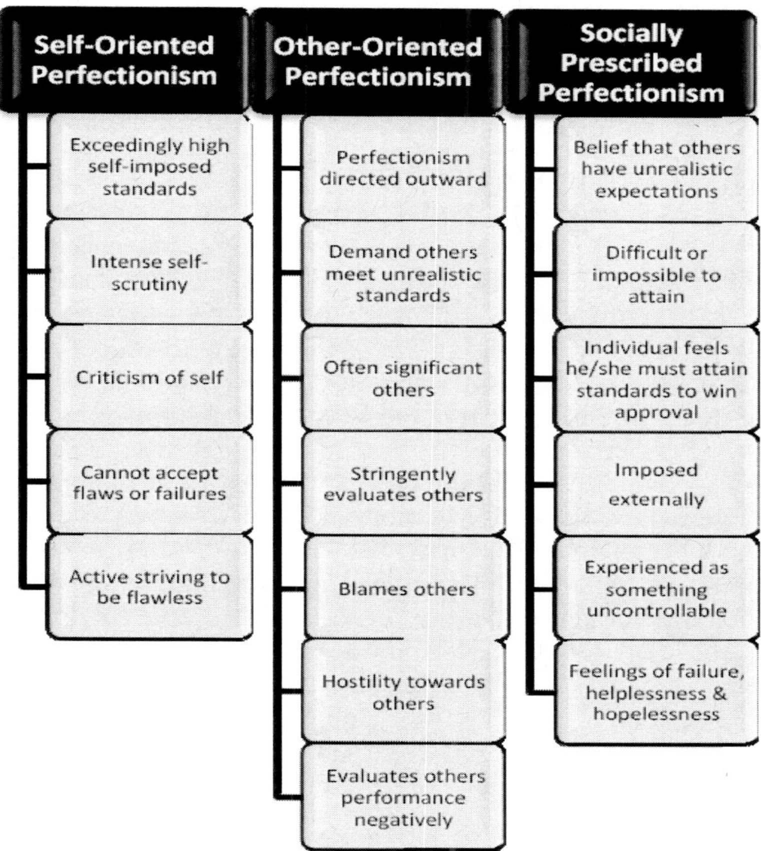

Figure 8-2. Three Subtypes of Perfectionism
(Adapted from Hewitt & Flett, 1991)

The socially prescribed perfectionism subtype incorporates the mirror effect from others. This type of officer believes that others have imposed unrealistic or exaggerated expectations. Their goals or objectives may in fact be improbable, impossible to obtain, or demand unreasonable time constraints. This officer feels that he must reflect back the correct behaviors or standards to gain approval and acceptance from others. This form of perfectionism results from imposed external goals and objectives. Stress increases when the police officer perceives the situation as uncontrollable. Consequences include failure, helplessness, and hopelessness, possibly resulting in depression and potential suicide.

Blatt et al. (1995) cited that perfectionism interferes with the treatment of the resulting depression. Perfectionists are extremely self-critical, they often find it difficult to establish and sustain interpersonal relationships. Blatt et al. (1998) concluded that individuals with increased levels of perfectionism and self-criticism are more vulnerable when experiencing failure. Their perfectionism and personally perceived failure has consequences for self-criticism, depression, and suicide.

Perfectionism and high expectations are symptomatic of irrational thinking (Ellis, 1998). Law enforcement is wide open to this fallacy and irrational thinking because of the mission mentality. One is bound to fail and experience disillusionment and stress: perfection is impossible to obtain. Law enforcement, as a culture, is an example of organizational perfectionism and an extremely stressful climate, "Zero tolerance for failure" is failure waiting to happen resulting in a possible suicidal solution in the making.

Hewitt et al. (1992) conducted two studies to measure the relationship between perfectionism and suicidal ideation. Hewitt found that suicide potential is associated with persons who perceive others have unrealistic expectations of them. Socially prescribed perfectionism correlates with suicidal threats and intent (Hewitt et al., 1994). Significant statistical analysis of these results revealed the importance and power of perfectionism. Self-oriented and socially-prescribed perfectionism distinctively discriminates against suicidal groups and suicidal ideation. In addition, perfectionism serves as a moderator variable between high stress and suicidal ideation.

Psychological research demonstrates that self-oriented and socially prescribed perfectionism contributes to feelings of hopelessness, helplessness, and despair. Perfectionism increases one's vulnerability to fear of failure, imperfection, and a sense of worthlessness. This kind of research has transferability to the competitive law enforcement culture. The triggering event to the perfectionist can be a simple annual supervisory/personnel rating.

Depression-prone people set rigid, perfectionist, or unattainable goals and objectives for themselves. When their universe collapses, they confront inevitable disappointments. These unreasonable aspirations and expectations start in early childhood; parents and significant others may drive the child toward high achievements. The precipitating event may have substantial significance to the suicidal individual. However, it is not always a specific event; it can be insidious stressors over a protracted period of time (Beck, 1976).

The depression-prone perfectionist may fear repeated recognition gaps between what a person expects and what they receive. For example, an important interpersonal relationship from career or other significant activities may cascade this type of police officer into a depression. The brief or protracted sense of loss may stem from the result of unrealistically high goals and grandiose expectations (Beck, 1976).

Unrealistic crime reduction expectation in police organizations may serve as an impetus to disappointment and depression. The officer may feel like a loser because of a protracted sense of personal self-worth attached to accomplishment to meeting his responsibilities and goals. Self-punishments may follow the perceived perception of these deficiencies in behaviors or performance. The personal feelings of psychological inadequacy or unworthiness lead to self-criticisms and depression. The following case study is an example of a young woman trying to aspire to perfectionism that ultimately leads to depression and suicide.

Case Study Illustration

Christine was the first of an early 1960s vanguard of female police officers hired for uniform patrol. She was a pioneer, a college graduate, and a future leader of her police department. Fellow officers often described Christine's personality as friendly and caring. Unfortunately, she found some peers unfriendly, a social change agent's reprimand. She was a liberated woman, ahead of the curve, and experiencing considerable stress. Christine was a perfectionist at everything in her life, setting the foundation in place for success.

Christine came to her judo classes demonstrating enthusiasm and determination to prove to her peers that she could handle the physical requirements of police work. She practiced overtime with her judo instructor, Jeb. They became good friends. Their friendship became increasingly important in Jeb's life, beyond judo classes.

Jeb separated from his wife after suffering considerable stress over the years, and then filed for divorce. He was about 20 years older than Christine; however, they entered into a romantic relationship that appeared obvious on and off the judo mats.

One officer was particularly demeaning and taunted Christine constantly. Jeb paired them in a judo match. Christine threw him to the mat with a thud. Charlie was embarrassed, and retreated in disgrace. After that incident, Christine gained considerable status. Stress and pressure still existed on a daily basis. Charlie and a few other officers created some distress in Christine's life, but she responded with kindness. She was hurt and disappointed by their disapproving behaviors, because she was not perfect in their eyes.

The critical event that triggered the suicide was a former female university roommate who had a sexual relationship with Christine during those years. She was stalking Christine and threatening to tell Jeb and the Chief of Police about her sexual identity crisis. Christine, now caught in a love triangle, saw no way out.

During that era of discrimination, the lesbian relationship was powerful information against a police officer. Certainly, it would provide her unreasonable adversaries with social controversy, and possibly the termination of Christine's career. This form of rejection and imperfection was more than the rising star could tolerate.

She hung the phone up after the telephone conversation from her former girlfriend, then walked to the bedroom, and wrote a brief good-by note. She removed her service revolver, fired once, and died instantly.

The suicide of Christine created a PTSD response in Jeb; the insider information multiplied the trauma. She had insulated and protected him from the emotional trauma of divorce, but now she was the source of Jeb's worst trauma.

Jeb, after years of stress in the military and police department, was on the edge of his own mid-life crisis. His pending divorce and separation from his only son was now an emotional issue again. He was the classic example PTSD and the collateral secondary damage of a suicide. Jeb was the walking emotionally wounded.

Jeb's emotional state was in disarray, he was moving toward a tragic event. He was making statements about killing his wife's new boyfriend. Then one day Jeb lost control of his grief over Christine's suicide. He intercepted his wife's boyfriend and pulled alongside his vehicle. He fired six rounds from his service revolver. Every round was a hit to the head and upper torso; Jeb was the best expert shooter on the department.

Jeb was recently promoted to sergeant and was on the short list for lieutenant. Now, charged with felony murder, he pled innocent, and was found guilty by a jury of second-degree murder. He was finally alone with his grief in prison.

Special Note: Jeb and Christine both sought perfection in their lives; the world is an imperfect place. Public ridicule and the information about her private life were now too much for Christine to tolerate. The hard-core clique certainly would use the information against her. Her suicide triggered the stressors of Jeb's past, which re-emerged in the present, and his wife's new boyfriend was the target of his rage over the disintegration of his family and the suicide of Christine.

Ironically, the shooting occurred after a conversation with Neal, a former rookie partner, who departed Jeb's home. He was visiting with a new girlfriend, Shannon, when Jeb made the threat to kill his wife' boyfriend. The statement put a chill on the social climate. Shannon said, "He is serious, Jeb is going to kill this man." Neal said, "That is just talk, Jeb would never hurt anyone." Shannon was right and Neal was in denial often seen in police officers.

Focus Points

The narcissist leader's manipulations form the basis for rationalizations that offer multiple opportunities for psychological violence. Narcissist leaders are accomplished politicians who are difficult to detect and identify before they harm police officers and civilians. The damage they do to police organizations is psychologically ruthless. The constant vigilance of ethical leaders concerning a potential hostile work environment remains part of the solution, rather than part of the problem.

The hostile work environment is a future sign of potential police violence and suicide. The bullying problem will persist until the source of the problem, which is poor narcissist leadership, ceases to exist. The typical administrative reaction is to ignore the abusive and bullying leaders; this is a huge mistake. The hope that the problem will eventually go away or resolve itself leads to many unintended consequences.

The apathetic response to bullying occurs because police commanders feel that the problem reflects adversely on them as leaders. Moreover, there is the tendency to close ranks because of the fear of admitting errors in judgment will lead to legal consequences. The failure to make a decision is a decision, which leads to legal culpability due to senior leaders' incompetence and negligence.

Just a few bullying/abusive leaders can create huge problems for good leaders, especially when they fail to take appropriate action and remedy the grievances. Police officers who experience alienation retaliate in many ways, i.e., excessive sick leave, citizen bullying, and abuse of family members. Police officer negative reactive behaviors may indicate a hostile work environment that is worth investigating.

Poor leadership skills create the hostile work environment. Morale dives to the bottom when officers feel their leaders have failed to take appropriate action on justice issues. The narcissist leader can create a high stress and hostile work environment, which leads to a high rate of police suspicion and distrust.

The narcissist leader only cares about his personal welfare, and is not concerned about subordinates. Driven by aggressive energy, people are pawns on a chessboard. They tune into the weaknesses of others, and exploit that knowledge to further their careers. The narcissist/bullying leader humiliates others and uses sarcastic remarks in public forums.

This kind of leader has little shame for the harmful consequences of his actions, and rationalizes his domineering behaviors against those believed to be weak. The narcissist's perfectionism imposes unreasonable standards on police officers. The identification and exploitation of other perfectionist personalities may suit their needs.

Police officers who have perfectionism traits are unrealistic and frequently fail to fulfill their expectations. These officers have considerable dissatisfaction with their accomplishments and results. The mission impossible attitude produces considerable stress, and may eventually lead to low self-esteem. The resulting depression provides incentive for disillusionment and suicidal ideation.

Conclusion

Narcissist leaders are not promoting high standards and rigorous management that benefits the police agency. Their abuse and bullying meets their needs for power games, control, and career advancement. These abusive/bullying leaders use the excuse that strong discipline is for the good of the department and their sanctimonious self-serving rhetoric plays well to superiors.

Perfectionism may eventually lead to depression and suicide, even in light of considerable successful performance. These officers are at risk for suicide and vulnerable to the narcissistic leader's bullying behaviors. Additional research regarding the relationships between bullying, abuse, and perfectionism could prove a significant contribution to the causes of police suicide.

CHAPTER 9

POLICE SUICIDE: PREVENTION PROGRAMS

"First, have a definite, clear, practical ideal; a goal an objective. Second, have the necessary means to achieve your ends, wisdom, money, materials, and methods. Third, adjust all your means to the end."

— Aristotle

Howard was a 43-year-old policy officer with two years at this agency and previous law enforcement experience in another part of the state. As a school resource officer, Howard was under investigation for inappropriate sexual behavior. The internal affairs investigators were vigorously pursuing allegations of sexual misconduct. Despite a grueling investigation, the investigators could not make their case.

During the investigative ordeal, Howard became depressed and his marriage ended in divorce. Ultimately, he lost his wife, family, and home due to the strain of the accusations. At one point, Howard departed his home, fired a shot in the sky, and sat on the hood of his patrol car ... ready to end it all.

Howard sought help from the agency psychologist who transported him immediately to the crisis center. His psychiatric treatment was successful, however, the pattern of allegations eventually cost Howard his job with the agency. The lifesaving intervention and treatment arrived in a timely manner. Howard is currently working as a police chief in another small town.

Source: This case study was adapted from James S. Herndon (2001), Department of Justice publication.

General observations about individuals contemplating suicide are relevant to police organizations. Timely prevention and intervention can reduce suicides and save lives. What kind of support system or programs exists within the police department that could have initiated the proper intervention before the officer committed suicide? If a suicide occurs, how does the agency respond in an appropriate and tactful manner?

Chapter Focus

This chapter explores the basic concepts of programming strategies. It discusses program development and the Johari Window. In addition, the chapter endeavors to explain that the Johari Window opens opportunities for insight into an officer's psychological and social domains. The graphics serve as an illustration and application of the Johari Window's communication components and related social dynamics.

Overview

Standing operating procedures (SOP) remain the starting point for a successful suicide prevention and intervention program. These procedures provide leadership direction for members of the law enforcement agency and information for minimum, not optimal outcomes. Representative fundamental areas include: (1) key responsible persons, (2) a trained crisis team, (3) identification of key external resources such as a psychologist, and (4) notification procedures. In addition, ongoing assessment of existing programs helps determine effectiveness and improve future interventions.

Violanti (1995) cited several essential remarks about police suicide and the role of police agencies: (1) the first step is to recognize that the suicide problem exists, (2) police agencies should be at the forefront of developing suicide intervention programs, (3) police organizations must develop effective suicide countermeasures, (4) police supervisors trained to recognize suicide warning signs offer opportunities to intervene before it is too late, and (5) police agencies ensure that appropriate referrals outside the organization are available. The process of intervention needs to be as easy and supportive as possible.

A suicide prevention program recognizes that the risk for suicide exists for law enforcement officers. Modified risk protocol applications for dealing with mental health issues have direct application for risk assessment (Fein, 1998; Kahan, 1993). The risk assessment process includes the following components: (1) identify the health problem, (2) assess the risk to police officers, (3) identify the specific risk factors, (4) examine the elevated exposure, (5) modify the work process, (6) reduce the exposure to the hazard, (7) introduce protective factors, and (8) treat the series of exposures and monitor. Refer to Table 1-9 for an example of the goals and assessment process (Amsel et al., 2001).

Table 9-1. Police Suicide Prevention Program Goals

(Adapted from Amsel, et al., 2001)

Suicide Prevention	•Reduce completed suicides. •Reduce number of suicide attempts.
Program	•Reduce distress causing suicidal ideas & behaviors. •Improve early detection & appropriate treatment referral of officers with suicidal thoughts, especially treatment for depression, alcohol abuse & poor coping styles
Goals	•Reduce potential of harm to other officers & the general public from a suicidal individual possibly making bad judgements & decisions. •Reduce stigma around mental health issues & increase acceptance of treatment options.
Primary Goal	•Prevent suicides by improving the knowledge & skills of those who evaluate police officers at risk for suicidal behavior.
Secondary Goal	•Help counselors identify & refer police officers whose suicidal ideation or suicide attempts indicate severe distress & probable vocational dysfunction.

Meaningful, nonthreatening, and timely programs enhance maximum officer participation. Resistance decreases with effective programming and supportive leadership. Police executives and leaders must work cooperatively to meet the needs of their officers. Trust is the motivating factor. Without trust, there will be little participation in any employee assistance program or mental health initiative.

Suicide prevention programs work if officers feel free to take advantage of the opportunities provided. Police administrators and supervisors must play a non-punitive role. Leaders communicate four clear messages: (1) seeking help will not result in job termination or punitive action; (2) all information will be respected and kept confidential; (3) other ways exist for dealing with a situation, no matter how hopeless it seems at the time; and (4) someone is available to help them deal with their problems (Hill and Clawson, 1988; Violanti, 1995). Police training and departmental policy, as well as the everyday examples set by police leaders, must communicate these four messages consistently. Asking for help signals strength, not weakness, and that must form the foundation of any prevention program.

Program: Feedback

Violanti (2007) suggested law enforcement officers are less inclined to find constructive and healthy alternatives for dealing with stressful circumstances. Some maladaptive coping strategies include "escape avoidance" and "distancing." Defensive techniques are eventually counterproductive to successful programs that offer assistance. Furthermore, these maladaptive strategies break down self-appraisal skills required for optimal suicide awareness programs.

One basic tool used to obtain information in the social and emotional climate is feedback from police officers and civilians. When leaders operate in a social vacuum, there are endless surprises and occasional serious and tragic consequences. Impersonal leadership that denies information to officers and threatens officers with the rubber gun squad will constantly operate in the dark. Threatening leadership, without the basic element of trust, will never access the blind and unknown windows of human opportunity.

Johari Window Communication

The Johari Window opens opportunities for insight into psychological and social domains. This social window encourages expansion of shared information and achieving accurate feedback, but requires personal risk for the leader. Psychological insight and rapport requires candid leaders who establish trust and mutual respect. Excellent leadership suggests information exchanges, rather than one-way dialogs that don't involve feedback (Baker, 2009; Luft, 1970).

Feedback requires information from police officers about how they feel toward and perceive leadership behaviors. Open leaders are willing to disclose and encourage opportunities to understand how others feel about suicide.

Impersonal or detached leaders deny officers opportunities to disclose feelings because of poor approachability, their facades, and the absence of leader feedback (Baker, 2009; Luft, 1970).

The goal is to obtain information not known to self, but known to others. The opportunity to gain information from this *blind spot*, and *unknown* windowpane portions from the four Johari windowpanes, or quadrants, proves essential to successful prevention and intervention. Sharing information from the *hidden area windowpane* (sometimes referred to as the facade) of the leader provides greater understanding for subordinates to follow and share feedback. Leadership self-disclosure encourages rapport and trusting relationships with individual officers, civilians, informal groups, and the police organization (Baker, 2009; Luft, 1970).

Peering into the Johari windowpanes allows police leaders to expose the façade or the *hidden area* (the issues others do not know about the leader). The purpose is to gain sufficient knowledge about the blind spot and unknown windowpanes (the issues the leaders do not know about). Refer to Figure 9-1 for examples of Johari windowpanes, or quadrants, and concepts (Baker, 2009; Luft, 1970).

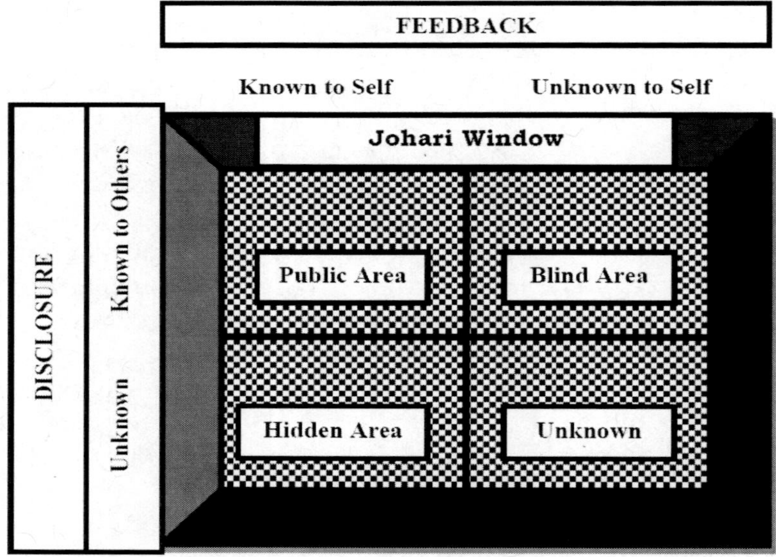

Figure 9-1. Johari Window

Adapted from: Joseph Luft, Group Process: An Introduction to Group Dynamics (California: National Press Books, 2ed., 1970; Baker, 2009)

Shrinking the windowpanes or quadrants around the blind spot ultimately offers insight into the unknown windowpane area and related issues. Insight provides opportunities to communicate, seize initiatives, and problem-solve with appropriate prevention and intervention remedies. Leaders need feedback about the unknown factors of suicide. Establishing communication and feedback develops relationships that allow the proper referral for officers and civilians looking for the right intervention resources (Baker, 2009; Luft, 1970).

The Johari windowpanes suggest that denial is a two-way communication and feedback quandary. For leaders and officers engaging the facade or hidden area, thereby blocking access to the blind spot and unknown windowpanes, the solution is in the open space. The warning signs are there; however, feedback is not present.

The open space is the key to personal power or windowpane where leaders have opportunities to be authentic and open to communication. Openness allows for the exchange of what one knows about himself and what others know. This form of personal leadership interaction and risk taking invites the necessary feedback for effective outcomes for suicidal officers. Successful leaders access the public area or windowpane and use it to launch admittance to a blind area or windowpane (at risk officers) and unknown (impeding crisis) areas or windowpanes. Once the relationship and rapport are in place, the leader is in the right position to take action. Refer to Figure 9-2 for examples of the Johari Window feedback opportunities for police suicide information.

The numbers of stealth suicides are surprising; many incidents go undetected. One explanation is that the officer was able to maintain a facade in front of peers. Connected to this theme is the notion that officers feel a need to engage in denial to avoid the psychological appearance of weakness under fire. Another rationale is that the police culture is socially and structurally conducive to maintaining the cover for feelings of inadequacies. In addition, leaders may not have opened the Johari Window of opportunity.

Responding leaders must exercise the highest degree of judgment when responding to a police suicide call. Excellent judgment is especially important when responding to family members and friends. Notification is a sensitive function, the mission requires a special person, and the selection process is important. The social support for survivors, the most important priority, and the last remembrance are the lasting impressions.

Critical Incident Stress Management Program

The Critical Incident Stress Management Program (CISM) is a compressive, integrated multi-component crisis intervention system. The origination and foundation of CISM is the collaborative work of Mitchell and Everly (1997), which dates back to the early 1970s. Their writings and training described a stress management strategy for those who might experience a critical incident or traumatic stressor. CISM was originally for emergency first responders; however, now it is applicable to all persons exposed to trauma. Certainly, police officers fall into that category.

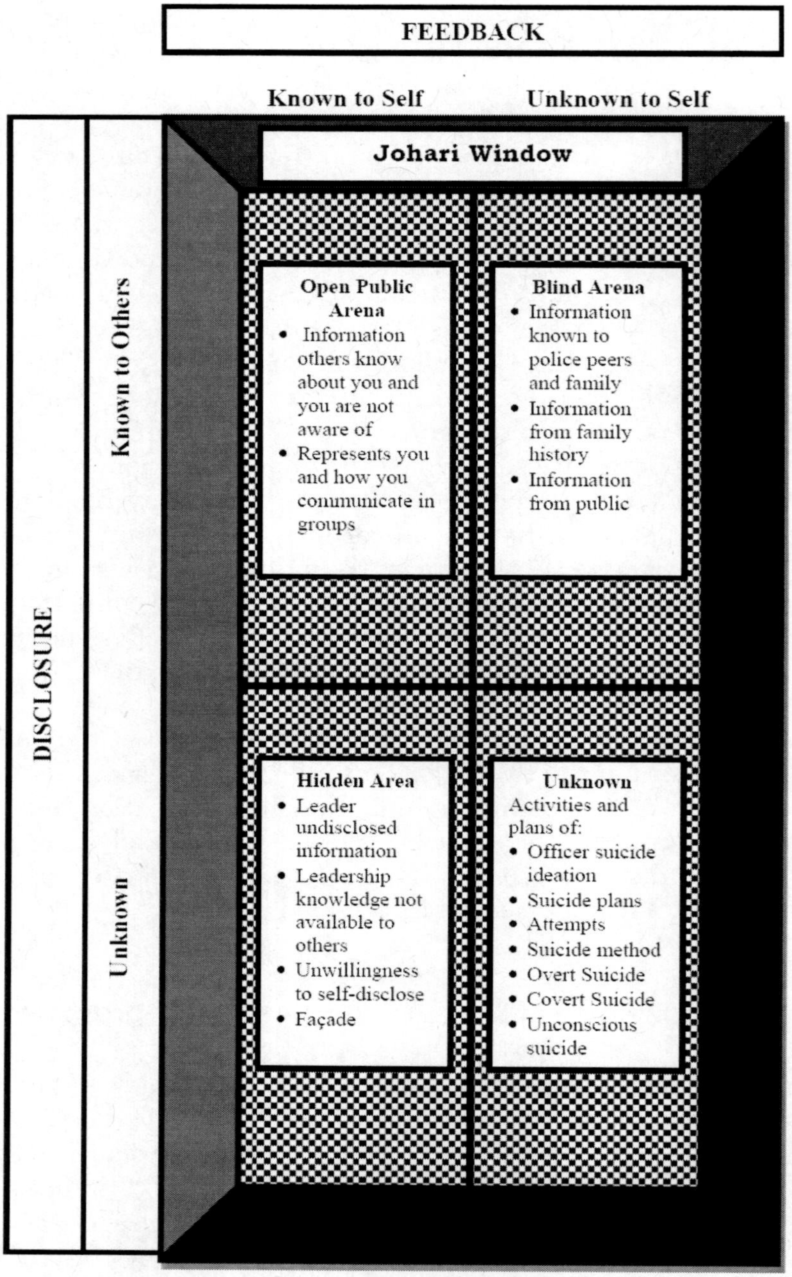

FEEDBACK

		Known to Self	Unknown to Self
DISCLOSURE	Known to Others	**Open Public Arena** • Information others know about you and you are not aware of • Represents you and how you communicate in groups	**Blind Arena** • Information known to police peers and family • Information from family history • Information from public
	Unknown	**Hidden Area** • Leader undisclosed information • Leadership knowledge not available to others • Unwillingness to self-disclose • Façade	**Unknown** Activities and plans of: • Officer suicide ideation • Suicide plans • Attempts • Suicide method • Overt Suicide • Covert Suicide • Unconscious suicide

Johari Window

Figure 9-2. Johari Window and Suicide Feedback Opportunities

Adapted from: Joseph Luft, Group Process: An Introduction to Group Dynamics (California: National Press Books, 1970; Baker, 2009 Modification)

CISM applies seven core crisis-intervention components. The goal is to mitigate crisis symptoms in traumatized persons. Examine the discussion of CISM principles below:

Pre-crisis preparation: This component includes stress management education, stress resistance, and crisis mitigation training for individuals and organizations. Disaster, terrorist, or other large-scale incident interventions include but are not limited to (1) demobilizations for emergency response personnel, a shift change decompression; (2) and crisis management debriefings for police officers, rescue personnel, general citizens, schools, or corporate organizations, town meetings, and Incident Command Staff advisement.

Defusing: This three-phase structured small group discussion is provided within hours of a crisis for purposes of assessment, triaging, and acute symptom mitigation.

Critical Incident Stress Debriefings (CISD): Refers to the International Critical Incident Stress Foundation's seven-phase structured group discussion customarily provided 24 to 72 hours, or 3 to 4 weeks after a major disaster. Post-crisis procedures mitigate acute symptoms, assess the need for follow-up, and provide a sense of post-crisis closure.

Counseling Services: Provide individual crisis intervention/counseling or psychological support throughout the full range of the crisis incident. In addition, they coordinate family crisis and organizational and pastoral crisis interventions. Finally, the follow-up and referral services for assessment and treatment when necessary are essential to the successful resolution of the crisis. CISM crisis interventions cover the full spectrum and temporal span of the incident from pre-crisis to acute-crisis and finally post-crisis phases.

Critical Incident Stress Debriefing

Critical Incident Stress Debriefing (CISD) continues to be a work in progress, and has direct application by emergency service workers, rescue workers, and police and fire personnel, as well as trauma/disaster survivors. One subcomponent of the CISD model applies the CISM strategies of Mitchell and Everly (1997). Groups of individuals, usually within 24 to 72 hours following a critical incident or 3 to 4weeks after a major disaster, critical incident, or similar catastrophic or traumatic experience receive the CISD briefing.

A critical incident is any negative situation that exceeds the normal experiences of an individual and that can potentially overwhelm the individual's ability to cope and function effectively. The traumatic event(s) may bring on unusually strong emotions and thoughts.

The formal CISD intervention is a seven-phase process, which includes leadership and assistance by a mental health professional and a peer facilitator. These phases include seven content and goal directed behaviors. Refer to Table 9-2 for an example of additional goal-directed behaviors.

Table 9-2. Goal-Directed Behaviors: Critical Incident Stress Debriefing (CISD Seven-Phase Process)
(Adapted from Mitchell, et al. 1997)

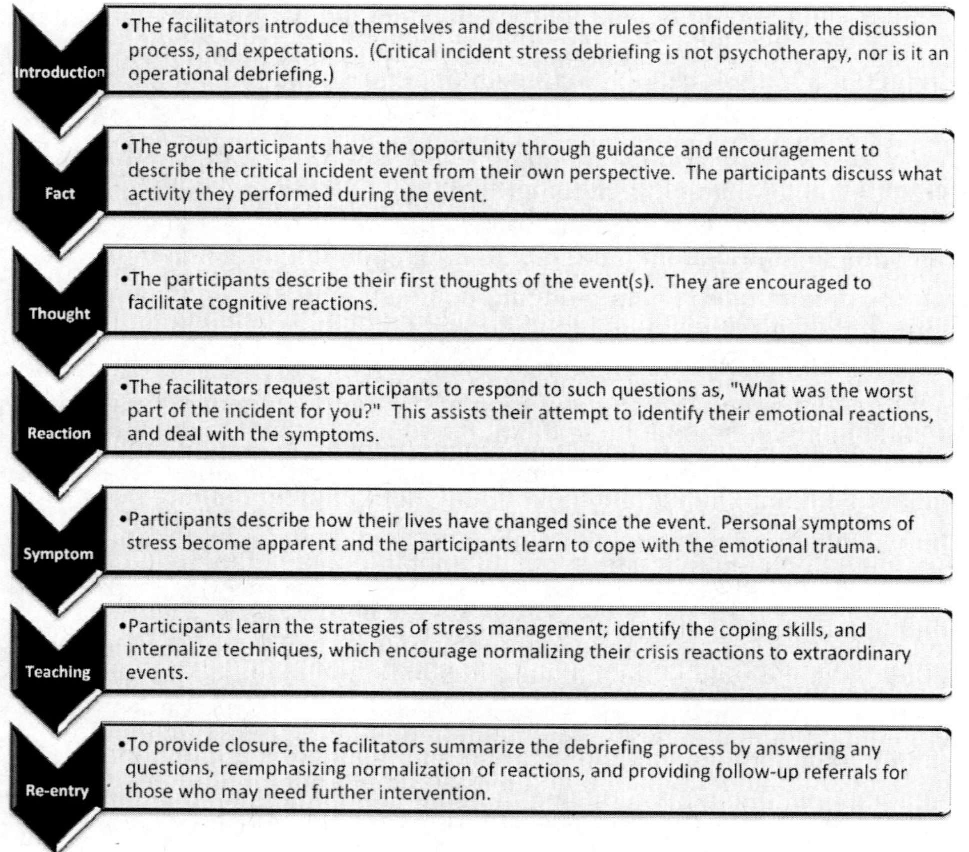

Phase	Description
Introduction	•The facilitators introduce themselves and describe the rules of confidentiality, the discussion process, and expectations. (Critical incident stress debriefing is not psychotherapy, nor is it an operational debriefing.)
Fact	•The group participants have the opportunity through guidance and encouragement to describe the critical incident event from their own perspective. The participants discuss what activity they performed during the event.
Thought	•The participants describe their first thoughts of the event(s). They are encouraged to facilitate cognitive reactions.
Reaction	•The facilitators request participants to respond to such questions as, "What was the worst part of the incident for you?" This assists their attempt to identify their emotional reactions, and deal with the symptoms.
Symptom	•Participants describe how their lives have changed since the event. Personal symptoms of stress become apparent and the participants learn to cope with the emotional trauma.
Teaching	•Participants learn the strategies of stress management; identify the coping skills, and internalize techniques, which encourage normalizing their crisis reactions to extraordinary events.
Re-entry	•To provide closure, the facilitators summarize the debriefing process by answering any questions, reemphasizing normalization of reactions, and providing follow-up referrals for those who may need further intervention.

There is still some misunderstanding of crisis-intervention debriefing strategies. One mistaken assumption is that a single CISD session can prevent PTSD developing in traumatized individuals. According to Everly and Mitchell (2000), CISD emergency intervention was never declared a substitute for psychological treatment, and definitely not as a stand-alone intervention.

They acknowledge that it is a form of crisis intervention and a component of the larger crisis intervention program. This is important to remember because these PTSD issues have associations and links to suicidal behaviors and the possibility of police suicide. Those individuals demonstrating pathways to PTSD need follow-up, intervention, and in-depth treatment referrals.

Informal Debriefing

Formal debriefings allow professional counselors, social workers, and other mental health professionals access to those who need help after a traumatic event. This forum allows the survivors/victims to talk about and vent their emotional reaction in a safe environment. Natural or informal briefings that take place before and after police shift deployments offer safe social zones. This informal natural model can offer similar interventions through peers, friends, and family.

The military has a "buddies on the battlefield program" to provide interpersonal communication and a support system about traumatic experiences. These discussions are going to take place naturally and may serve as universal responses following devastating traumatic events. Accomplished in an informal manner, natural briefings provide a compassionate milieu in response to stressful experiences.

Fullerton et al. (2000) suggested that there are potential advantages of a natural briefing over a formal briefing. Mental health professionals have generally believed that survivor groups need to find their own resources of emotional support. Survivor groups can mutually assist each other, offer a potential resource for bonding, and form the foundation of the healing process.

Police Family Support

The police officer's family bereavement process remains an important consideration and deserves a high priority. Restorative Retelling Group (RRG) offers a strategy for close family members of police officers. They are vulnerable after their family member's homicide or suicide and may be experiencing intrusive thoughts or flashbacks about the final moments of the death of their loved one. The family's preoccupation about their loss may take many forms; looking at a photograph, a particular time location, or nighttime dreams.

The commitment to overcoming trauma must move beyond telling the story. The transformation will most likely develop when the preoccupation with the violent death moves to a form of acceptance. Rynerson et al. (2002) developed a systematic community-based support system for family members who suffer a violent death. Time-limited interventions consist of ten weekly, two-hour sessions with a closed-group format:

(1) "The first 10-session group is entitled the *Criminal Death Support Group*. The objective of this intervention during the early period of spotlighted media exposure (whether local or national), the raw recounting of events and the judicial findings are to provide reasons for clarification and advocacy for the demands resulting from public retelling of the victim's death.

(2) The second 10-session group is entitled *Restorative Retelling*. These sessions meet after the investigation and trial are completed. The objective of this intervention is to moderate the internalized trauma of the violent death experience. When factual and imaginary retellings become prolonged and obsessive, the recounting includes reframing the resilient reconnection with positive life memories of the deceased.

This reconnection with vital imagery is the basis for restorative retelling. The group focuses on commemorating the vital living memory of the deceased. Then writing and drawing exercises follow, allowing the survivors to restore meaning and purpose in life beyond the violent death."

The external counseling programs may be more acceptable to police officers. External or internal programs must have the confidence and trust of the officers, and not be a tool of discipline for the police agency. The stigma associated with referrals can act as a major deterrent. The negative labeling of officers who seek help is extremely counterproductive.

Chaplain Services

Police leaders are in an excellent position to assess the need for religious clergy. There is less stigma and acceptance to seeking religious help. This is not the time for indoctrinating one's religious beliefs, but an opportunity to open the door to possibilities.

Police agencies need to identify a police officer's religious preferences then follow-up with a list of police chaplains. This resource may not apply to everyone, but it may be helpful in the initial referral phase. Atheists are not likely to respond, but, in a severe crisis, may reach out to someone they know as a religious helper.

D'Angelo (2001) recommended that a healthy spiritual relationship can be a resource for police officers who are coping with troubled interpersonal relationships and marital difficulties. The major contributor to police officer suicides is the inability or refusal to request outside help. Spiritual counseling may help people deal with issues of shame, including the shame associated with suicidal thoughts. Feelings of isolation and alienation may find relief in spirituality and lead to reaching out for help.

Police Referral Programming

Police agencies tend to emphasize facts and investigative procedures. The facts are important; however, so are feelings. The emotional considerations are always essential to superior communication. Haberfield (2001) recommended expanding the definition of critical incident stress, and supplementary training modules include the Feelings, Inputs, Tactics Model (FIT) applications.

FIT has several advantages for law enforcement officers. The importance of counseling, peer support, or other stress reducing strategies is essential, but FIT offers a missing component. Police officers may define these terms as signs of weakness that stereotype them as less capable of doing dangerous assignments. Introducing FIT and Maslow's theory of human needs serves as a bridging platform to link those programs. Haberfield (2001) suggested that the mandatory FIT program target police academies and in-service training programs to address many of the hidden stressors.

Stressful or critical incidents are in the eye of the beholder. Refer to the following case study as an example. CISM strategies, debriefings, and FIT programs provide strategies to meet the needs of individual officers who experience critical incidents.

Case Study Illustration

Suicide by cop not only affects the officers involved in the shooting, but also can negatively affect those officers on the scene who do not shoot. Alice is a 30-year-old female who has been a police officer for 2 years. While working a single car, she received a gun run from the dispatcher.

The subject fled and a brief chase ensured culminating in the subject running off the side of the road, bailing out of his car, and pointing a gun at an officer responding to the scene. Alice arrived on the scene, heard gunfire, and drew her weapon to cover her fellow officer. She saw the subject shot and lying on the ground and appropriately backed off, holstered her weapon, and helped secure the scene.

All of her actions on an in-cruiser video demonstrated correct actions on her part. Alice, however, felt her reactions were inappropriate. She was unsure if she should have shot and questioned her actions. She began having vivid dreams with themes of fear, self-doubt, and helplessness.

She questioned her adequacy as a police officer and berated herself for not shooting the subject in spite of obvious negative crossfire implications. She became anxious at the subject for "putting us in the position of shooting him." Her sleep patterns disturbed, she now thought about resigning from her job. She lost objectivity and experienced self-doubt.

All of these emotions were relatively short-lived and she was able to recover adequately with expert debriefing and a few follow-up sessions with the department psychologist. Returning three months post incident, she was once more functioning effectively on the job. Six months post incident she reported "rarely thinking about it," and having it "pretty much out of my mind."

Her nightmares subsided, interest levels returned, and she even reported feeling generally better prepared to handle the unexpected. Over time, she felt the incident made her stronger and had no feelings of hyper-vigilance, numbing, guilt, failure, or problems with concentration or attention that were previously reported. Her take on the incident at this point was rationally stated as "he forced the situation; he put us in a position of shooting him. He took away our control and I'm angry about that."

Source: This case study was adapted from J. Nick Marzella (2001), Department of Justice publication.

Special Note: Alice may be experiencing Secondary Traumatic Stress (STS), she was not the shooter, but witnessed the results. Just merely being present has consequences for the officer arriving at the scene. Each officer experiences different symptoms of critical incident stress. Attending officers individual needs through excellent programming and debriefings is essential for positive outcomes.

Marzella (2001) found that access to a department psychologist or a psychologist familiar with policing was important and effective, as was support from coworkers and family. When possible, those doing the debriefing should be familiar with the department or at least chosen by the department. This practice seems to have more credibility than those bent on relating their own war stories. The psychologist should have excellent verbal skills as well as listening, empathic understanding, and interviewing expertise. Attending to officers' emotional needs is important to help them through difficult times.

Focus Points

A suicide prevention program recognizes that the risk for suicide exists for law enforcement officers. Standing operating procedures (SOP) remain the starting point for a suicide prevention and intervention program.

Troubled officers typically resist seeking help, but often give clues and warning signs.

The process of intervention needs to be as easy and supportive as possible. Trust is the motivating factor for participation in prevention and intervention programming.

Asking for help signals strength, not weakness, and that must form the foundation of any prevention program. One basic tool for obtaining information in the social and emotional climate is feedback from police officers and civilians. Leaders need feedback about the unknown factors of suicide.

The "Johari Window" opens opportunities for insight into psychological and social domains. Leaders and officers engaging the facade or hidden windowpane are blocking access to the blind spot and the unknown.

The Johari Window suggests that denial is a two-way communication and feedback quandary. The solution to communication is in the open window of opportunity. The warning signs appear in the combination of windowpanes. However, if observers do not seek on open window, the tragedy of police suicide remains a possibility.

Many police officers may feel comfortable with personal contacts. The chaplain or other clergy are very effective in cases where the officer is reluctant to talk to counselors. The chaplain's high visibility in the department is an important factor. Police officers are likely to trust and engage people they know.

Police departments create a number of innovative referral prevention and intervention programs. Counseling programs may assist in preventing the effects of stress, alcohol abuse, and drug treatment. The key requirements for the success of these programs are confidentiality and trust.

Conclusion

Police senior leaders, managers, and superiors have major responsibilities regarding the welfare of their officers. The human side of law enforcement is generally more difficult to handle than the daily routine of technical issues. Characteristically, when police officers experience serious, long-term emotional problems that can lead to suicide, two reactions occur that hinder the helping process. First, everyone from the affected officer, friends, and coworkers to the department's hierarchy initially deny that a problem exists. Applying excellent leadership and the Johari Window allow the feedback information that opens the door to program interventions.

CHAPTER 10

POLICE RESEARCH CONTROVERSIES

"Knowing yourself is the beginning of all wisdom."

— Aristotle

Police leaders may not be able to predict every police suicide; some give little warning of their state of mind. Police suicide or any suicide is not about counting the losses; it is about saving lives. The human factor remains immeasurable; the loss of one life is always significant. The rippling effect causes shock waves across the community and law enforcement agency. Family and friends suffer immeasurable loss. The question remains: How many will police agencies and counselors prevent?

Chapter Focus

This chapter explores basic scientific methodology and statistical problems concerning police suicide. It discusses research obstacles to adequate statistical analysis methods. In addition, this chapter endeavors to explain the suicide rate for police officers and the statistical quandary. The military PTSD case studies serve as illustrations and possible applications to police suicide.

Overview

Police suicide research presents unique opportunities to help citizens from the private sector. Federal, state, and local government resources offer fewer prospects to fund police intervention strategies. In addition, private sector suicide interventionists benefit from the exchange of data-generating research. The collaboration of researchers, psychologists, and law enforcement executives may improve opportunities for prevention and intervention strategies. This chapter explains the present state of research and eliminates some of the misunderstandings involving police suicide.

Research Enigma

Science is the process of thinking and asking the right questions. Police suicide studies confront numerous methodological and statistical issues that confound analysis. The proverbial elephant parable describes the research quandary concerning related data collection and statistical analysis.

The first blind man has contact with the body, the second the tusk, the third the trunk, the fourth the knee, the fifth the ear, and the sixth, the tail of the elephant. The six blind men interpret different perspectives regarding the elephant's description. Individual perceptions compartmentalize thinking and deny reliable information concerning the totality of the whole. This analogy explains how our sensory perceptions influence research and can lead to miscalculations.

This is especially the case when the research of the component parts of a whole, and their relationships in making up the whole, remain insufficiently synchronized. For example, the elephant analogy is appropriate to problems associated with police suicide research in the United States. These measurement limitations in the literature and media obscure scientific understanding. Refer to Figure 10-1 for analysis of the police suicide research problems in the United States according to Bergen et al. (2001).

Figure 10-1. Police Research Methodology Issues
(Adapted from Bergen et al., 2001)

Early Research

Researchers started to focus on violence and suicidal behavior in the workplace in response to the 1990 New York City police suicides. Police suicide reached new statistical highs with eleven deaths. Moreover, police suicides represent the leading cause of police fatalities in New York City. While that statement is accurate for New York City, it may not represent what is happening nationally.

The New York phenomenon should not serve as a scientific generalization. Large cities similar to New York such as Los Angeles, Detroit, and Chicago may not reflect an accurate representation. Police research might identify common patterns by examining a representative sample. Dividing the number of suicides (12) by the average number of sworn officers (5,272), then multiplying this quotient by 100,000 and then dividing by the number of years in the study (8) leaves a false impression concerning the national rate of police suicides (Aamodt and Stalnaker, 2001).

Focused scientific inquiry and systematic research would serve mid-size and smaller police agencies. Research conducted by the Federal Bureau of Investigation reveals that the average police department employs less than 50 officers. In addition, 75% of police agencies have less than 25 sworn officers. The focus on police suicide should address regional and local variations and the nature of police organizations.

We mourn all suicidal deaths. However, when suicide involves police officers who are bound to serve and protect, it is difficult to understand why they would harm themselves. Those closest to the officer attempt to correct their cognitive dissonance, and may even try to deny the reality of suicide. Researchers may drift in the emotional waves that interfere with scientific inquiry. There are two extremes in cases of police suicide: denial at the interpersonal level and misinterpreting the data on the scientific level of analysis. Both perspectives influence data objectivity.

The literature reports that one major obstacle is the underreporting of police suicide. Researchers argue that the misclassification of suicide represents the larger problem. A suicide cover-up is always possible including documenting the officer's death was accidental or even a homicide to protect the officer, family, and department. Insurance companies will not pay benefits to families of individuals who commit suicide. Therefore, the incentive to "doctor" reports exists because of investigator denial and financial loss to the family. The stigma to the officer and department offers another motivational factor (Burge, 1982).

These considerations may serve as a basis for the misclassification of police suicides; however, insufficient data exist to provide statistical evidence. Researchers agree that there are many consequential statistical and collection problems associated with police suicide reporting and documentation.

The Statistical Quandary

Statistics describe large-scale trends, and police suicide data may have political ramifications. The findings have value in illustrating, rather than proving or disproving, theories about the causes of police suicide. The greater significance may be in reflecting trends and changes, but only when calculated collectively with other police departments. Police agency statistics serve as simple snapshots in time for a department when they stand-alone.

The Center for Disease Control (CDC) estimates that Americans commit suicide at a rate of 12 per 100,000 residents. In addition, the CDC reports suicide is the ninth leading cause of death in the United States. The most common measure of comparison is determining the number of suicides per 100,000 of the targeted populations statistically. This is accomplished by using the following formula: The total officer suicides are divided by the number of officers in the agency or total sample; the resulting percentage is multiplied by 100,000 and that number divided by the number of years involved in the study (#suicides/#officers x 100,000/# years).

However, generalizations from values in small samples are at the origin of much misunderstanding in social science research. Police suicide research and the literature encounters the resulting reliability and related validity scientific concerns. The failure to examine large samples results in a common statistical problem of small numbers (Vogt, 1999). Small sample values deviate significantly from real population values.

Meta-Analysis: Strategic Picture

Meta-analysis offers a methodological technique that offsets statistical limitations addressing police suicides. Statistical analysis that applies meta-analysis addresses multiple studies. Combining related research requires identifying a common hypothesis. Meta-analysis overall averages are more powerful estimates than those derived from a single study. One weakness of the meta-analysis method is that sources of bias are not controlled. In addition, if poorly designed studies serve as data sources for meta-analysis, then the results are not valid and reliable (Cooper and Hedges, 1994).

An earlier review of the research and survey of the literature reveals that police officers do not have the high suicide rate previously reported. Aamodt and Stalnaker (2001) initiated a scholarly discourse and debate concerning the accuracy and validity of law enforcement suicides. Their analysis exposed flaws in the existing data. Furthermore, these data proved that law enforcement officers *do not* have a higher suicide rate when compared with people of a comparable age, race, and gender. The popular view that suicide rates are unusually high in law enforcement seems inconsistent according to their research.

Aamodt and Stalnaker (2001) found that law enforcement personnel are less likely to commit suicide when compared with other groups. They tabulated the national literature and media reports into one statistical aggregate. After completing their meta-analysis study of suicide rates, they concluded that the best probable estimate of law enforcement suicides is 18.1 per 100,000. When the authors compared for a similar population of Caucasian men between the ages of 25 and 54, law enforcement officers improved their statistical standing considerably.

Aamodt and Stalnaker (2001) concluded that the police personnel rate for suicide is 18.1% greater than the general population of 11.4%; however, it is not as high as would be expected when the comparisons are to a similar group of people in the general population. The evidence showed that law enforcement officers are 27% below the average population once the suicide rate for sex, race, and age (25-54) are controlled. Moreover, the authors included all published data regardless of adequacy of the studies' scientific control of the variables, which obviously affects the validity of study findings. Another important consideration was the use of a comparison group that included individuals who were unemployed or suffered mental illness (Aamodt and Stalnaker, 2001).

Loo (2003) recommended several superior methodology strategies and thought that police suicide researchers should address longer time frames. Moreover, complete suicide statistics that include more variables and categories include: (1) year, (2) sex, and (3) ethnic groups. In addition, the rates for population comparison groups are most helpful. Loo suggested that variations in police suicide rates across law enforcement agencies may cause inaccurate statistical results.

A department may have no suicides one year and perhaps one or two the next year. Because of this, Loo (2003) recommended that researchers report modes and ranges of police suicide and averages. One example might be a police department that reported one suicide over 50 years ago. The suicide rate might appear high for that year, but low if a yearly average was calculated.

Campion (2001) made some insightful observations that complemented previous contributors' excellent research. Their joint effort shed new light on the police suicide mystique regarding the rate of suicide and related factors. Campion's observations counter the media's attempt to promote victimization, cover-up, the code of silence, and tendency to disregard research that counters or negates their position. Police suicides rank fourth behind dentists, doctors, and entrepreneurs who constantly encounter the public, but do not have the same easy access to weapons.

Campion concludes that police suicide is a rather infrequent occurring event when one considers that 99.98% of officers in his study did not commit suicide. Police suicide, when compared as a yearly average over 19 years, is slightly higher (by 0.0004%) than the rate of the general population (not adjusted for race, sex, or age). His research refuted the earlier statistical analysis of police suicides as excessive.

Police suicide research should focus on an appropriate comparison group. The target sample would primarily include white, 21- to 55-year-old working-class men who have access to weapons. Improved methodology and sampling would assist in obtaining better reliability and validity for the police research data.

Group adjustments are necessary for officer diversity including gender, racial, and ethnic composition. In New York City, 89 police officers committed suicide between 1985 and 1998. This means that the NYPD had an annual suicide rate at nearly 16% per 100,000. Eight of these suicides were female officers comprising 15% of the police force. The annual rate for female officer suicides was 9.6 per 100, 000, indicating female officers have a higher risk than the civilian female population (Amsel et al., 2001).

Another reason for altering the sampling process includes an increase in the African American population serving as NYPD police officers. These minority officers represented 10 of the 89 officers who committed suicide, for a rate of 13.8 per 100,000. This population was nearly twice the annual rate for civilian African Americans of 7.2 per 100,000 (Amsel et al., 2001). Expanding the population database offers an opportunity to develop a more representative population.

Research Synopsis

Police research identifying academy recruits at higher risk for suicide continues to lack clarity. Hem et al. (2001) published a systematic critique of police suicides. They identified 41 original studies that were inconsistent and inconclusive. Most of the studies reported on limited and specific police populations. In addition, previous research literature advocated that police officers do not have as high a rate of suicide as previously reported.

O'Hara and Violanti (2009) collected descriptive police suicide data from 50 states that provided a statistical snapshot for 2008. They reported that considerable controversy exists concerning the accuracy and validity of suicide previous studies. Their research confirmed a lower police suicide rate than originally advocated. Unfortunately, the topic of police suicide has given rise to speculation and exaggerated statistics.

Military Research Opportunities

The military is another population worthy of study since this research continues to reveal many applications to policing. The armed forces experience accelerates combat stress. Military trauma exposure generally takes place in a short time frame, while policing trauma unfolds over years of career service. The cross-referencing of military research continues to expand the present state of knowledge concerning PTSD and suicide.

The military has experienced a recent upsurge in suicides. Police operate in a similar paramilitary high-stress and trauma environment. The stress and trauma of combat operations offer unique opportunities to study individual resilience and hardiness. One of the ways to offset the present police research limitation would be to include military research on PTSD and suicide.

The military presents an opportunity to follow several subjects in a career path from recruitment to retirement. This research would include military personnel who have completed multiple combat deployments. For example, Helmkamp (1996), in his study of suicide among males in the U.S. Armed Forces, established that military security and law enforcement personnel had a significantly increased rate ratio for suicide. The study of Vietnam veterans with PTSD found that nearly 50% indicated a current sense or belief of a foreshortened future. In addition, over 64% had a coexisting diagnosis of major depression.

The emphasis would be on those members of the military that made a successful adjustment to combat trauma versus those that experienced PTSD and suicidal ideation. Another comparison group would be those military personnel that committed suicide early and late in their careers. There is a great deal to learn about trauma and suicide by comparing military personnel and paramilitary police personnel populations.

Returning veterans from Afghanistan and Iraq also offer unique opportunities to study high rates of trauma exposures that influence Combat Post-traumatic Stress Disorder (CPTSD). This population is at a very high risk for trauma incidents. Direct combat exposure is one of many trauma opportunities in a war zone. There are many other stressors including exposure to suffering soldiers and civilians, death and destruction, and suicide bombers.

According to the U.S. Veterans Administration, war stress reactions include the following personal stressors: guilt concerning personal actions or inactions, anger and rage, and numerous other threats and the related loses. War stress reactions include withdrawal, restlessness, psychomotor deficiencies, confusion, sweating, nausea, and inactivity, and fatigue, heightened sense of threat, severe suspicion, distrust, and nightmares.

PTSD is a risk factor for suicide among veterans. Those at the highest risk for suicide are those who were wounded. Combat-related guilt is another risk factor for veterans who suffer PTSD. Military research findings indicate there are two points where soldiers become psychologically incapacitated. The first is after traumatic stressors on the battlefield identified as "acute combat stress." These soldiers are unable to return to the battlefield (Shaw, 1987; Swank and Marchand, 1946). The remaining soldiers after the initial combat trauma remain highly efficient and combat proficient. These combatants maintain this composure for approximately 60 days. A second trauma reaction, *combat fatigue*, follows the 60-day period.

During this 60-day interval, a period of resiliency, the combatants prevailed. This presents two peaks of traumatic responses. Friedman (1996) described the period between the two peaks as a period of "negative resilience." The combatants' apparent adaptation conceals negative reactions of disassociation, numbing, and denial. This might suggest that negative resilience may serve as a temporary coping mechanism to sustain some sense of power and control.

Police officers express their trauma experience as "used to" traumatic exposure or the "routinized traumatization of war" (Laufer, 1988). This seems to suggest that resiliency that the traumatized participants believe as true may only be temporary. Military personnel or police officers may be masking the trauma exposure by adapting the use of repression and denial. The twin peak effect may account for delayed on-set of traumatic related symptoms.

Peterson et al. (2008) suggested that 500,000 veterans still suffer from PTSD from their service in Vietnam. According to statistics gathered by the National Center for Post-traumatic Stress Disorder, the lifelong prevalence for PTSD among combat veterans is 30.9%. Nearly half of all male combat veterans, as well female veterans who served in Vietnam, experienced "clinically serious stress reaction symptoms."

The National Vietnam Veterans Readjustment Survey (NVVRS, 1986-1988) established some interesting statistics. Almost half of all Vietnam combat veterans with PTSD experienced arrest or served time in jail at least once, 34. 2% of combat veterans were arrested and served jail sentences more than once; 11.5% of these PTSD veterans sustained felony convictions.

Schnurr et al. (2004) re-analyzed the NVVRS data and concluded that several key risk factors emerged. The important risk factors among PTSD Vietnam combat veterans were (1) family instability, severe punishment during childhood, and (3) depression. The military risk factors included: (1) war zone exposure, (2) immediate dissociation at the time of the traumatic event, (3) and depression.

Future incidents, depending on the intensity, duration, and frequency of the trauma, might destroy the resiliency factor. After some minor triggering event, the soldier or police officer may move into the second peak experiencing combat fatigue, burnout or PTSD. During this peak of trauma, the emotional reaction may include hospitalization, PTSD, or suicide (Roszell et al., 1991).

The future holds the possibility of additional research beyond Afghanistan and Iraq that will prove useful. The scientific data offer the possibility for law enforcement and the general population applications. The estimates are that 20% of these combat veterans will experience PTSD. In addition, it is estimated that 40% of the returning National Guard and USAR reservists will experience mental health symptoms. The exact statistical estimates are unknown as to how any veterans will suffer from PTSD return from Afghanistan and Iraq (Peterson et al. 2008).

Special Note: The knowledge developed from the CPTSD veterans may be of considerable value to the scientific knowledge base. Research funding would serve our soldiers, police officers, and citizens well. The transfer of the related trauma data to the mental health practitioners and public domain may save lives lost to suicide and related homicides.

Case Study Illustration

An armed robber permanently injured a young police officer. His partner was shot and dies due to an error on his part. Because of the extent of his injuries, he retired on disability. To control the chronic pain of his injuries, he had to take a multitude of various medications. Although the officer maintained friendships within the department, he struggled with survivor's guilt. He was unable to forgive himself for the death of his partner. After 5 years of battling depression, pain, and guilt, the officer committed suicide.

Although suicide is preventable in many cases, it is inevitable in some. A physical injury may end an officer's career. Disabled police officers must choose to accept their new lifestyle and apply new goals to keep them motivated. There will be officers who cannot achieve this acceptance and sadly, a life will be lost to suicide.

In departments across the country, there are daily reminders of the dangers of police work. Officers injured in the line of duty may sustain injuries as mild as scratches and bruises or as severe as bullet wounds. Wounded officers' emotional scars can vary as much as their physical scars. Many may be thankful that they survived; others may wish that they had not. The severity of the injury may cause chronic pain and emotional distress for years to come. Some officers may overcome the event, while others will remain bitter and angry. No two people will handle their trauma or their pain the same way.

Source: This case study was adapted from Teresa T. Tate (2001), Department of Justice publication.

Special Note: Many suicides like this may go unreported as police suicide because of the civilian or retired status. In addition, the active or retired military police suicides fail to register as a part of suicide statistics. Even dying in police uniform status may not classify the death as a suicide. The reporting system is far from perfect; denial and misclassification as police homicide or accidental death is a possibility.

Focus Points

Studies on police suicide generally focus on the number of suicides, the methods employed, and the impact of having service weapons readily available. Police suicide research must address unanswered questions and assist leadership in policy development that supports prevention, intervention, and training.

Answers to inquiries concerning police suicide have been elusive, and many issues remain unclear. Rather than dwelling on the rates and the means of suicide, perhaps analysts should determine what steps might have interfered with officers who ultimately took their own lives.

Police suicide studies confront numerous methodological and statistical issues that confound analysis. There are many statistical and collection problems associated with police suicide. A generalization from values in small samples is at the origin of much misunderstanding in social science research. In addition, media reports interfere with scientific inquiry and the flow of accurate information. Improved methodology and sampling would assist in obtaining better reliability and validity for the police research data.

The initial limited research on police suicide indicated a higher rate than the general population. Meta-analysis offers one methodological technique to offset statistical limitations addressing police suicides. State-of-the-art research studies found that law enforcement personnel are less likely to commit suicide than the general population.

Police suicide intervention strategies are not ideal; additional research will further enlighten the enigma. However, the good news is that law enforcement agencies now acknowledge the potential risk, after years of denial. Open and forthright discussions concerning sensitive topics and research inspire endeavors to prevent future police suicides. The military studies offer the opportunity to assist in that endeavor.

The present state of research on police suicide is mounting. An improved police attitude is helpful for the development of police intervention and prevention programming. Research does not reflect the role of the social environment and shifts focus to individual officers.

Police suicide remains an enigma; however, with the efforts of dedicated researchers, there has been some illumination. Human behavior is challenging and often unpredictable.

Conclusion

Perhaps it is time to look beyond descriptive statistics that rank statistical suicide comparisons for professions. Studies on police suicide generally focus on the number of suicides, the methods employed, and the impact of having service weapons readily available. Police suicide research needs to define questions that support prevention, intervention, and training. Police leaders plan for contingencies that may or may not happen to avoid or anticipate events. One police suicide can devastate a police organization and generate emotional ramifications throughout the community.

CHAPTER 11

POSITIVE LEADERSHIP: FINAL FOCUS POINTS

"It is one of the most beautiful compensations of life that no man can sincerely try to help another without helping himself."

— Ralph Waldo Emerson

James, a 42-year-old police officer struggling with alcohol abuse, was in an emotional spiral into depression. His wife feared that her husband's drinking was out of control. She reasoned that her departure would shock stop James' alcohol abuse. She believed the he would quit the heavy drinking and seek treatment. She did not want a divorce; however, she was unable to find another solution to his alcohol addiction. The officer's partner was aware of the situation, but chose not to intervene. The officer committed suicide a week later.

Source: This case study was adapted from Teresa T. Tate (2001), Department of Justice publication.

Special Note: The opportunity to act and save a life may appear several times, or only present itself once. Suicidal ideation may pass or result in the officer's death, so this brief widow of opportunity requires action. Hoping for the best possible outcome and doing nothing may result in a lifetime of regrets. Important research questions remain unanswered: Did the suicidal officer seek help prior to the life-taking event? Did his subtle pleas for help go unheeded? Did the officer turn away from a strategically-planned intervention and why?

Chapter Focus

The purpose of the Final Focus Points is to examine research application issues associated with police suicide. This chapter concludes with an emphasis on the foundations for the prevention and intervention of police suicide, which include: (1) intervention strategies, (2) police suicide prevention, and (3) reiteration of conceptual issues. The Final Focus Points expand initial focus points described in the Introduction, and tie together the ten chapter themes.

Overview

Recently, police stealth suicides have become a major consideration and are worth examining. O'Hara and Violanti (2009) collected descriptive police suicide data from 50 states that provided a statistical snapshot for 2008. They reported that considerable controversy exists concerning the accuracy and validity of previous studies. Their research confirmed a lower police suicide rate than originally advocated and refuted previous exaggerated frequency rates.

These researchers reported that only 12% of officers demonstrated a clear warning of suicide, while 64% "slipped under the radar" and did not provide a noticeable indication of suicide. It appears that these officers were able to maintain a facade and disguise their symptoms from other officers.

The above-cited recent police suicide statistics differ considerably from civilian statistics on suicide concerning warning signs and indicators. Why did the officers *not express* their desire to commit suicide or seek professional assistance? Were police officers more recently adept at concealing suicidal ideation, thereby, creating subtle obstacles to timely intervention and treatment?

Police chief executives plan for contingencies that may or may not happen to avoid or anticipate events. One police suicide can devastate a police organization and generate emotional ramifications throughout the community. Police leaders cannot second-guess; they must act on the current information and err on the side of life. Appropriate intervention occurs during a specific period, but within police organizations, denial often delays assistance.

Police chief executives are developing programs to counter stressors and suicide in their agencies. The focus is primarily at external change with programs to assist officer problems associated with professional responsibilities. These programs are reactive, rather than proactive, and include professional referrals to group counseling, psychological services, and individual counseling.

The concept of *vision* applies to law enforcement. Effective police executives, senior leaders, commanders, middle managers, and first-line supervisors need to look forward into the future, but there remains one core requirement for police leaders. Critical thinking offers direction and provides a compass and map for reaching the desired destination. The key to establishing vision is strategic planning, training, and program development (Baker, 2005b).

Program assessment is the best means for opening the channel of communication and feedback. This strategy allows critical information about the principle stressors and the possibility for prevention and intervention of police suicide. The potential police suicide requires immediate attention, program planning, and policy development.

Strategic Planning

Strategic long-term planning is global in nature and offers opportunities for quality research to verify the accuracy of strategic data. The loss of one police officer's life is one too many. Police suicide is preventable with some careful crisis intervention programming and planned procedures.

Police officers planning to commit suicide generally conceal their motives and intentions. There are testing instruments, clinical techniques, and screening methods, but none can conclusively predict suicide. Police murder-suicide also lacks a conclusive predictor. Some of the clues for murder-suicide are acute indications of hopelessness and obsessive preoccupations involving jealousy, paranoia, and fantasies of reunion or deliverance and salvation during episodes of major depression, psychosis, or bipolar disorder (Jacobs et al., 1999). Jacobs also indicated that alcohol or substance abuse is likely to increase the risk of murder suicide when other circumstances are concurrent.

Police departments cannot conduct surveillance and a suicide watch on every officer who is having on-the-job or domestic problems. The majority of police officers will cope with these issues. Every officer is unique; it is not possible to predict suicide. There are no absolute formulas, but there are indicators when an officer might need professional help. There are some indexes that suggest the recognition of risk, i.e., significant loss, particularly of a loved one; loss of police employment; or the officer's reputation. This chapter serves as a reexamination of those general risks and indicator factors.

Final Focus Points

Positive Strategy 1 – Introduction to Police Suicide

The possibility of depression as a previously existing condition may become aggravated due to traumatic stress. Depression is the primary factor and diagnosis in 70% of completed suicides. Styron (1990) described depression as a mystery, a gray drizzle of horror that takes on the quality of physical pain, an evil trick played upon the sick brain by the inhabiting psyche, which colors psychological events negatively. There is no hope of escape and it is entirely natural that the victim begins to think ceaselessly of oblivion.

Pam (2001) suggested that "Fifty percent of all depressions are alleged to be precipitated by stress-related events. Especially pernicious is early life stress, which permanently sensitizes the central nervous system, and cause a perpetual overreaction to events and acts to precondition or program later life afflictions. Depression appears to be predominantly a recurrent illness that shapes circuitry patterns in the brain, has dangerous physical concomitants and, characterized by loss of appropriate adaptability, sleep disturbance, diminished libido, inability to experience pleasure or happiness, lack of concentration and perspective, hopelessness, and impaired short-term memory."

Researchers linked depression to a genetic component that manifests its symptoms in families. Some research scientists view depression as a chemical imbalance. Others suggest that depression is a neurological disorder that sets up neural roadblocks to the processing of information. This defective circuitry fails to generate positive feelings and inhibit disruptive negative ones (Marano, 1999).

Janik and Kravitz (1994) reviewed the personnel of 134 police officers. Their target population was officers who were the subject of fitness-for-evaluations. They were attempting to predict variables that might contribute to an officer having made a suicide attempt. The researcher scanned the reports for officers having marital problems, alcohol and drug abuse, administrative harassment, and cumulative stressors. A multivariate analysis of these data to determine which variables best predicted suicide attempts revealed that marital problems and job suspension were the only statistically significant predictors. An officer experiencing marital problems was 4.8 times as likely to have attempted suicide. If job suspension was a variable, the odds of an attempted suicide were 6.7 times that of those officers who did no attempt suicide.

The average police suicide or profile is a white male, age 35, who serves in the patrol division, has marriage problems, and has experienced a recent loss or disappointment. The profile includes the following risk factors: (1) alcoholism, (2) impending retirement, (3) administrative inconsistencies, (4) aging/physical illness, (5) mental problems, (6) negative public image, (7) exposure to death/injury, (8) drug abuse, and, (9) firearms availability (Turvey, 1995).

O'Hara and Violanti (2009) reported approximately 102 police suicides in 2008. Their data indicated that law enforcement personnel, ages 35-39 were at a higher risk for suicide, with 29% of the suicides in this group. In addition, officers with 10-14 years of service were at an increased risk for suicide. Those serving at the lower ranks were at a higher risk. Furthermore, the use of firearms was the primary means and cause of death.

Proactive leadership intervention and prevention of police suicide requires assessment of social/psychological indicators. Psychological profiles may assist in reading the risk factors of suicidal ideation. Psychological autopsies serve as the basis for typologies, which may identify valuable indicators. Refer to Figure 11-1 for the scientific requirements for the psychological autopsy.

The evaluation of risk factors associated with police suicide includes the use of control groups (suicide vs. no suicide). The best indicator of the validity and reliability of psychological autopsies is the consistency of findings across studies. For example, psychiatric disorders reported in suicides tend to aggregate in families (Berent et al., 1988).

Psychological autopsies have empirical history associated with epidemiological case-control methodology. Case design can be applied to identifying personal characteristics or behaviors related to outcome occurrence. "Research designs of this nature select and compare attributes of case groups with known outcomes (suicide) with control groups matched on some specific criteria" (Friedman, 1994).

Depression remains the key red flag of police suicide. Police leaders need to read the signs of depression. Poor performance remains the most important indicator of depression and inner turmoil. The fitness evaluation is an opportunity to review the officer emotional climate and make an assessment for intervention and referral. Understanding the risk factors may save an officer's life and career.

Positive Strategy 2 – Police Suicide: Risk Assessment

Pre-employment psychological tests offer opportunities to assess suitability and serve as a superior officer screening process. Many federal, state, and local law enforcement agencies fail to administer psychological evaluations for entry-level applicants (Curran, 1998). The pre-employment testing procedures are absent particularly in smaller agencies and where politics triumph in the hiring process. A reliable pre-employment psychological examination assists in revealing possible depression and other forms of psychological pathology.

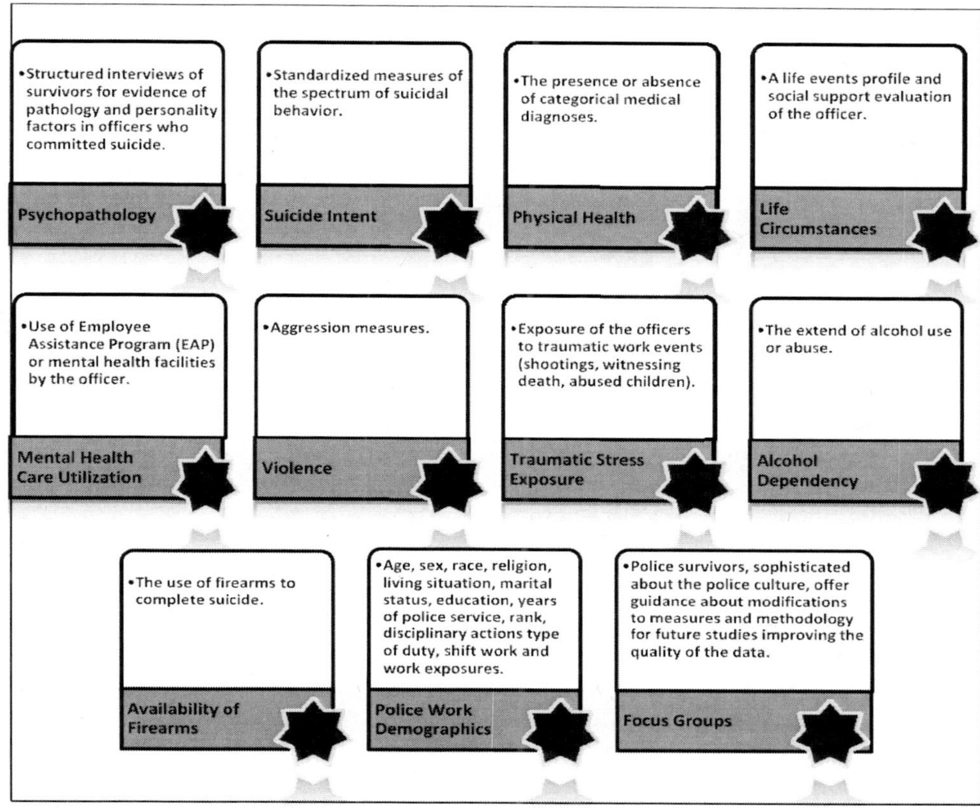

Figure 11-1. Police Suicide Psychological Autopsy Measures

(Adapted from Beskow et al., 1990; Robbins, et al., 1959; Friedman, 1994)

Does personality predispose officers to suicidal behaviors? Goldfarb and Aumiller (2004) suggested police selection procedures are not regulated and universal. These researchers recommended that police agencies hire people whose individual characteristics indicate that they are likely to be resilient police recruits. This is an important recruiting consideration because of police officer traumatic event exposures.

One perspective is to forecast forward in the police screening process for employment. The opportunity for many false negatives and false positives is always a factor. This may result in errors in screening police candidates. It would be wise to err on the side of the rights of citizens and public safety. Those recruits with tendencies toward depression and other psychological disorders would thrive better in an environment with less stress and violence in their daily encounters. Avoiding the triggering events that may aggravate their life-threatening status may avert a potential suicide.

Law enforcement agencies should provide a target specific foundation for developing a satisfactory match for aspiring officers. Human resources objectives strive to match their selection criteria in response to the police agency. Selected officer applicants should be psychologically resilient and match agency qualifications.

The early alert system starts with pre-employment psychological testing. Generally, larger departments have entry level psychological testing; financial concerns deter testing in smaller agencies. Ironically, small agencies can least afford the civil suits that may emerge from psychological disorders. Psychological screening is at best a general indicator, and provides a gauge to assess and intervene in higher risk cases.

For example, there is an alarming increase in Narcissistic Personality Disorder (NPD), which appears in the Diagnostic and Statistical Manual of Mental Disorders. Researchers at the National Institute of Justice conducted a representative sample of 35,000 Americans and determined that 1 out of 16 suffered from NPD at some point in their lives. These individuals are capable of generating a considerable amount of havoc and stress in police organizations. It appears members of this youthful population may file applications for police service.

Twenge and Campbell (2009, p. 2) make the observation that indicates a broader problem with narcissism in American culture. "The rise in narcissism is accelerating, with scores rising faster in the 2000s than in previous decades. By 2006, 1out of 4 college students agreed with the majority of the items on a standard measure of narcissistic traits. Narcissistic Personality Disorder (NPD), the more severe, clinically diagnosed version of the trait, is also far more common than once thought. Nearly 1 out of 10 Americans in their twenties, and 1 out of 16 of those of all ages, has experienced the symptoms of NPD. Even these shocking numbers are just the top of the iceberg; lurking underneath is the narcissistic culture that has drawn in many more. The narcissism epidemic has spread to the culture as a whole, affecting both narcissistic and less self-centered people."

Narcissism shares several related issues in common with other destructive behaviors including gambling, binge drinking, and possible sexual indiscretions. These high-risk destructive behaviors have time delayed short-term benefits and long-term costs (Twenge and Campbell (2009). Psychologists assess narcissism personality traits using the Narcissistic Personality Inventory (NIP). The effort involved in this form of psychological testing is worth the long-term results.

The Minnesota Multiphasic Personality Inventory (MMPI) is the most common pre-employment police psychological assessment. MMPI research data concerning the prediction concerning suicide is unsatisfactory (Clopton, 1979). However, in the revised edition MMPI-2 Structural Summary Format, Green and Nichols (1995) identified a cluster of scale items, and item information concerning Sc2 (Emotional Alienation), DEP (Depression Content Score), Sc4 (Lack of Ego Mastery Score; Cognitive), D3 (Brooding), and five other items as true. This level of specification offers a more comprehensive predictive target for suicide (Clopton, 1979; Kraft, 2001).

Personality testing is one important method used to find excellent psychological qualities for police candidates. Certainly, screening out those who do not have resilient personality qualities would be an important objective. The selection process assumes that there are personality traits that distinguish the potentially outstanding officer from the satisfactory officer. Bartol (1996) argued that screening in the best police candidates is improbable and screening out based on personality is far more effective. Future research directed at selecting those officers who possess the best resilience personality characteristics should receive the highest priority.

Proactive police leaders demand psychological testing at the entry level as it may assist in identifying those officers who are at the highest risk. The primary effort includes preventing suicidal police officers through improved research. Examining police organizations and culture from within ultimately means improved effectiveness in police testing. Early alert police screening has future implications for screening out those police candidates who are at risk for depression and suicide. Testing officers who display the red flags and profile indicators of suicidal behavior may assist in saving lives.

Positive Strategy 3 – Police Subculture: Social Climate

Inherent in police work is the emotional risk that may overwhelm the senses. The bond with danger and excitement has implications for personality and internalization of professional identity. Police culture reinforces the values, beliefs, and norms that reinforce the hero model. Police culture encourages risk taking and rewards bravery. These values and attitudes may lead to neglecting family life.

Researchers estimate that the incidence of domestic violence among police officers is significantly higher (25-40%) than the general population, which is approximately 16%. Unfortunately, police training teaches skills that not only make effective officers, but also can contribute to domestic violence. Police officers may learn how to avoid detection and cover up offenses. Research suggested that violence is addictive and the use of physical force, employed in police work, may find crossover applications in the home (Jacobs et al., 1999).

Alcohol abuse is serious indicator in police operations that typically leads to other problems: (1) high absenteeism and lateness, (2) intoxication on duty, (3) complaints from supervisors, (4) complaints from citizens of misconduct, (5) traffic accidents, and (6) an overall decrease in work performance (McCafferty et al., 1992).

The common denominator that adds the synergistic effect is alcohol use and its influence on PTSD and the suicidal ideation equation. Joiner and Rudd (1995) found that the effects of depression with six other psychological problems work together to increase the severity of suicidal ideation. There is evidence that supports that depression and anxiety increase the probability of suicidal ideation (Rudd et al., 1993). Moreover, depression and alcohol abuse also increase suicidal ideation (Bongar, 1991), and many individuals diagnosed with PTSD have co-morbidity assessments (Green et al., 1989).

One researcher found that 67% of the police officers sample admitted drinking on duty. Furthermore, the study indicated that that several instances of intoxicated off-duty police officers injuring other with firearms (Van Raalte, 1979). Lester (1995) reported a positive association between increased alcohol use and higher levels of suicide. In addition, alcohol abuse can lead to reduced inhibitions, and other excessive risk taking.

Allen (1986) noted that the identification with risk-taking behaviors can lead to psychological confusion for police officers. Positive risk taking can lead to police professional growth and development. Negative risk taking may lead to the failure to perceive the consequences for the officer's actions. Then, negative risk taking may begin the cycle of depression and suicidal ideation.

Negative risk taking is dangerous; it leads to an additional need for excitement that may become compulsive or addictive. In addition, behaviors, which find professional esteem and assessed as desirable, may serve as early warning signs of self-destruction (Allen, 1986). These high-risk negative behaviors are dangerous to the officer and to those officers who may attempt rescue. Police officers who constantly pursue danger and the limelight are worth tracking for potentially suicidal ideation.

Proactive leadership requires identifying those officers who are at risk for alcohol abuse, domestic problems, and excessive risk taking. These officers require special assistance referrals to employee assistance programs, counselors, and other mental health officials. Implementing a health promotion program that includes fitness and stress reduction techniques offers positive coping mechanisms.

These alcohol abuse and domestic violence risk factors set in motion some of the preconditions for police suicide. Police rules and regulations should provide automatic referrals to selected services and support systems. Alcohol and drug abuse testing for those who are on duty should be mandatory. The discipline process should follow immediately for those officers in violation of department rules for drinking on duty.

Positive Strategy 4 – Police Suicide: Stress Factors

Police work is stressful because mistakes can turn fatal for officers and citizens. The police constantly face violence, death, and cruelty. This psychological hazardous exposure may contribute to elevated suicide rates among police officers (McCafferty et al., 1992). This hypothesis has merit and it is worth pursuing; additional research may reveal useful information for this position.

Police officers who experience critical incident trauma are at elevated risk of adverse mental health outcomes including: (1) adjustment disorder, (2) acute distress disorder, and (3) PTSD. Reactions to traumatic incidents can impair police performance and have adverse consequences for police organizations; latent consequences for families are under-recognized and infrequently addressed. Hidden impairment reveals itself when tragedy emerges and the psychological impact of trauma requires immediate proactive police leadership and counseling support.

There may be relationship between PTSD and depression. Depression is frequently present in cases of PTSD as part of a syndrome or as a condition that might be part of the traumatic event. This is especially the case when depression was present in the life history. Further research concerning the link between PTSD and depression may provide some answers.

Measuring the impact of the officer stress over time remains an essential and difficult task. The long-term consequences of police stress and its relationship to depression invite future investigation and research. Delayed PTSD occurs at least six months after the traumatic event, or even years later after repressing an extremely traumatic event. The individual officer may unlock these memories after an unrelated stressor or major event that reactivates the officer's extreme feeling of helplessness. Refer to Table 11-1 for an analysis of the relevant types of PTSD.

The preliminary means of assessment for PTSD is psychological testing. The Davidson Trauma Scale (DTS) is a 17- item self-report instrument used to measure the presence, frequency, and severity of PTSD symptoms. The Traumatic Stress Schedule (TSS) is a brief instrument for measuring the occurrence of traumatic events. Lay interviewers can administer the TSS. In addition, there are numerous clinician-administered and self-report instruments available to meet specialized needs for assessing PTSD.

One area worthy of additional attention is the depression and suicide association with PTSD. Research indicates that depression is commonly associated with PTSD; approximately 48% also had current or past depression. Those individuals who experience PTSD at some point in their lives are almost seven times as likely as individuals without PTSD to experience depression. One study identified that 44.5 % of people with PTSD, within one month after experiencing a traumatic event, received a diagnosis of depression. Refer to Table 11-1, for an explanation of the PTSD and depression disorder comorbidity (Breslau, 2002; Breslau e. al., 1997; Jakupcak et al., 2006; Kessler et al., 1995; and Shalev et al., 1998). Refer to Table 11-2 for an analysis of PTSD and its relationship to depression.

O'Donnell et al. (2004) conducted research on a group of 360 injury survivors for PTSD and depression. Their research measured the relationship between PTSD and depression. Depression frequently follows traumatic events. This presents the question of whether PTSD and depression are separate disorders in the aftermath of trauma or part of a single general traumatic stress construct. The objective of their research was to ascertain if they are separate disorders or concurrently appear with PTSD. Their findings supported the existence of depression as a separate construct in the acute, but not the chronic, aftermath of trauma.

Fear and the resulting distress from critical incident exposure activate brain systems. The stimulation includes the amygdale and hypothalamic-pituitary-adrenal axis. This combination of brain activities has a role in triggering and regulating physiological activation (Yehuda, 2002). The activation of these processes, if prolonged or particularly intense, appears to contribute to psychophysiology and cognitive behavioral abnormalities associated with PTSD (Pole, 2007).

Table 11-1. Types of PTSD
(Adapted from DSM-IV – TR, 2000)

Posttraumatic Stress Disorder:
*Common type of anxiety disorder
*May develop as a result of many different types of stressors

Delayed Posttraumatic Stress Disorder:
*Symptoms occur six months or later subsequent to traumatic event
*Major life events or stress may trigger delayed PTSD that stems from feelings of helplessness that were initially experienced during traumatic event

Complex Posttraumatic Stress Disorder:
*Disorders of extreme stress not otherwise specified (DESNOS)
*Exposure to chronic traumas that last for months to years at a time, such as repeated physical or sexual abuse
*May experience extreme anger, persistent sadness, suicidal thoughts, and other strong emotions
*May feel helpless, ashamed, and guilty
*May become convinced they are completely different from others

Circumscribed Posttraumatic Stress Disorder:
*Single incident trauma rather than chronic problems with trauma
*Trauma event could range from one-time incident of bullying that is extremely distressing to a severe experience, such as a kidnapping or a physical or sexual assault
*Different from complex posttraumatic stress disorder, which stems from chronic abuse

Table 11-2. The PTSD and Depression Connection
(Adapted from Breslau, et al., 2002)

People with Depression
More likely to have traumatic experiences than people without depression
May increase likelihood that PTSD develops
Possibility there is some kind of genetic factor that underlies development of both PTSD and depression

Distressing PTSD Symptoms
May cause depression to develop
May feel detached
May feel disconnected from friends & family
Little pleasure in activities once enjoyed
Difficulty experiencing positive emotions

Experiencing PTSD Symptoms
Experiencing PTSD symptoms may make someone feel:
Very sad
Lonely
Depressed

Effective police leadership communicates the following message: PTSD is not the fault of individual officers. Most importantly, it is not a matter of courage or weakness. The stress reaction and related psychophysiology are normal responses to abnormal crisis field situations. Proactive leadership requires that it is necessary to get some assistance and the police agency will support police officers.

Police senior leaders have command responsibilities that ensure the training of middle managers, supervisors, and peer leaders. The training emphasizes that PTSD is a normal event, and officers do not need to suffer alone. The training manager coordinates PTSD training and organizes peer support teams. Police agencies who have policy statements dealing with officers exposed to critical incidents have fewer instances of long-term PTSD and less severe symptoms (Mullins, 2001).

Stress factors vary according to the size of the department and urban policing requirements. Controlling variables and interpreting data for police stress factors is problematic. In the interim, proactive leadership attempts to reduce unnecessary administrative stress exposure and prevention programming seems prudent. Stress-protective training may have some crossover value for suicide prevention, but scientific data have not verified it at this point.

Positive Strategy 5 – Suicide by Cop: Crisis Intervention

Suicide by cop (SbC) is fraught with definition and data collection problems. The criteria used to define the SbC critical incident remain problematic. Keram and Farrell (2001) suggested that the frequency of SbC is significant enough to influence a potentially demoralizing influence in a law enforcement agency. The trauma related consequences make the case for senior leader and middle manager crisis management coordination.

Violanti and Drylie (2008) defined "copicide" as an incident involving the use of deadly force by a law enforcement agent(s) in response to the provocation of a threat/use of deadly force against the agent(s) or others by an actor who voluntarily entered into the suicide drama and has communicated verbally or nonverbally the desire to commit suicide. SbC or copicide encompasses many other descriptive terminologies that have similar meanings; however, it is important not to confuse these terms with *police suicide.*

One study indicated that approximately 10% of police shootings might involve SbC incidents (Wilson et al., 1998). Some researchers include a broader estimate of 9-28% of officer SbC shootings (Keram and Farrell, 2001). According to Parent (2001), law enforcement officers kill approximately 400 citizens each year. Of this deadly use of force population, at least 10% percent as a general estimate are SbC cases. Hutson et al. (1998) estimated higher frequencies of SbC shooting incidents at a range of 25 to 28% of all fatal police shootings.

The statistics cited above indicate that SbC is a threat possibility for the mental health of officers and police agencies. The negative resiliency factor of SbC can undermine the police officer and the organization's ability to recover morale. Therefore, proactive police leadership and planning requirements dictate an appropriate response. There is a tendency to overlook secondary victims and minimize the officer's distress and grieving process.

Disenfranchised grief is distress experienced by an officer over a traumatic SbC shooting when he or she does feel it is not permissible to grieve. Negative resilience can result from disenfranchised grief; this often the result of an organizational climate where emotional expression is stifled. This might develop in military units or police organizations where emotions such as fear, horror, helplessness, and distress find thwarted expression. Disenfranchised distress has a negative effect on the person grieving and the police organization. The denial, numbing, or disassociation that results can produce a negative rather than a positive resilience factor (Doka, 1989; Friedman, 1996).

Therefore, SbC crisis management programming serves the law enforcement agency well, and adding this to the suicide prevention program makes sense because of the possible PTSD and devastating psychological outcomes. The prevention and intervention process requires similar police suicide responses, and the SbC officer can receive the same proper agency assistance. SbC incidents are life-altering events that require direct agency assistance for the involved officer. The initial phase of assistance involves coaching and mentoring, the second phase requires counseling intervention, and the third requirement is follow-up.

Positive Strategy 6 – Leadership: Crisis Intervention

The general symptoms and signs of stress are behavioral, psychological, and physical. Some symptoms may be evident to police supervisors; many are not easy to detect. Recognizing stress indicators is an important first step in identifying the causation. Then, leaders are in the best position to help their officers.

Indicators of stress such as body symptoms (backache, fatigue, chest pain) indicate potential psychological problems. Some police emotional factors include panic, irritability, and panic. The officer may have motor symptoms that include muscular tightness, tics, and immobilization, and may experience cognitive states of mind including feelings of dread, worry, and fear of death.

Limiting high profile and dangerous assignments are essential to saving officers from their propensity to seek excitement and adventure. Police leaders rotate officers from high-risk assignments frequently. Police officers must understand that they cannot ride the emotional roller coaster forever.

High-risk assignments like undercover work, SWAT, and vice intelligence units necessitate innovative leadership and organizational support. The recruitment, selection process, training, and monitoring indicates interactive management and supervision requirements. The susceptibility factors of stress risk of these officers should receive leadership and research analysis as to content, type, and frequency of exposures. Then, risk and exposure decrease by the application of adaptive, proactive coping strategies that enhance the perceived control over the exposure (Anshel, 2000).

Changing shifts, rotating shifts over several months, or a permanent shift reduces stress on the body. Training in nutrition, health care, and providing exercise programs can help reduce the negative effects of stress. Providing the opportunities to vent emotions in debriefings and active listening may release negative emotions.

First-line supervisors, police sergeants, and corporals are in the best position to apply leadership interventions. They are very close to officers and are in the best position to intervene and prevent police suicide. Peer leaders are even closer to the officer who is experiencing emotional difficulties. Their training and proactive responses can make a difference.

Police officers are adept at masking the signs and symptoms of stress. They have considerable skill at disguising stress and fear because police officers must demonstrate courage. Handling hot police calls requires suppression of emotions and being in control of themselves and the situation. This kind of emotional suppression and response may invite long-term consequences.

Positive Strategy 7 – Counseling: Crisis Intervention

Suicide prediction for law enforcement officers at risk is a difficult task for police leaders and counselors. Leaders examine the risk factors and must take action; second-guessing is not an option. The complex variables between trauma and suicide ideation and attempted or completed suicide continue to make prediction difficult (Bongar, 1991). The preemptive decision is superior to inaction.

Proactive police leaders must apply the elements of scientific analysis to police suicide issues. This requires cooperation from law enforcement, counselors, and personnel officers to develop timely policies and programs. Privacy and confidentiality rights are always the concern, but common areas of cooperation are necessary in this important endeavor. There are research limitations in the area of counseling intervention programs assessment.

Certified stress management programs that include peer support allow the officer in need to engage the counseling referral. Police officers are more likely to seek peer assistance and advice from peers. A trained peer support officer is the ideal person to direct the emotional traffic of the officer in crisis. The peer support officer has police credibility and serves as a pivotal point for referral to mental health specialist. The peer support program assists officers who are the most reluctant to seek professional assistance.

The Peer Support Program (PSP) should serve as an integral part of the Critical Incident Stress Management Program (CISM). Central to the CISM programming elements are (1) pre-incident education, (2) critical incident stress debriefings, (3) family debriefings, and (4) peer training. Peer counselors are one way to remove the threat of coming forward and open the informal social network.

Positive Strategy 8 – Police Suicide: Abuse and Bullying

A few bullying leaders can create huge police personnel problems for good leaders. Psychological problems can escalate when effective senior leaders fail to take appropriate action and remedy grievances. Police officers experiencing alienation engage the workplace in many ways—i.e., excessive sick leave, citizen bullying, and abuse of family members. Failure to take action on bullying and abuse creates a feeling of injustice, which may create an impetus to social retaliation. Unfortunately, police workplace violence and suicidal ideation can rapidly appear.

A policy on abuse and bullying should encourage a positive attitude and mandate a compassionate approach to leadership that respects the human rights and dignity of police officers. A firm policy that defines abuse and bullying is necessary, and leaders not tolerating these behaviors remain the starting point. Policy enforcement must be fair and equitable, and must protect the accuser with the grievance from further bullying.

The first step is identifying the bullying problem. The second step is recognizing and defining abusive and bullying behaviors. The third step is to identify a distinct pattern of the narcissistic leader's personality. The fourth step is developing a constructive solution to the problem.

Police executives can identify these abusive and bullying behaviors. The remedy should come sooner, rather than later, before extreme damage to the climate occurs. Leaders may need to identify a series of related behaviors such as (1) micromanagement, (2) controlling behaviors, (3) unrealistic expectations, and (4) blaming others for their mistakes.

Micromanagement excess involves checking on the physical location of the officer(s) unexpectedly, and even asking others to report after conducting surveillance. The bullying/narcissist leader accuses the subordinate of inefficiency, ineffectiveness, and even personal disloyalty. The bully constantly monitors officer activities and primarily supervises through e-mail rather than personal contact. The officers may feel like they are constantly under investigation and documentation.

The abusive leader must over-control the subordinate. The methods vary however, and the penalties are severe and disproportionate for violating what the leader defines as absolute conformity. The attitude is one of supremacy and dominance. Sometimes condescending or patronizing behaviors disguise passive-aggressive behaviors.

The narcissist leader spends considerable time casting doubt and engages in character assassination. The ongoing campaign of propaganda includes a consistent and persistent attack on the victim's sanity, character, and credibility. The objective is to create doubt in the minds of peers, friends, and anyone who might be willing to control the abused officer(s).

The narcissist leader has high expectations for others and continuously attacks and belittles the officer(s). These narcissist/bullying leaders repeatedly berate and criticize, undermining self-esteem. These verbal attacks create a sense of inadequacy when the abused officer(s) fails to live up to unrealistic expectations and the "excuse for abuse" is now established.

The bullying and abusive behaviors occur when the officer fails to serve all of the narcissist leader's needs and perfection on every minuscule detail. The narcissist leader will use guilt statements like "You are letting me down," to justify the punishment. Penalties in the form of emotional abuse or disciplinary procedures follow the failure to meet unrealistic expectations.

The narcissist leader blames the officer(s) for failures in field operations, personal relationships, and failed missions. He has difficulty enjoying life because everyone else is ruining it for him, exclaiming, "I can't help being angry." This excuse will often justify or cover-up their frequent temper tantrums. This narcissist/bullying leader is very capable of playing the martyr or victim when necessary to gain the sympathy of members of the chain of command who they report to regularly.

The narcissist leader feels the need to curry power, influence from above to abuse, and bully subordinates. This type of personality establishes a network of power relationships to garner influence that advances career aspirations. This poor excuse for a leader uses the close association with management to frighten others into submission.

Tracking abuse and bullying in police agencies is an important leadership requirement. The hostile work environment is a future sign of violence, which may emerge from the officer as suicide or homicide. Just one abusive and bullying leader can create havoc in the entire police organization. The narcissist leader creates a high stress climate, which leads to a high rate of distrust.

Narcissist leaders are not promoting high standards and rigorous management practices that benefit the agency. This kind of leader uses the excuse for abuse as the need for strong discipline. Their sanctimonious, self-serving rhetoric makes sense to superiors. They are excellent politicians who are difficult to detect and identify. This form of defective leadership can harm the mental health of police officers and civilians. Such defective leadership seeks to exploit certain personalities and use their weaknesses to achieve intimidation and conformity.

A policy on abuse and bullying should encourage a positive attitude and mandate. The mandate is compassionate and respects the human rights and dignity of police officers. A firm policy that defines abusive and bullying behaviors is necessary. The policy should be fair and equitable to protect the officer from further abuse and bullying.

The first proactive leadership progression of prevention and intervention is to train police leaders and officers how to recognize the red flag behaviors of abuse and bullying. The second progression involves an independent and autonomous assessment survey, which addresses the social climate. The third progression plan is assessment evaluation for gathering and analyzing the data annually. The fourth progression should lead to leadership remedial actions and solutions then assess the effectiveness of the solutions.

Positive Strategy 9 – Leadership and Prevention Programming

A police officer's career journey takes many twists and turns along the way. Some officers move rapidly through the ranks, spending little time on the streets. Fast track individuals make sergeant in the first five years, serving administrative careers. Promotions quickly restrict officers to serving office time. Street officers are in the field and experience a considerable amount of stressors. The accumulated trauma exposure of these two types of officers remains difficult to assess. This difficulty makes it impossible to rate which officers are more resilient.

Police career stressors add up over the years, especially with high profile and dangerous assignments. Leadership responsibilities generally preclude traumatic and critical events. However, the vast majority of street officers experience a considerable amount of trauma, critical incidents, and multiple stressors. Some officers have very high rates of trauma exposure, while others serve in low to medium stress environments.

Proactive leadership monitors officer trauma exposure. The importance of a career perspective becomes an issue that spans an officer's lifetime of exposure. The Life-Course Theory cites three significant dimensions in a police career that influence traumatic exposure. The three critical elements of trauma exposure are *frequency*, *seriousness*, and *length of exposure* (Turkewitz and Darlynne, 1993).

Life-Course Theory offers central themes concerning aging and development processes that unfold throughout a lifetime. The life-course model applies to a police career and beyond the multiple dimensions and duration of a "person's existence." History and social conditions that affect personal outcomes influence an officer's human development. Social trajectories in different realms of life are interconnected. Most important, these social paths have reciprocal effects on one another (Elder, 1985; Riley, 1986; Paton, 2009).

The effort to take full advantage of human potential requires sensitivity and timely intervention. The human developmental needs and capabilities of a particular stage in the life span are extremely relevant. The social, psychological, and biological needs of an individual change from the beginning to the end of life. These needs may intersect, connect, and change one's life and social trajectories (Elder, 1985; Riley, 1986; Paton, 2009).

Programming requires flexibility to meet a wide range of social and psychological requirements. New York City has considerable experience and expertise in handling their employee assistance programs (EAPs). The NYPD programs meet the needs of a large police agency, acknowledging that mid-size and smaller police agencies dominate in the United States. These agencies might adapt some of these programs; in most cases, a regional approach would be cost-effective. Life-Course Theory applications add another dimension to EAPs. Refer to Figure 11-2 for an outline of the NYPD programs adapted from Michael O'Neill (2001), Department of Justice publication.

NYPD applies a number of strategies to deal with police suicide and prevent future tragedies. This police organization continues to strive for new approaches to remedy police problems. Reducing the stigma attached to seeking help is paramount and accomplished through continuing education and training. NYPD has stringent confidentiality requirements for those seeking help from the employee assistance program. The exception to confidentiality is for those members of the department who commit criminal acts or pose a potential threat of physical injury to others (O'Neill, 2001).

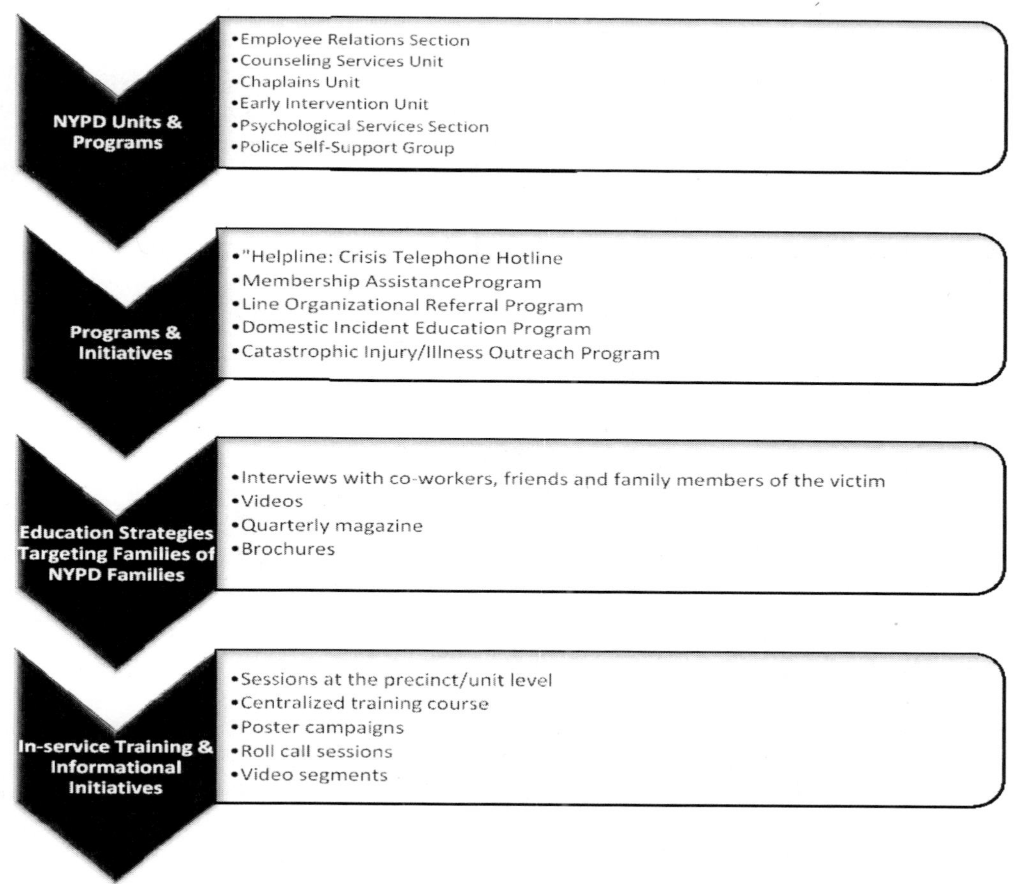

Figure 11-2. NYPD Overview of Employee Assistance Unit/Programs

(Adapted from O'Neill, 2001)

Positive Strategy 10 – Strategic Internal Research

Several strategic focal points for suicide crisis management need to be addressed for maximum effectiveness: (1) the starting point remains training senior leaders, middle managers, and supervisors, then police recruits and their wives, (2) develop a peer support program on suicide prevention and intervention, (3) develop an employee wellness program, and (4) develop an employee assistance program, and encourage continuing education programs. These efforts will not prevent every police suicide; however, just reducing the losses is a worthy, compassionate goal.

Strategic internal research identifies department strengths and weaknesses, and addresses mental health issues. Strategic planning examines capabilities, officer support systems, and external counseling services. In addition, external researchers and consultants help find further practical solutions. Strategic goals encourage scanning for weaknesses in the police organization and developing training programs to address those limitations.

The basic qualities of strategic planning include: (1) global considerations, (2) systemic police mental health issues, and (3) liaison planning with mental health counselor and resources. Strategic planning includes large scope mental health issues that affect police officers. Multiple long-term targets are expansive and set the stage for assessment such as: (1) critical incident analysis, (2) symptoms of depression, (3) PTSD, and (4) police organizational stressors. Examining risk factors may save lives and provide an improved social climate.

Evaluation and assessment are necessary to direct the programming process and reorient the planning process. It answers three crucial questions:

1. *Has the police agency arrived?*
2. *Where is the police agency now?*
3. *Where does the police agency go next?*

Evaluation and assessment provides the map for developing strategic goals and objectives; furthermore, it provides the plans for directing officers to specific tasks.

If police leaders plan their vision and journey well, evaluation will be part of the process. Evaluation research is essential to the measurement of suicide prevention programming, effects, goals, and objectives that support the accomplishment of the welfare of police officers. Excellent theoretical research may change of many of the applied police suicide remedial actions. Some police organizations are initiating innovative programming. The feedback from new police suicide prevention programs need thorough applied research and evaluation procedures.

Violanti (2003) cited several logical points concerning prevention. There is a lack of sufficient knowledge concerning why police suicide occurs. This research information gap concerns the lives and personal experiences of those officers who choose suicide as a solution. The challenges of intervention and prevention are many; opportunities to provide support do exist.

Perhaps additional research on personality, selection, and psychometric testing would provide some insight into the type of recruit that would have emotional survival ability in law enforcement employment. One of the most important areas of research is personality and its relationship to suicidal ideation and the consequential fatalities. The universal application of psychological testing may reveal some of the answers.

Psychological assessment should not end at the MMPI; additional testing offers more opportunities to predict police suicide. Developing a cross-configuration with other test scales adds to the likelihood of screening in desirable police applicants. Other psychometric assessments for suicide include Personality Assessment Inventory (PAI), the Adult Suicidal Ideation Questionnaire (ASIQ), and the Firestone Assessment of Self-destructive Thoughts (FAST). Targeting specific diagnostic suicide assessment during the police selection and intervention stage may best assist in recognizing the potential risk.

Identifying potential police candidates who are prone to suicide is a key prevention strategy. Even though some applicants have other excellent attributes, they may be a risk to themselves and others. Improved psychological testing and vigilance is a worthy prevention effort. Continuing research concerning psychological screening may serve applicants, police culture, and the community well.

Psychological research offers opportunities to examine personality and the related behaviors that might identify those predisposed psychologically to commit suicide. Pre-employment profiles may assist in identifying self-destructive and threatening behavior to others. Merely administering the tests is not enough; the expertise of a qualified examiner is essential.

Since great majorities of individuals communicate their intent prior to acting on their impulses, Morey (1996) considered that our ability to detect suicidal thinking using test instruments increases our ability to assess and intervene in higher risk cases. Thus, Morey (1996) created a suicide ideation scale based on the PAI that provides a gauge of how serious an individual may be in thinking about suicide.

Scores on this scale (SUI) ranging from 85T to 99T indicate that an individual is having intense and recurrent thoughts about suicide. This type of suicidal individual might receive help from suicide precaution or supervision. In addition to the individual suicide ideation scale, Morey (1996) developed a configuration of other test scales to add additional weight to our predictive power.

These additional scores consist of 20 features that researchers found load on completed suicides Some of these factors include severe psychic anxiety, severe anhedonia (an inability to feel pleasure), diminished concentration, insomnia, acute alcohol use, and poor impulse control.

The ASIQ identifies the principle that the more serious forms of suicidal thought, including greater specificity of methods and plans, portend outcomes that are more serious. This instrument has 25 items and a 7-point rating scale with critical items such as "I thought about what to write in a suicide note."

The ASIQ instrument differentiates between levels of risk involving constructs of ideation, intent, attempt, and completion. The cutoff score of 31 was demonstrated to have a moderately high level of specificity of 84%. (The specificity of an instrument is the measure of its ability to detect positive or accurate hits with a measure.)

A multi-measure scale of self-destructive tendencies is the FAST developed by Firestone (1997). This self-reporting instrument has 84 items with 11 levels of progressively self-destructive thoughts cited from Kraft (2001). Refer to Figure 11-3 for an example of the FAST 11 levels of progressively self-destructive thoughts.

The Suicide Probability Scale (SPS; Cull and Gill, 1989) can offer valuable information on the clinical signs and symptoms associated with suicidal risk. The SPS is a 36-item self-reporting measure that assesses four primary factors including hopelessness, suicidal ideation, hostility, and negative self-evaluation. Scores on this instrument provide information on an individual's level of risk from subclinical through mild to severe.

Validity research data show the correct classification percentages for suicide attempters were 98.2, 83.0, and 29.2% in the high, intermediate, and low presumptive risk base rates, respectively. Alpha reliability ranges in the 0.90s. The FAST categories of Hopelessness (Level 7) and Giving Up (Level 8) had the highest correlation with the SPS Suicide Ideation subscale where r = 0.77 and r = 0.82, respectively.

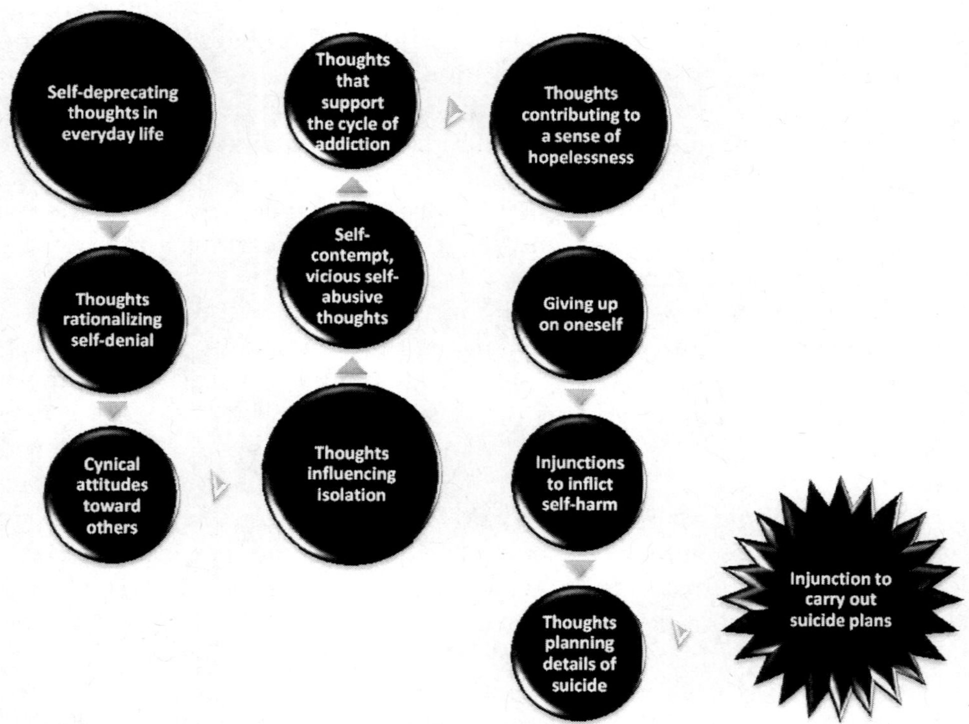

Figure 11-3. FAST 11 Levels of Progressively Self-Destructive Thoughts
(Adapted from Firestone and Firestone, 1997)

Suicide testing serves as an early warning index system for intervention and follow-up counseling, but officers can refuse to take the tests. Another problem is subterfuge when replying to the questions. Officers sincerely seeking help offer opportunities for this form of psychological testing. Suicide testing may lead to additional research, prevention, and intervention programming.

Case Study Illustration

A police sergeant departed his home and said good-bye to his wife and three daughters. His 20-minute drive and destination, the police department ... he never arrived. The sergeant was a supervisor in the major crimes division, and he failed to appear for his tour of duty. His supervisor and fellow investigators started a search for him when he failed to check in for the morning shift.

That morning, two citizens walking along a path in a forest preserve discovered his body. The location was not far from his home, a place where he jogged on a regular basis. They discovered his body lying against a tree, next to him was his 9-mm duty weapon. The sergeant fired one shot to his head; he died instantly. Inside his shirt pocket was a short note. The sergeant stated that he was depressed and unable to handle the stress any longer. That was the only clue the sergeant left ...or was it?

The whole police department was completely devastated. How could this be? After the initial shock, officers gathered in their offices searching for answers. The remarks and questions concerned how stress and depression caused this tragedy. The sergeant was one of the most decorated officers in the department. What had gone wrong in this well-respected homicide investigator's life to cause such hopelessness?

Police officers were replaying in their minds the last few weeks of the sergeant's life. There were no foreseeable events that indicated his intent to commit suicide. The most troubling question loomed in their minds: With our experience in suicide investigations, how did we miss the clues? The police officers were asking a variety of questions, but the suicide was a complete shock to everyone.

Psychologists divide the clues into four categories: (1) direct verbal, (2) indirect verbal, (3) behavioral, and (4) situational. There were no available clues from any of the categories that might have led anyone to believe that the sergeant might kill himself. Family members reported nothing out of the ordinary; his behaviors were not atypical.

Police officers remembered some incidents that appeared insignificant at the time. The sergeant tried to locate a substitute instructor for his police academy class. He cleaned his office comprehensively, and shredded some papers. He visited his parents the night before the suicide. His behaviors appeared normal at the time, but the facts now seem relevant that the sergeant's suicide involved extensive planning.

Special Note: How did the police department react to the sergeant's suicide? Apparently, the initial reaction created emotional strain and concern. One police officer became depressed after attending the wake, and said the sergeant had "the right idea." The department's rapid intervention prevented another suicide tragedy. There is always the possibility of multiple suicides after the first one.

The department's social workers worked many hours meeting with employees informally, providing an important outlet to vent their feelings. The police chaplain engaged officers in the counseling process, meeting with many employees individually. The Northern Illinois Stress Debriefing Team held separate debriefings for supervisory and non-supervisory personnel. The team members distributed worksheets on coping with stress and provided support on what police officers might feel and react in the future.

Counselors made the point that stressful reactions might not appear immediately, but could emerge in the following months. It will take a considerable amount of time to recover from the trauma of this suicide. This case study demonstrates that suicide intervention after the event is important. Secondary victims, including family members and fellow officers, need support. Others may need life-saving support; it may prevent them from following the original suicide scenario.

Source: This case study was adapted from Robert W. Marshall (2001), Department of Justice publication.

Conclusion

Goldfarb (2001) provided a formula based on the variable of Durkheim's Theory for suicide. Durkheim's (1951) concept of anomie advocated that a breakdown in the cultural/societal rules that bring order to one's life increases the rate of suicide. He noted that the effect of social pressures had more of an impact on suicide statistics than emotional disorders such as psychosis and depression. Goldfarb suggested the following formula as an index of suicide:

Suicide = [Anomie *Altered State] [Desperation+ Depression]
Desperation = Time Pressure * Perceived Pain
Spirituality + 1

Goldfarb (2001) recommended utilizing this formula and check list when assessing or treating suicidal officers because it encourages the clinician to keep focused on the whole person. Moreover, it drives the treatment toward the client's difficulties. The formula clearly drives the issues that are causing the problems that can be organized, prioritized, and centered on the correct treatment plan.

Control over all possible variables remains improbable. Generally, one incident will not catapult an officer to commit suicide; the terminal act requires a combination of internal and external issues. Several variables interact to facilitate the final decision, and the officer cannot find a solution. However, the deadly blueprint emerges as:

Suicidal Threats + Depression + Rage + Suicidal Fantasies +
Domestic Violence + Accessibility to a Weapon +
Alcohol/Drug Abuse = Potential Suicide.

In the case of a suicide, the follow-up support to the family and survivors means everything to everyone concerned. The grieving process remains the most important issue; police leaders can make a real difference in the recovery process.

Chapter 12

Epilogue: Future Implications

"It is not enough to wish to become the master, it is not even enough to work hard at achieving such mastery. Correct knowledge as to the best means of achieving mastery is also essential."

— Aldous Huxley

Officer Jakes arrived on the scene; heard shots fired, but could not return fire because a fellow officer was in his crossfire. He felt helpless and angry: "Why did he put me in this position?"

Officer Jakes said the subject had a "determined look" on his face and thinks he wanted to die. Shortly after the suicide by cop (SbC), Officer Jakes found himself being more irritable than usual with his wife and family.

The officer felt detached, desensitized, hypercritical, and analyzed everything. His family responded in both a supportive yet concerned manner. They realized policing is "not a game" and can be deadly serious.

This critical incident is the third one Officer Jakes has been involved in; however, it is the first SbC. Reflecting on the situation, he recounts several changes in his life. He reports cherishing time with his family and being more protective of them. Insignificant events seem even smaller to him now and he better prioritizes his life.

While he hated to see the situation occur, he realized "the world is screwed up." He becomes irritated when he thinks of any impending lawsuits born from this situation.

Although the officer's anger has dissipated over time, he still reports "waiting for the next one," exhibiting some signs of hyper-vigilance. Even with additional training, Officer Jakes feels more vulnerable on the street. He summarized the incident by stating, "The guy put us in a position to kill him; he is the problem."

Source: This case study was adapted from Nick Marzella (2001), Department of Justice publication.

Special Note: Each officer involved in the same SbC scenario reacted somewhat differently, given his or her involvement. Several officers arrive as a SbC incident scenario is unfolding. The secondary trauma is a possibility even for the officers who did not shoot. The reactions are unpredictable. One officer at this shooting scenario experienced traumatic symptoms and PTSD. Another officer experienced a less severe reaction to the incident. Why did this officer appear more resilient to critical incident stress when compared to others at the scene? The issue of positive resiliency is of primary importance. Research on resilience and hardiness is an important contribution to policing, fire, and emergency rescue service workers.

Chapter Focus

This final chapter emphasizes future research for developing innovative research training and programming that will assist in preventing PTSD and police suicide. The main goal of the chapter is to look forward into the future and examine where to go next.

Overview

Human resources management is a core leadership responsibility. Police leaders develop the vision for meeting future staffing requirements. Thus, strategic recruitment planning policy is an essential step to selecting the best officers. The most important influence on the quality of police officers is the testing and selection process.

The recruitment of psychologically qualified officers helps ensure excellent police service to the community. The proper selection of officers is the most important proactive precautionary measure to preventing police suicide. Proactive police leadership provides guidance, coaching, and mentoring. Police leaders who apply the Life-Course Theory perspective optimize careers of their officers and minimize the effects of trauma (Elder, 1985; Paton et al., 2003, 2009).

We must continue the research journey and stop the tragedy of police suicide. Everyone must understand the basic steps in suicide prevention, and provide the teamwork to bring forth successful outcomes. Several research areas offer future implications: (1) police leadership and organizational change, (2) simulation training, and, (3) resiliency research.

Leadership: Future Organizational Change

Police agency leadership has a profound impact on officer resilience and ability to cope with trauma. Effective leadership strives to mitigate the adverse affects of trauma and deter the consequences of long-term exposure to trauma and related hazards. The management and organizational milieu can offer a proactive risk management approach, vulnerability assessment, and resilience training.

Paton et al. (2009) cited several important police organizational changes: (1) the need for a paradigm shift in the conceptualization and management of critical incident stress risk, (2) the need to move beyond the relationship between the officer and event in a single point in time, and (3) to adopt a broader career-length approach. This is difficult to achieve because the counseling focus is on the officer and the critical event. However, the career approach compliments the officer's resiliency and recovery process.

Paton et al. (2009) acknowledged that many career transitions offer predicable pathways that respond to negotiation, appropriate programming, and support. However, sudden traumatic events that occur without warning or past experiences create unpredictable consequences that influence officers and their organization. Risk management requires proactive management that responds to the immediate and long-term impact of organizational and environmental changes.

Planning is essential to managing critical incident stressors effectively. This means that police leaders act proactively with some vision toward the future. The planning process considers career transitions. Risk management planning assumes that some career transitions are in response to changes in the policing environment and can affect the future risk of their officers.

The adaptation of police organizations to critical incidents is an important precursor to organizational resilience. Many of the experiences and transitions police officers encounter are predictable. Police leadership that anticipates the career stage consequences develops policy rules and procedures that enhance the pathway. However, some transitions remain unpredictable, including the impact of catastrophic crisis events.

The "Life Stage Principle" advocates that the way personal experiences and social events affect individual officers influences them by where they are in their career and the time span when events occur. The authors suggest that observers often collapse the officer and critical incident into one single event that begins and ends with clear deliberate moments in time. Critical risk management is an evolving process that accommodates officer integration into the organizational structure and immersion in the police culture (Elder, 1985; Paton et al., 2003, 2009).

This Life Stage Principle considers the impact of both prior experiences and experiences learned from the job that influence an officer's interpretation of the fluid and sometimes unpredictable environment. The ideal broader career-length perspective offers acknowledgment of the residual effects of decades of challenging encounters that affect the lives of police officers as they maneuver through their life/career transitions. Stressful events recur throughout the officer's career; measuring those exposures remains the challenge. Moreover, the trauma may affect the officer's retirement and eventually lead to suicide (Elder, 1985; Paton et al., 2003, 2009).

Simulation Training: Future Implications

Proactive police leadership and training reduces trauma, stress, and police suicide before it occurs. Police training must offer practical solutions for adjusting expectations of police candidates who enter the field. When the training addresses the field realities, rather than unnecessarily high expectations, the stress levels may be manageable, and this may influence suicide rates.

Violanti (2007) recommended that training programs for self-appraisal skills are necessary for optimal suicide awareness programs. This excellent researcher recommended training in healthier self-care, rather than focusing on the surveillance of others. Interpersonal training should start at the recruit level. Training would focus on field challenges, personal skills, and individual talents. Preparing recruits for trauma by building the necessary resiliency skills that lead to well-adjusted career patterns should be the priority.

The academy program should emphasize content information that prepares officers for dealing with stressful issues in the real world. Antonovsky (1987) and Maddi (2006) offered the following solutions for police academy training: (1) developing a meaningful purpose in life, (2) encouraging a belief in one's ability to influence the outcome, (3) encouraging a belief that one can learn and develop as a result of experiences, and most importantly, (4) the willingness to accept uncontrollable outcomes. These life skills are difficult to address in police academy classrooms.

Police training offers the opportunity to desensitize police recruits to traumatic field experiences. The police academy that provides realistic training and approximates operational requirements serves recruits well. Training simulations impose meaning and coherence for future operational experience that allows real-world applications (Paton, 1994). Training that approximates critical incidents and simulation-based training exposes officers to challenging situations to practice skill levels.

Simulations encourage the integration of theory and field applications. They provide a broad range of opportunities to apply the officers' knowledge to realistic scenarios. Lessons learned from the critique and reactions of others participating allow the trainee to apply the knowledge from a critical incident perspective (Paton and Jackson, 2002). The application of critical thinking skills offers the opportunity to transfer expertise to different field scenarios.

Learning simulations allow officers to develop, review, and rehearse operational skills. The secondary benefit is to anticipate and rehearse stress management skills. The high-pressure training scenarios in a safe, controlled, and supportive environment encourage positive feedback. Simulations instill the understanding and teach variable reactions under replicated standards and conditions (Paton and Flin, 1999). Training goals and related training objectives according to active learning criteria find venues for application and assessment.

Resilience Assessments: Future Implications

Critical incidents have the capacity to triumph over officer resilience. Officers experience emotional trauma during and in the aftermath of critical incidents from which PTSD and depression can emerge. Several lesser stress reactions are also possible, depending upon the individual officer and the scenario. Some officers are less susceptible to higher exposures to experiences in the field.

One interesting area of research is the "resilience to stress factor"; not everyone has the same vulnerability. Resilience to stress refers to those individuals who do not develop PTSD and depression after experiencing traumatic events. The understanding of resilience-related factors may lead to a better selection process when hiring police recruits and intervention and prevention measures.

Screening in police recruits that possess resilience is an important goal; however, it remains a difficult task. Finding officers who are psychologically fit for serving in police organizations and remain calm in a crisis remains an essential personnel recruiting mission. The ability to interact with diverse kinds of people successfully and manage the daily stressors requires a well-adjusted person. Finding the right person for the role of police officer might assist in offsetting the negative results of serving in a high stress social milieu.

Personality characteristics and a calm disposition would encourage personal adjustment to the police environment. For example, personality characteristics such as extraversion, hardiness, and self-efficacy contribute to the officer's resilience. These personality characteristics influence positive job performance in high stress work environments. These personalities also experience less adverse affects while responding to critical events (Linley and Joseph, 2004; Paton, 2005).

Costa and McCrae (1989) defined five broad personality characteristics as a useful taxonomy for classifying personality. The Five-Factor Model classifies and describes: (1) Extraversion, (2) Neuroticism (or emotional stability), (3) Conscientious, (4) Agreeableness, and (5) Openness to Experience (or culture). Research on this model generally confirms that personality characteristics, factors, and dimensions appear stable and persist during adulthood (Soldz and Vaillant, 1999). Refer to Table 12-1 for additional explanation of the Five-Factor Model.

Related to the concept of positive resilience is the term *hardiness*, which stems from existential philosophy. Hardiness refers to an authentic ideal personality type, a person who lives the ideal identity. This personality type lives a vigorous and proactive life with a strong sense of meaning and purpose, and believes in its own ability to influence things (Maddi, 2001). This kind of personality would make the ideal proactive leader who could foster the resiliency of officers and the police organization.

Yehuda et al. (2006) found that exposure to trauma does not necessarily lead to impairment and result in the development of psychopathology. The most important psychological factors to resilience related factors were positive affectivity, optimism, cognitive flexibility, coping, social support, emotional regulation, and mastery. These factors emphasize that the majority of people exposed to traumatic events do not develop lasting PTSD related trauma. In addition, human against human abuse like violence, torture, bullying, etc., seems to produce the highest incidents of traumatic reactions.

Police officers vary in their responses to critical incidents. The prevalence for PTSD and the related depression has a limited debilitating range of approximately 7 to 20%. Officers who experience same/similar events react differently; however, a small proportion does experience pathological outcomes. Furthermore, 80-93% involved in the same event did not react pathologically; they may even exhibit a capacity to adapt and experience beneficial outcomes from the same experience (Carlier et al., 1997, 2000; Hodgins et al., 2001).

In addition, some officers may actually experience post-traumatic growth, and not only recover, but even benefit from the traumatic experience. If the traumatic event or a series of events is severe enough, reactions may produce a significant reconsideration of previously held assumptions. Calhoun and Tedeschi (1998) defined post-traumatic growth as significant beneficial change in cognitive and emotional life beyond previous levels of adaptations, psychological functioning, or life awareness that occurs in the aftermath of psychological traumas that challenge previously-existing assumptions about self, others, and the future.

The trauma survivor successfully finds a way to manage the initial debilitating factors of the trauma and related distress. Moreover, disengagement from previous goals and assumptions must occur and the distress must persist for some time. The traumatized officer may be able to construct new ways to create narratives that emerge into positive life schema changes. People or officers who are extraverted are more likely to engage in this process and report post-traumatic growth (Calhoun and Tedeschi, 1998).

Table 12-1. The Five-Factor Model: Personality Dimensions

(Adapted from Costa & McCrae, 1989)

The Five Factor Model	Personality Characteristics
Extraversion *Introverts, on the other hand, describe themselves as withdrawn, calm, discreet, and rather cautious.	• Sociable • Talkative • Open toward other people • Tend to be adventurous and out-going • Able to respond effectively to atypical events and to provide support for others • Attributes that would be important for aspiring police officers
Neuroticism (or emotional stability)	• Nervous and sad • Hostile • Insecure • Self-conscious • Worried about health • Unrealistic ideas • May be unable to control their impulses • Adapt poorly to stressful situations (which increases vulnerability to adverse stress outcomes) • Attributes would reduce the capacity of someone to discharge the duties of a police officer
Conscientiousness	• Habitually reliable • Careful and hard-working • Well-organized & purposeful • Would help the person fit with the administrative and organizational facets of their role
Agreeableness	• Opposite pole of antagonism • Friendly • Understanding • Caring & empathic • Altruistic • Good-natured • Interpersonal trust • Willingness to cooperate • Compliance
Openness to Experience (or culture)	• Appreciation for new experiences • Preference for variety and change • Curious & creative • Imaginative • Predisposed to making independent judgments

Past traumatic exposures could influence the future resiliency of these police officers. There is contradictory research concerning the prior service traumatic evidence. Huddleston (2006) determined that 85% of 315 police recruits surveyed experienced at least one traumatic event. Additionally, 54% of the police experienced two traumatic events, and 26% experienced three or more traumatic events. Buchanan et al. (2001) indicated that 70% of police officers in that study experienced traumatic events prior to police service.

Identifying High-Resiliency Officers

The need for national requirements for police officer psychological testing is apparent. This basic standard represents a necessity for protecting communities, but also the mental health of future police applicants. Policing demands a great deal of psychological resiliency. Mandated psychological testing increases the department's statistical odds of finding model officers and preventing police suicide. Hiring a police officer is a considerable financial and psychological investment; therefore, it makes sense to protect that investment.

The traits of introversion and extroversion in the police population continue to receive considerable attention. For example, Hewitt and Flett (1991) discovered that officers exhibited greater levels of self-confidence in their abilities, and those who held themselves in high regard were generally more satisfied in the profession. In addition, those holding a more positive outlook on life were more hopeful about the future and were happier individuals (Scheier et al., 1986). Individuals with an internal locus of control, as compared to an external locus, would perform better on tasks requiring initiative and autonomy, as they tend to look to themselves for direction (Spector, 1982). This internal locus of control is an important psychological component for police officers to possess, and it is often associated as a characteristic of conscientiousness (Costa and McCrae, 2003).

The officer's perception of stress is another important component of positive resiliency and psychological survival. An individual's perception of job stressors influences his or her locus of control directly, and these stress perceptions then influence job satisfaction. The officer's internal locus of control represents a desirable characteristic because of its value as a mechanism for coping with stress in the field. Extraversion is associated with positive and active coping, whereas neuroticism expresses itself as a negative, avoidant strategy (Kaczmarek and Packer, 1997).

Those officers exhibiting extraversion seem capable of seeking social support (e.g., Anshel, 2000), which strongly connects with job satisfaction (Crank et al., 1993). Related to extraversion, officers who are more optimistic also have higher levels of self-esteem and self-confidence and experience less strain in stressful situations (Kobasa, 1979; Lefcourt, 1992). Officers with an internal locus of control and who have extraversion personality traits may have a greater ability to survive in high stress and critical incident environments.

In opposition to extraversion, characteristics such as neuroticism increase the probability of officers using ineffective coping strategies that lead to increased levels of distress (Shakespeare-Finch, 2006). Thompson and Solomon (1991) also reported a consistent relationship between neuroticism and psychological distress. These researchers found that extraversion serves as a protective effect on police officers who had been involved in body recovery duties.

Future assessment and testing should consider developing methods to identify officers with the qualities of resiliency to stressors. This population would be at a lower risk for PTSD disorders, depression, and suicide. The other related area of research that is important is identifying those characteristics that are significantly to predisposing police applicants to early childhood abuse, high stress and depression related family backgrounds. The police recruits' prior experience with trauma may affect their resilience in future exposure to critical or traumatic incidents.

This case study is an example of running on the excitement and internal chemistry that is addictive. The drive for career perfection and subculture requirements to the exclusion of self and family is a dangerous pursuit. High-risk assignments like undercover work require the officer to assume another identity. The adjustment to a new vice or drug culture requires new and specific demands. The officer is having an identity crisis, trapped between two cultures and trying to balance a family life. The following case study is an example of the ability to "rebound back" from traumatic stress and demonstrates resiliency after considerable trauma.

Case Study Illustration

Lieutenant Brown spoke to the police academy class about his Vice, Intelligence, and Organized Crime Unit. The lecture became intriguing as he spoke about undercover narcotics assignments. One officer's interest was piqued when he mentioned being out there alone, without a badge, and most of the time without back up. The lone-ranger assignment really struck a deep cord inside Officer Jones, and he wanted this assignment.

It was the great escape from routine patrols and groupie end of shift "choir practices." This was an opportunity to demonstrate bravery and build a police legend." Jones had the reputation as an officer for handling hot calls at another police agency. It was time to prove his bravery and value in his new department.

The lieutenant mentioned it was difficult to find the right person for undercover assignments. He was looking for officers to fill a limited number of positions; Jones was the only volunteer for the undercover assignment. After a brief explanation about his qualifications, the lieutenant had a certain glint in his eye. Jones knew in that moment that the undercover assignment would take place right after his police academy graduation.

The graduation ceremony would commence without Jones. His wife was very upset about the new assignment. He was in a dangerous sort of heaven, but his family was going to be in emotional hell. Leaving his gold badge in the dresser, Jones kissed his wife good-by and hit the streets, wide-eyed and innocent. Jones was now facing danger, but loving every minute of the excitement. Along the way, he lost his innocence; his personality would change.

As he played the role, changing his identity and appearance, it led to a continuous struggle to keep his real identity. The cases came his way, buying controlled dangerous substances, and running on his own internal drugs of adrenaline and testosterone.

Ironically, the most difficult part was not being able to talk to anyone about the stress. Jones met one sergeant in the field to pick up the field notes and reports.

One night, the big marijuana buy would take place, 20 kilos, and the possible location of a farm site. He met the dealer through an informant; his partner was to take to an unknown location. They met at a local pool hall, and drove around in paranoid circles; he was trying to make sure he was not under surveillance.

The surveillance team included several cars and helicopter backup. Officer Jones was concealing electronic surveillance equipment, which failed to operate properly. The surveillance team lost Jones after approximately 30 minutes.

Officer Jones was on his own, as he pulled into a hotel complex. He meets several suspects in a hotel room, they agree on the price, and the deal is going to take place outside. One of the group's members returns with a duffle bag full of marijuana. Officer Jones is supposed to face arrest with the group member, but the team is not in place.

He remembers his orders from the Lieutenant Brown about not letting that much money leave his control. Officer Jones identifies himself and places the suspect under arrest and calls headquarters. He arranges for the arrest of the others in the hotel room and drives the suspect to police headquarters. The police department was on total alert search for the lost officer and his green Mustang.

His wife was on total alert waiting to find out if her husband was coming home alive. The next week, Officer Jones departed for an undercover narcotics buy. His wife asked, "Where are you going?" Officer Jones mentioned the location and departed after a telephone call from his sergeant. Our team members were waiting to leave on the hill as or lieutenant approached.

The lieutenant from the Crimes against Persons Unit arrived with a robbery suspect. He turned one of the suspects over to a uniformed officer. The lieutenant then returned to locate the second suspect locked in the trunk. As he pulled the rear seat off to access the trunk, the suspect shot him. The lieutenant stood up and fell over dead. The shift was changing, everyone close to incident fired into the car trunk, killing the suspect.

Lieutenant Brown turned to the narcotics team, and said, we cannot help here we have another mission. The team departed for their assignment reluctantly, the heroin buy was set to go in minutes.

This time Jones was part of a backup team for a narcotics buy to take place near an apartment complex. His sergeant and the DEA agent would make the "buy and bust" and the team would support on a prearranged signal. Suddenly gunshots flashed in the night, something was wrong, it was not part of the plan. The backup team swarmed the area, hoping that the sergeant and DEA agent survived the shooting.

The bodyguard for the drug dealer pulled a weapon in the middle of the drug deal. The sergeant shot the bodyguard in a split second. The rescue squad arrived and transported the body. The paper work and collecting and preserving the evidence took several hours. The media coverage was intense; the team was unaware of the coverage.

Officer Jones arrived home near dawn to find his wife wide-eyed in front of the television set with the radio on at the same time. She was thrilled to see him alive and well because the police officer's name was withheld pending family notification. Then with anger, she said, "You should have called me."

Threats on the officer's life, suicide, and murdered informants found dumped in the Potomac River; the undercover assignment was taking its toll on his wife. The final breaking point was the death of a state trooper wife in a car bombing meant for him.

The triggering event was when she hid behind the brick pillar in the underground parking lot clutching her baby girl. "You start the car," she said. Jones started the car and left the engine running. Sliding into the front seat of his Mustang, she looks into his eyes, "You have the right to risk your life, but not our lives."

Officer Jones realized that not addressing his family needs would eventually lead to an emotional collapse. Temptations are many; alcohol, promiscuous sex, and family stress top the list. The rotation of undercover officers out of these units should take place frequently; officers should not serve longer than two years.

After two years of working narcotics, prostitution, and gambling, it was time to bail out and find family again. It was time to break the addiction of living on the edge. Officer Jones was hooked on his own form of internal chemistry; it took three years to break the dependency from that undercover assignment.

There is a price tag for living on the edge, not every officer survives. Approximately one year later, his replacement died in a police encounter with a drug dealer, ironically, in the same hotel that Jones made his drug purchase. The surveillance team lost Officer Jackson in a similar scenario. His wife and children paid the ultimate price of police service.

Special Note: The police subculture is seductive and attractive to those who want to serve. The main danger is losing yourself and your identity in the process. The cycle of change from idealism to cynicism can be a rapid transition. Living in any subculture has consequences that are intended and unintended. The police lifestyle is full of risks and trauma; it takes an inner-directed person to survive.

The resiliency factor is an important consideration. This officer survived five years of high-risk assignments, threats on his life, and near death experiences. Officer Jones eventually made the transition to another career as a teacher and writer. Any police officer can misplace his or her life and lose their sense of identity during the police journey. The resiliency factor is an important factor in surviving the policing experience.

Focus Points

Police leaders who address entry level mental health requirements improve the quality of the police subculture. Their disruptive behaviors can detract from police missions and increase considerable stress in police organizations.

Police officers who disengage early in their careers present financial burdens to police organizations. The emotionally walking wounded are not productive police officers. These officers avoid the conflict and stress and displace emotional burdens to other officers.

Emotionally damaged officers may be vulnerable to stressful incidents and incur future mental health problems. There are many financial issues and related emotional costs if officers with unresolved issues remain in law enforcement agencies.

The quest must persist for initiating viable training programs and solutions. The police-training academy, including idealistic values that are part of the curriculum, may have latent negative and unintended consequences. Academy program development might better serve officers if curriculum emphasizes content that prepares officers for dealing with stressful issues and enhances self-awareness skills, which serve as an internal monitoring system. Street encounters and pragmatic solutions may contradict those police academy values.

Recruiting officers with resilience and hardiness remains an essential component of any critical incident, stress risk management strategy. The organization's responsiveness to changing and often challenging environments nurtures and helps maintain officer resilience.

Police officers experience positive and negative emotional outcomes while encountering challenging field events. Positive and negative post-trauma emotional experiences vary extensively over the course of a career.

Moreover, family, police culture, and community support have significant and independent influences on trauma outcomes. This officer started to realize that there were issues that are more important than career and professional reputation. The little things now mattered, and family was first in a new set of priorities.

Controlling the variables and comparing individuals is difficult because of the *frequency*, *intensity*, *duration,* and individual *resiliency*. Police officers may experience different stress outcomes in response to individual resilience and vulnerability variables.

Conclusion

In the future, police agencies need to provide the cultural and organizational leadership that provides the optimal structure conducive to positive resiliency. The combination of proactive leadership, selection of police personnel, and reducing the level of organizational distress offers the best hope for successful career transitions. The commitment to investigate, monitor, respond, and evaluate change, no matter what the tempo, is a win-win situation for the department, officers, and their communities. In other words, the concept of officer and department resilience is reciprocal. One entity depends on, as well as nourishes, the other.

References

Aamodt, M., Brewester, J. A. & Raynes, B. (1998, September). Is the police personality predisposed to domestic violence? Paper presented at the Domestic Violence by Police Officers Symposium, FBI Academy, Quantico, Virginia.

Aamodt, M. G. & Stalnaker, N. A. (2001). Police officer suicide: Frequency and officer profiles. In D. C., Sheehan, D. C., & Warren, J. I. (Eds.) Suicide and Law Enforcement (pp. 383-398). Department of Justice, Federal Bureau of Investigation. Washington, DC: U.S. Government Printing Office.

Adorno, T. (1950). The Authoritarian Personality. New York, NY: Harper Publishing.

Allen, S. W. (1986). Suicide and indirect self-destructive behavior among police. In J. T. Reese & H.A. Goldstein (Eds.), Psychological services for law enforcement (pp. 413-417). Washington, DC: U.S. Government Printing Office.

Allen, S. W. (2004). Dynamics in responding to department personnel. In V. B. Lord (Ed.) Suicide by Cop: Inducing officers to shoot. Practical Directions for Recognition, Resolution, and Recovery (pp. 246-255). Flushing New York, NY: Looseleaf Law Publications, Inc.

Amaranto, E., Steinberg, J., Castellano, C., & Mitchell, R. (2003). Police stress interventions. Brief Treatment and Crisis Intervention 3(1): 47-53.

American Association of Suicidology. (2001), Fact sheet: *Suicide and Depression:* www. Suicidology.org.

American Psychiatric Association. (2000). Diagnostic and statistical manual of mental disorders, (DSM IV-TR 4th ed., Text Revision). Washington, DC: American Psychiatric Press.

Amsel, L. V., Placidi, G. P. A., Hendin, H., O'Neil, M., & Mann, J. J. (2001). An evidenced-based educational intervention to improve evaluation and preventive services for officers at risk for suicidal behaviors. In D. C. Sheehan, & J. I. Warren, (Eds.) Suicide and Law Enforcement (pp. 17-30). Department of Justice, Federal Bureau of Investigation. Washington, DC: U.S. Government Printing Office.

Anshel, M. H. (2000). A conceptual model and implications for coping with stressful events in police work. *Criminal Justice Behavior*, 27(3): 375-400.

Antonovsky, A. (1987).Unraveling the mystery of health (pp.1-14). Josey-Bass Publishers: San Francisco.

Arnetz, B. B., Nevedal, D. C., Lumley, M. A., Backman, L., & Lubin, A. (2009). Trauma resilience training for the police: Psycho-physiological and performance effects. *Journal of Police and Criminal Psychology* 24(1): 1-9.

Aussant, G. (1984). Police suicide: Royal Canadian Mounted Police Gazette, 46(5), 14-21.

Baker, T. E. and Baker, J. (1995). Research problems: Police suicide. *The Chief of Police* 10, (3), 35-41.

Baker T., & Baker, J.P. (1996, October). Preventing police suicide. *FBI Law Enforcement Bulletin,* 65(10), 24-27.

Baker, T.E. (2005a). Introductory criminal analysis: Crime prevention and intervention strategies. New Jersey: Pearson/Prentice-Hall, 4.

Baker, T.E. (2005b). Effective police leadership: Moving beyond management. New York: Looseleaf Law Publications, 86.

Baker, T. Published Reviewer: Hackett, D. P. & Violanti, J. M. (2008). Police suicide: Tactics for prevention. Springfield, Illinois: Charles C. Thomas, Publishers, LTD. *The Journal of Police and Criminal Psychology,* 2009.

Baker, T. E. (2009). Intelligence–led policing: Leadership, strategies and tactics. New York, NY: Looseleaf Law Publications, 127-129.

Bartol, C.R. (1996). Police psychology: Then, now and beyond. *Criminal Justice and Behavior*, 23, 70-89.

Beck, A. T. (1976). Cognitive therapy: And the emotional disorders. New York: NY: Meridian, Penguin Group.

Berent, L. (1981). The algebra of suicide. New York: Human Sciences Press.

Berent, D. A., Perper, J. A., Kolko, D. J., & Zelenak, J. P. (1988). The psychological autopsy: Methodological considerations for the study of adolescent suicide. *Journal of the American Academy of Child and Adolescent Psychiatry,* 27, 326-366.

Bergen, G. T., Deutch, A., & Best, S. (2001). Police suicide: Why are the rates in some places so low. In D.C. Sheehan, D. C., & J. I. Warren (Eds.) Suicide and Law Enforcement (pp. 407-416). Department of Justice, Federal Bureau of Investigation. Washington, DC: U.S. Government Printing Office.

Beskow, J., Runeson, B., & Asgard, U. (1990). Psychological autopsies: Methods and ethics. Suicide and Life-Threatening Behavior, 20, 307-323

Blatt, S. J. (1999). Researcher links perfectionism in high achievers with depression and suicide. *American Psychologist,* 49(12), 1003-1020.

Blatt, S. J., Quinlan, D. M., Pilkonis, P. A., & Shea, M. T. (1995). Impact of perfectionism and need for approval in the brief treatment of depression: National Institute of Mental Health Treatment of Depression Collaborative Research Program revisited. *Journal of Consulting and Clinical Psychology,* 63, 125-132.

Blatt, S. J., Zuroff, D. C., Sanislow, C. A., & Pilkonis, P. A. (1998). When and how perfectionism impedes the brief treatment of depression: Further analysis of the National Institute of Mental Health Treatment of Depression Collaborative Research Program. *Journal of Consulting Research and Clinical Psychology,* 66, 423-428.

Bonafacio, P. (1991).The psychological effects of police work. New York, NY: Plenum Press.

Bongar, L. (1991). The suicidal patient: Clinical and legal standards of care. Washington: DC, American Psychological Association.

Brandl, S.G. & M.S. Stroshine (2003). Toward an understanding of the physical hazards of police work. *Police Quarterly* Vol. 6, (2) 172-191.

Breslau, N. (2002). Epidemiologic studies of trauma, posttraumatic stress disorder, and other psychiatric disorder. *Canadian Journal of Psychiatry*, 47, 923-929.

Breslau, N., Davis, G.C., Peterson, E.L., & Schultz, L. (1997). Psychiatric sequelae of posttraumatic stress disorder in women. *Archives of General Psychiatry*, 54, 81-87.

Brewster, J., & Broadfoot, A. (2001). Lessons learned: A suicide in a small police department. In D.C. Sheehan, & J. I. Warren (Eds.) Suicide and Law Enforcement (pp. 45-56). Department of Justice, Federal Bureau of Investigation. Washington, DC: U.S. Government Printing Office.

Brown, G., & Beck, A. (2005). Cognitive therapy for the prevention of suicide attempts. Journal of the American Medical Association, 294(5): 563-570.

Brown, J.M., & Campbell, E.A. (1994). *Stress and policing: Sources and strategies.* United Kingdom, London: John Wiley.

Brown, G. K., Ten Have, T., Henriques, G. R., Xie, S. X., Hollander, J. E., & Beck, A. T. (2005, August). Cognitive therapy for the prevention of suicide attempts: A randomized controlled trial. *Journal of the American Medical Association*, 294(5): 563-570.

Buchanan, G., Stephens, C.V., & Long, N. (2001). Traumatic experiences of new recruits and serving police officers. *Australasian Journal of Trauma and Disaster Studies.* 2001-2 (on-line serial) URL. http://www.massy.ac.nz/%7Etrauma/-issues/2001-2/buchanan.htm.

Burge, J. H. (1982). Suicide and occupation: A review. *Journal of Vocational Behavior*, 21, 206-222.

Calhoun, L.G., & Tedeschi, R.G. (1998). Posttraumatic growth: Future directions. In R.G. Tedeschi, C.L. Park, C.L., & Calhoun, L.G., (Eds.) Posttraumatic growth: Positive change in the aftermath of crisis (pp. 215-238). Mahwah, NJ: Lawrence Erlbaum.

Campion, M.A. (2001). Police Suicide and small department: A survey. In D.C. Sheehan, & J. I. Warren (Eds.) Suicide and Law Enforcement (pp. 417-430). Department of Justice, Federal Bureau of Investigation. Washington, DC: U.S. Government Printing Office.

Carlier, I. V. E., Lamberts, R. D., & Gersons, B. P. R. (1997). Risk factors for posttraumatic stress disorder in police officers: A perspective analysis. *Journal of Nervous and Mental Disease*, 185, 498-506.

Carlier, I. V. E., Lamberts, R. D., & Gersons, B. P. R. (2000). The dimensionality of trauma: A multidimensional scaling comparison of police officers without posttraumatic stress disorder. *Psychiatric Research,* 97, 29-39.

Carpenter, B. N., & S. M. Raza (1987). "Personality characteristics of police academy applicants: Comparisons across subgroups and with other populations." *Journal of Police Science and Administration*, 15(1): 10-17.

Carter, D. L. (1994). Theoretical dimensions of the abuse of authority by police officers. In T. Barker and Carter, D. L. (Eds.) Police deviance, 3rd Edition, 276-277, Cincinnati, Ohio: Anderson Publishing Company.

Carver, C. S., Scheier, M. F., & Weintraub, J. K. (1989). Assessing coping strategies: A theoretically based approach. *Journal of Personality and Social Psychology*, 56, 267-283.

Clopton, J.R. (1979). The MMPI and suicide. In C.S. Newark (Eds.*), MMPI clinical and research trends* (pp.149-166). New York, NY: Praeger.

Collins, J.C. (2001) Good to great: Why some companies make the leap...and others don't. New York, NY: Harper Collins Publishers.

Cooper, H., & Hedges L.V. (1994). The handbook of research synthesis. New York, NY: Russell Sage.

Cox, T. (1978). Stress. Baltimore, MD: University Park.

Costa, P.T., Jr., & McCrae, R.R. (1989). The NEO-PI/NEO-FFI *manual supplement.* Lutz, FL: Psychological Assessment Resources.

Costa, P.T., Jr., & McCrae, R.R. (2003). NEO-Five Factor Inventory. Lutz, FL: Psychological Assessment Resources.

Crank, J.P., Regoli B., Hewitt, J.D., & Culbertson, R.G. (1993). An assessment of work stress among police executives. *Journal of Criminal Justice*, 21, 313-324.

Crits-Cristoph, P., & Barber, J. P. (1991). Handbook of short-term psychotherapy. New York, NY: Basic Books.

Curran, S.F. (1998). Pre-employment psychological evaluation of police officers. Police Chief, LXV(10), 88-95.

Cull, S. F., & Gill, W. (1989). The Suicide Probability Scale Manual. Los Angeles: Western Psychological Services.

D'Angelo, J. J. (2001). Spirituality and police suicide: A double edge sword. In D.C. Sheehan, & J. I. Warren (Eds.) Suicide and Law Enforcement (pp. 503-510). Department of Justice, Federal Bureau of Investigation. Washington, DC: U.S. Government Printing Office.

Davidson, M., & Veno, A. (1980). Stress and the policeman. In C, L. Cooper & Marshal J. (Eds.), *White collar and professional stress.* United Kingdom, London: John Wiley.

Doka, K. (1989). Disenfranchised grief: Recognizing hidden sorrow. Massachusetts: Lexington Books.

Durkheim, E. (1951). Suicide: A study in sociology. New York, NY: A free Press.

Eggert, L. , Randel, B., Thompson, E. & Johnson L. (1997). Gatekeeper training. In The Washington State Youth Suicide Prevention Program: Report of 1995-1997 (pp. 51-75). Seattle WA: University School of Nursing.

Elder, G.H. (1985). Perspectives on the life course. In G. H. Elder (Eds.), Life course dynamics (pp. 23-49). Ithaca, NY. Cornell University Press.

Ellis, A. (1998). How to control your anxiety: Before it controls you. New York, NY: Citadel Press, Kensington Publishing, Corp.

Evans, G., and Farberow, N. (1988). The history of suicide. New York: Facts on File.

Everly, G. S. & Mitchell, J. T. (2000). "The debriefing controversy and crisis intervention: A review of lexical and substantive issues." *Journal of Emergency Health*, 2(4): 211-225.

Farberow, N. L. (1980). The many faces of suicide. New York, NY: McGraw-Hill.

Federal Bureau of Investigation (2007). Uniform crime reporting: Law enforcement officers killed and assaulted. Available at http://www.fbl.gov/ucr/killed/2007/.

Fein, L .J. (1998). Surveillance, monitoring, and screening in occupational health. In R. B. Wallace (Eds.) Public Health and Preventive Medicine (pp. 669-674). Stamford, California: Appleton and Lang.

Feldner, M. T., Monson, C. M., & Friedman, M. J. (2007). A critical analysis of approaches to targeted PTSD prevention: Current status and theoretically derived future directions. *Behavior Modification* 31(1):80-114.

Figley, C. R. (1995). Compassion fatigue: Toward a new understanding of the costs of caring. In B. H. Stamm (Eds.), Secondary Traumatic Stress: Self-care issues for clinicians, researchers, and educators (pp. 3-27). Lutherville, MD: Sidran Press.

Firestone, G. (1997). Clinical epidemiology of suicide. *Journal of Clinical Psychiatry,* 48(12): 33-38.

Foa, E. B., & Meadows E. A. (1997). Psychosocial treatments for post-traumatic stress disorder: A critical review. *Annual Review of Psychology,* 48: 449-480.

Freeman, A., Pretzer, J., Fleming, B., & Simon, K. M. (1990). Clinical applications of cognitive therapy. New York: Plenum Press.

Friedman, M. (1996). *Emergent self-management for security and emergency personnel in situations of continuous traumatic exposure.* Paper presented at the European Conference: Stress in Emergency Services, Peacekeeping Operations and Humanitarian Aid Organizations, UK.

Friedman, P. (1968). Suicide among police: A study of 93 suicides among New York City policemen, 1934-40. In E.S. Shneidman, (Eds.), Essays in self-destruction (pp.414-419). New York, NY: Science House.

Friedman, G. D. (1994). Primer of epidemiology. New York, NY: McGraw-Hill.

Fullerton, C. S., Ursano, R. J., Vance K., & Wang, L. (2000). Debriefing following trauma." *Psychiatric Quarterly*, 71(3): 259-276.

Gaines, L. K. and Van Tubergen, N. (1989). Job stress in police work: An exploratory analysis into structural causes. *American Journal of Criminal Justice*, 13(3), 197-214.

Galea, S., Ahern, J., Resnick, H., Kilpatrick, D., Bucuvalas, M., Gold, J. (2002). Psychological sequelae of the September 11 terrorist attacks in New York City. *The New England Journal of Medicine*, 346: 982-987.

Calhoun, L. G., & Tedeschi, R. G. (1999). Facilitating posttraumatic growth: A clinician's guide. Mahwah, NJ: Lawrence Erlbaum.

Garcia, L., Nesbary, D. K. & Gu J. (2004). Perceptual variations of stressors among police officers during an era of decreasing crime. *Journal of Contemporary Criminal Justice*, Vol. 20 (1), 33-50.

Geberth, V. J. (1993). Suicide by cop. *Law and Order,* July, 105-108.

Gilmartin, K. M. (1986). Hypervigilance: A learned perceptual set and its consequences on police stress. In J. T. Reese & H. A. Goldstein (Eds.) Psychological Services for Law Enforcement. Washington, DC: U.S. Government Printing Office.

Glasser, W. G. (1975). Reality therapy. New York, NY: Harper & Row Publishers.

Glasser, W. G. (1998). Choice theory: New psychology of personal freedom. New York, NY: HarperCollins Books.

Goldfarb, D. A. (2001). Themes of police suicide: An analysis of forensic data, media coverage, and case studies leading to protocol assessment and treatment. In D. C. Sheehan, & J. I Warren (Eds.) Suicide and Law Enforcement (pp. 211-222). Department of Justice, Federal Bureau of Investigation. Washington, DC: U.S. Government Printing Office.

Goldfarb, D.A., & Aumiller, G.S. (2004). The heavy badge – 10 reasons cops are different. Retrieved October 5, 2005, from http://www.heavybadge. com/ 10reason.htm.

Goleman, D. (2006). Social intelligence: The new Science of human relationships. New York: Bantam Publications.

Gotlieb, I., & Hammen, C. (2002). Handbook of depression. New York: The Guildford Press.

Gould, L. A. (2000). A longitudinal approach to the study of police personality: Race/gender differences. *Journal of Police and Criminal Psychology*, 15(1): 41-51.

Green, B.L., Lindy, J.D., & Grace, M.C. (1989). Multiple diagnoses in posttraumatic stress disorder: The role of war survivors. *Journal of Nervous and Mental Disease*, 177, 329-335.

Grollman, E. A. (1988). Suicide: prevention, intervention, post intervention (Boston, MA: Beacon Press.

Haberfeld, M. M. (2001). From critical incident stress to police suicide: Prevention through mandatory academy and on-the-job training programs. In D. C. Sheehan, & J. I. Warren (Eds.) Suicide and Law Enforcement (pp. 83-96). Department of Justice, Federal Bureau of Investigation. Washington, DC: U.S. Government Printing Office.

Hambrick, Donald C. and Chatterjee, A. (2007) It's all about me: Narcissistic CEOs and their effects on company strategy and performance. *Administrative Science Quarterly* 52, 3, 2007, pp. 351-386.

Harvey, A.G., R. A. Bryant, & Tarrier, N. (2003). Cognitive behavior therapy for post-traumatic stress disorder. *Clinical Psychology Review*, 23(3): 501-522.

Helmkamp J.C. (1996). Occupation and suicide among males in the US Armed Forces. *Annals of Epidemiology*, 6, 83-88.

Hem, E., Berg, A. M., & Ekeberg, O. (2001). Suicide in police—a critical review. *Suicide & Life Threatening Behavior*, 31, 224-233.

Hendin, H. (1995). Suicide in America. New York, NY: W. W. Norton.

Herndon J. S. (2001). Law enforcement suicide: Psychological autopsies and psychometric testing. In D. C. Sheehan, & J. I Warren (Eds.) Suicide and Law Enforcement (pp. 223- 234). Department of Justice, Federal Bureau of Investigation. Washington, DC: U.S. Government Printing Office.

Herbert, S. (1998). Police subculture reconsidered. *Criminology*, 36(2), 343-369.

Hersey, P., Blanchard, K., & Johnson, D. (2008). Management of organizational behavior: Leading human resources (9th Ed.) Upper Saddle River, NJ: Prentice-Hall.

Hewitt, P. L., & Flett, G. L. (1991). Perfectionism in self and social context: Conceptualization, assessment and association with psychopathology. *Journal of Personality and Social Psychology*, 60, 456-470.

Hewitt, P.L., Flett G.L. & Donovan, W.T. (1992). Perfectionism and suicidal potential. *British Journal of Clinical Psychology*, 31, 181-190.

Hewitt, P. L., Flett, G. L., & Weber, C. (1994). Dimensions of perfectionism and suicidal potential. *Cognitive Therapy and Research*, 18, 439-460.

Hill, K. O., & Clawson M. (1988). The health hazards of street level bureaucracy: Mortality among the police. *Journal of Police Science and Administration*, 16(4), 243-248.

Hodgins, G. A. Creamer, M. & Bell, R. (2001). Risk factors for post-trauma reactions in police officers: A longitudinal study [Electronic version]. *Journal of Nervous and Mental Disease*, 189, 541-547.

Hoff, L .& Adamoskwi, K. (1998). Creating excellence in crisis care: A guide to effective training and program designs. San Francisco, CA: Jossey-Bass.

Homant, R. J., Kennedy, D. B., & Hupp, R. T. (2000). Real and perceived danger in police officer-assisted suicide. *Journal of Criminal Justice*, 28, 43-52.

Homant, R. J., Kennedy, D. B. (2001). A typology of suicide by police incidents. In D.C. Sheehan & J. L. Warren (Eds.) Suicide and Law Enforcement (pp. 578-585). Department of Justice, Federal Bureau of Investigation. Washington, DC: U.S. Government Printing Office.

Huddleston, L. M., Paton, D. & Stephens, C. (2006). Conceptualizing traumatic stress in police officers: Pre-employment, critical incident and organizational influences. *Traumatology*, 12, 170-177.

Hutson, H. R., Anglin, D., Yarbrough, J., Hardaway, K., Russell, M., Strote, J., Canter, M., & Blum, B. (1998). Suicide by cop. *Annals of Emergency Medicine*, 32(6), 665-669.

Jacobs, D., Brewer, M., & Klien-Benhiem, M. (1999). Suicide assessment: An overview and recommended protocol. In D. Jacobs (Eds.), The Harvard Medical School guide to suicide assessment and intervention (pp. 3-39). San Francisco, CA: Jossey-Bass.

Jakupcak, M., Roberts, L.J., Matell, C., Mulick, P., Michael, S., Reed, R. (2006). A pilot study of behavioral activation for veterans with posttraumatic stress disorder. *Journal of Traumatic Stress*, 19, 387-391.

Janik, J., & Kravitz, H. M. (1994). Linking work and domestic problems with suicide. *Journal of Suicide and Life Threatening Behavior*, 24, 267-274.

Joiner, T.E., & Rudd, D.M. (1995). Negative attributional style for interpersonal events and the occurrence of severe interpersonal disruptions as predictors of self-reported suicide ideation. *Suicide and Life Threatening Behavior*, 25, 297-304.

Jung, C. G. (1975, 2nd Ed.). Psychology and Religion: West and east. (The collected works of C. G. Jung, Vol. 11, Princeton, New Jersey: Princeton University Press.

Kaçzmarek, A., & Packer, J. (1997). Determination of a job related test battery for the psychological screening of police applicants. Payneham, South Australia: National Police Research Unit.

Kahan, J. (1993). Mental health in the work place. New York, NY: Van Nostrand Reinhold.

Kappeler, V. E. and Potter, G. W. (2005, 4th Ed.). The mythology of crime and criminal justice., Prospect Heights, Illinois: Waveland Press.

Keram, E. A. & Farrell, B. J. (2001). Suicide by cop: Issues, outcomes, and analysis. In D.C. Sheehan & J. L. Warren (Eds.) Suicide and Law Enforcement (pp. 587-597). Department of Justice, Federal Bureau of Investigation. Washington, DC: U.S. Government Printing Office.

Kessler, R.C., Sonnega, A., Bromet, E., Hughes, M., & Nelson, C.B. (1995). Posttraumatic stress disorder in the National Comorbidity Survey. *Archives of General Psychiatry*, 52, 1048-1060.

Klerman, G. (1987). Clinical epidemiology of suicide. Journal of *Clinical Psychiatry*, 48 (12), 33-38.

Kobasa, S.C. (1979). Stressful life events, personality, and health: An inquiry into hardiness. *Journal of Personality and Social Psychology*, 37, 1-11.

Kraft, T. R. (2001). Suicide risk Assessment for police officers. In D.C. Sheehan & J. L. Warren (Eds.) Suicide and Law Enforcement (pp. 243-256). Department of Justice, Federal Bureau of Investigation. Washington, DC: U.S. Government Printing Office.

Krystal, H. & Neiderland, W. G. (1968). Clinical observations on survivor syndrome. In H. Krystal (Eds.) *Massive psychic trauma*. New York, NY: International University Press.

Lasiuk, G. C., & K. M. Hegadoren. (2006, February). "Post –traumatic stress disorder part I: Historical development of the concept." *Perspective in Psychiatric Care,* 42(1).

Laufer, R.S. (1988). The serial self: War trauma, identity and adult development. In J.P. Wilson, Z. Harel, & Kahana, B. (Eds.), *Human adaptation to stress from the holocaust to Vietnam*. New York, NY: Plenum.

LeBuffe, P. (2000). Assistant Director, Institute of Clinical Training and Research, QPR Institute. Devereux Foundation. Villanova, PA.

Lefcourt, H.M. (1992). Perceived control, personal effectiveness and emotional states. In B.M. Carpenter (Eds.), *Personal coping: Theory, research and application* (pp. 111-131). Westport, CT: Praeger.

Lester, D. (1993). A study of police suicide in New York City, 1934-1939. *Psychological Reports*, 73(3), 1395-1398.

Lester, D. (1995). The association between alcohol consumption and suicide and homicide rates: A study of 13 nations. *Alcohol,* 30, 465-468.

Linley, P.A., & Joseph, S. (2004). Positive change following trauma and adversity: A review. *Journal of Traumatic Stress*, 17, 11-21.

Loo, R. (2003). A meta-analysis of police suicide: Findings and issues. *Suicide and Life Threatening Behavior*, 33, 313-25.

Lord, V. B. (2001). Law enforcement assisted-suicide: Characteristics of subjects and law enforcement intervention techniques. In D.C. Sheehan & J. L. Warren (Eds.) Suicide and Law Enforcement (pp. 607-616). Department of Justice, Federal Bureau of Investigation. Washington, DC: U.S. Government Printing Office.

Lorr, M. & Strack, S. (1994). "Personality profiles of police candidates." *Journal of Clinical Psychology*, 50(2): 200-208.

Lotz, R., & Regoli, R.M. (1977). Police cynicism and professionalism. *Human Relations*, 30, 2, 175-186.

Luft, J. (1970, 2nd Ed,). Group processes: An introduction to group dynamics. Palo Alto, CA: National Press Books.

Lynch, J. (2002). Workplace bullying implications for police organizations. Critical Issues in Policing Paper, NCJRS, National Criminal Justice Center, 198269: 1-42, http://www. ncjrs. gov/App/publications/Abstract.

Maddi, S. R. (2001). The story of hardiness: Twenty years of theorizing, research, and practice. *Consulting Psychology Journal*, 54, 175-185.

Malekoff, A. (2001). On making connections and being flexible: A group worker's diary of the first ten days following September 11, 2001. *Social Work with Groups,* 24(3/4): 3-10.

Mallory, T. and Mays, G. (1984). The police stress hypothesis: A critical evaluation. *Criminal Justice and Behavior*, 11(2), 197—224.

Marano, H. E. (1999). Depression: Beyond serotonin. *Psychology Today*, 32, 11-23.

Maris, R. W., Berman, A. L., Maltsberger, J. T., & Yufit, R. I. (1992). *Assessment and prediction of suicide.* New York, NY: Guilford Press.

Marshall, R. W. (2001). Police suicide: We may never know the answer. In J.T. Reese, & E. Scrivner (Eds.) Law Enforcement Families: Issues and answers (pp. 115-123). U.S. Department of Justice, Federal Bureau of Investigation. Washington, DC: U.S. Government Printing Office.

Marzella, J. N. (2001). Psychological effects of suicide by cop involved officers. In J.T. Reese, & E. Scrivner (Eds.) Law Enforcement Families: Issues and answers (pp. 627-636). U.S. Department of Justice, Federal Bureau of Investigation. Washington, DC: U.S. Government Printing Office.

McCafferty, F. L., McCafferty, E., and McCafferty, M. A. (1992, March). Stress and suicide in police officers: The paradigm of occupational stress. *Southern Medical Journal* 85(3), 233-243.

Menniger, K. A. (1938). Man against himself. New York: Harcourt, Brace.

Mitchell, J. T. (1983). When disaster strikes: The critical incident stress debriefing process. *Journal of Emergency Services*, 8, 36-39.

Mitchell, J. T., & Everly, G. S. (1997, 2nd ed.). Critical incident stress debriefing (CISD): An operations manual for the prevention of traumatic stress among emergency service and disaster workers. Ellicott City, Maryland: Chevron.

Mitchell, J. T. (1994). Critical incidents stress interventions with families and significant others. In J.T. Reese, & E. Scrivner (Eds.) Law Enforcement Families: Issues and answers (pp. 195-204). U.S. Department of Justice, Federal Bureau of Investigation. Washington, DC: U.S. Government Printing Office.

Morey, L. C. (1996). An interpretive guide to the Personality Inventory Assessment Inventory (PIA). Odessa, Fl: *Psychological Assessment Resources.*

Monahan, J. (1992). Mental disorder and violent behavior: Perceptions and evidence. *American Psychologist*, 47,511-521.

Monahan, T. F. (2001). Suicide by cop: Strategies for crisis negotiators and first responders. In D.C. Sheehan & J. L. Warren (Eds.) Suicide and Law Enforcement (pp. 637-645). Department of Justice, Federal Bureau of Investigation. Washington, DC: U.S. Government Printing Office.

Mullins, W. C. (2001). The relationship between police officer suicide and posttraumatic stress disorder. In D.C. Sheehan & J. I. Warren (Eds.) Suicide and Law Enforcement (pp. 257-265). Department of Justice, Federal Bureau of Investigation. Washington, DC: U.S. Government Printing Office.

Norvell, N. K., Hills, H. A., & Murrin, M. (1993). Understanding female and male law enforcement officers. *Psychology of Women Quarterly*, 17, 289-301.

Obst, P. I. & Davey, J. D. (2003)."Does the police academy change your life?: A longitudinal study of changes in socializing behavior of police recruits. *International Journal of Policing Science and Mana*gement, 5(1):31-40.

O'Donnell, M. L., Creamer, M., & Pattison, P. (2004, August). Posttraumatic stress disorder and depression following trauma: Understanding comorbidity. *American Journal of Psychiatry*, 161: 1390-1396.

O'Hara, A. F. & Violanti, J. M. (2009). Police Suicide—web surveillance of national data. *International Journal of Emergence Health*, 11(1), 17-24.

O'Hara, A. K. (2008). Badge of life program. Citrus Heights, CA. badgeoflife@yahoo.com.

O'Neill, M. (2001). Police Suicides in New York City Police Department: Causal factors and remedial measures. In D.C. Sheehan & J. I. Warren (Eds.) Suicide and Law Enforcement (pp. 139-149). Department of Justice, Federal Bureau of Investigation. Washington, DC: U.S. Government Printing Office.

Oyster, C. K. (2001). Police reactions to suicide by cop. In D.C. Sheehan & J. I. Warren (Eds.) Suicide and Law Enforcement (pp. 647-652). Department of Justice, Federal Bureau of Investigation. Washington, DC: U.S. Government Printing Office.

Palm, K. M., Polusny, M. A., & Follette, V. M. (2004). "Vicarious Traumatization: Potential hazards and interventions for disaster and trauma workers." *Prehospital and Disaster Medicine*, 19(1): 141-153.

Pam, E. (2001). Police-homicide in relation to domestic violence. In D.C. Sheehan & J. I. Warren (Eds.) Suicide and Law Enforcement (pp. 357-363). Department of Justice, Federal Bureau of Investigation. Washington, DC: U.S. Government Printing Office.

Parent, R. B. (2001), Suicide by cop in North America: Victim-precipitated homicide. In D.C. Sheehan & J. I. Warren (Eds.) Suicide and Law Enforcement (pp. 653-662). Department of Justice, Federal Bureau of Investigation. Washington, DC: U.S. Government Printing Office.

Paton, D., Burke, K. Violanti, J. M., & Gehrke, A. (2009). Traumatic stress in police officers: A career-length assessment from recruitment to retirement. Springfield, Illinois: Charles C. Thomas, Publishers.

Paton, D. (2005). Posttraumatic growth in protective services professionals: Individual, cognitive and organizational influences. *Traumatology*, 11(4), 335-346.

Paton, D., & Flin, R. (1999). Disaster Stress: An emergency management perspective. *Disaster Prevention and Management*, 8, 261-167.

Paton, D. (1994). Disaster Relief Work: An assessment of training effectiveness. *Journal of Traumatic Stress*, 7, 275-288.

Paton, D., Burke, K. Violanti, J. M., & Gehrke, A. (2009). Traumatic stress in police officers: A career-length assessment from recruitment to retirement. Springfield, Illinois: Charles C. Thomas, Publishers.

Paton, D., Violanti, J.M., & Smith, M.A. (2003). Promoting capabilities to manage posttraumatic stress: Perspectives on resilience. Springfield, Illinois: Charles C. Thomas, Publishers.

Peterson, A. L., Baker, M. T., & McCarthy, K. R. (2008, July). Combat stress casualties in Iraq: Part I behavioral health consultations at an expeditionary medical group. *Perspectives in Psychiatric Care*, 44(3): 146-158.

Pinnizotta, A. J., Davis, E. F., & Miller, C. E. (2005). Suicide by Cop: A devastating dilemma. *FBI Law Enforcement Journal*, 74(2), 8-20.

Pogrebin, M. R., & Poole, E. D. (1991). Police and tragic events: The management of emotions. *Journal of Criminal Justice*, 19(3), 395-403.

Pokorny, A. D. (1983). Prediction of suicide in psychiatric patients: Report of a prospective study. *Archives of General Psychiatry*, 40, 249-257.

Pole, N. (2007). The psychophysiology of post-traumatic stress disorder a meta analysis. *Psychological Bulletin* 133: 725-746.

Perrou, B. (2001). Antecedent (pre-death) behaviors as an indicator of imminent violence. In D.C. Sheehan & J. I. Warren (Eds.) Suicide and Law Enforcement (pp. 365-371). Department of Justice, Federal Bureau of Investigation. Washington, DC: U.S. Government Printing Office.

Prial, E. M. (2001). Death at the hands of the police: Suicide or homicide? In D.C. Sheehan & J. I. Warren (Eds.) Suicide and Law Enforcement (pp. 663-676). Department of Justice, Federal Bureau of Investigation. Washington, DC: U.S. Government Printing Office.

Ramos, O. (2008). A leadership perspective for understanding police suicide: An analysis based on suicide attitude questionnaire (pp. 20-27). Boca Raton, FL: Universal-Publishers.

Rangell, L. (1988). The decision to terminate one's life: Psychoanalytical thoughts on suicide. *Suicide and Life Threatening Behavior*, 18(1), 28-46.

Regier, D., & Kaelber, C. (1995). Epidemiology catchment area program. In Tsuang, M., Tohen M., & Zahner, G.E.P. (Eds.), Textbook in Psychiatric Epidemiology. New York, NY: JohnWiley.

Reiser, M. & Geiger, S. P. (1984). Police officers as victims. *Professional Psychology: Research and Practice.* 15(3), 315-323.

Riley, M.W. (1986). Overview and highlights of a sociological perspective. In A.B. Sorenson, F. Weinert & Sherman, L.R. (Eds.), *Human development and the life course.* Hillsdale, NJ: Erlbaum.

Robbins, E., Murphy, G. E., Gassner, S., & Kayes, J. (1959). Some clinical considerations in the prevention of suicide based on a study of 134 successful suicides. *American Journal of Public Health,* 49, 888-889.

Roszell, D.K., McFall, M.E., & Malas, K.L. (1991). Frequency of symptoms and concurrent psychiatric disorder in Vietnam veterans with chronic PTSD. *Hospital and Community Psychiatry*, 42, 293-296.

Rothbaum B. O., Hodges, L., Ready, D. Graap, K., & Alarcon, R. (2001). "Virtual reality therapy exposure for Vietnam veterans with post-traumatic stress disorder." *Journal of Clinical Psychiatric*, 62(8): 617-622.

Rudd, D.M., Dahm, F., & Rajab, M.H. (1993). Diagnostic comorbidity in persons with suicidal ideation and behavior. *American Journal of Psychiatry*, 150, 928-934.

Ryan, A. H., & Brewster, M. E. (1994). Posttraumatic stress disorder and related symptoms in traumatized police officers and their spouse/mates. In J.T. Reese, & E. Scrivner (Eds.) Law enforcement families: Issues and answers (pp. 217-225). Washington, DC: U.S. Printing Office.

Ruzek, J. I. (2002). Dissemination and early intervention practices in the context of mass violence or large-scale disaster. *Behavior Therapist*, 25(2): 32-36.

Rynerson, E., Favell, & Saindon, M. (2002, October). Group interventions for bereavement after violent death. *Psychiatric Services* 53: 1,340.

Scheier, M.F., Weintraub, J.K., & Carver, C.S. (1986). Coping with stress: Divergent strategies of optimists and pessimists. *Journal of Personality and Social Psychology*, 51, 1257-1264.

Schnurr, P.O., Lunney, C. A., & Sengupta, A. (2004). "Risk factors for the development versus the maintenance of post-traumatic stress disorder." *Journal of Traumatic Stress Disorder*, 17: 85-95.

Schwartz J. A., & Schwartz, C. B. (1991). The personal problems of the police officer: A plea for action. Washington, DC: Government Printing Office, 130-141.

Selye, H. (1976). The stress of life (2nd ed.). New York, NY: J. B. Lippincott.

Sewell, J. D. (1983). Law Enforcement critical life events scale. *Journal of Police Science and Administration*, 11, 113-114.

Seltzer, J., Croxton, R., & Bartholomew, A. (2001). Psychiatric autopsy: Its use in police suicide. In D.C. Sheehan & J. I. Warren (Eds.) Suicide and Law Enforcement (pp. 275-284). Department of Justice, Federal Bureau of Investigation. Washington, DC: U.S. Government Printing Office.

Shaffer, M. (1983) Life after stress. Chicago Illinois: Contemporary Books.

Shakespeare-Finch, J. (2006). Individual differences in vulnerability to posttrauma deprivation. In J. Violanti & Paton D. (Eds.), Who gets PTSD? Issues of posttraumatic stress vulnerability (pp. 33-49). Springfield, IL: Charles C. Thomas.

Shalev, A.Y., Freedman, S., Peri, T., Bandes., D., Sahar, T., Orr, S.P., & Pitman, R.K. (1998). Prospective study of posttraumatic stress disorder and depression following trauma. *American Journal of Psychiatry*, 155, 630-637.

Shaw, J.A. (1987). Unmaking the illusion of safety: Psychic trauma in war. *Bulletin of the Menninger Clinic*, 51, 49-63.

Shneidman, E. S. (1968). Orientations toward death. In E. S. Shneidman , N. L. Faberow, & R. E. Litman. *The psychology of suicide*. New York, NY: Science House, P.7.

Shneidman, E. S. (1987). A psychological approach to Suicide. In G. R. Vandenbos & B. K. Bryant (Eds.), Cataclysms, crisis, and catastrophes: Psychology in action. Washington, DC; American Psychological Association, 167.

Shneidman, E. S. (1994). Theory note: Clues to suicide reconsidered. *Suicide and Life Threatening Behavior*, 24, 395-397.

Shneidman, E. S. (1995). Suicide as a psychache: A clinical approach to self-destructive behavior. Northvale, NJ: Jason Aronson.

Shneidman, E. S. (1996). The suicidal mind. New York, NY: Oxford University Press.

Shneidman, E. S. (2004). Autopsy of a suicidal mind. NY: Oxford University Press.

Slovenko, R. (2002). Psychiatry in law. *Law and Psychiatry,* 2, 784.

Soldz, S., & Vaillant, G.E. (1999). The big 5 personality traits and the life course: A 45 year longitudinal study. *Journal of Research in Personality*, 33, 2, 208-232.

Slosar, J. R. (2001). The importance of perfectionism in law enforcement suicides. In D.C. Sheehan, & J. I. Warren (Eds.) *Suicide and Law Enforcement* (pp. 539-547). Department of Justice, Federal Bureau of Investigation. Washington, DC: U.S. Government Printing Office.

Spector, P.E. (1982). Behavior in organizations as a function of employee locus of control. *Psychological Bulletin*, 91, 482-497.

Stamm, B. H. (1997). Work-related Secondary Traumatic Stress. *PTSD Research Quarterly*, 8(2), 1-6.

Stricker, G. & Gold, J R. (1993). Comprehensive handbook of psychotherapy integration. New York, NY: Plenum Press.

Styron, W. (1990). Darkness visible. New York, NY: Random House.

Swank, R.L., & Marchand, W.E. (1946). Combat neuroses: Development of combat exhaustion. *Achieves of Neurology and Psychology*, 55, 236-247.

Tate, T. T. (2001). Police suicide: Assessing the needs of survivors. In D.C. Sheehan, & J. I. Warren (Eds.) Suicide and Law Enforcement (pp. 173-180). Department of Justice, Federal Bureau of Investigation. Washington, DC: U.S. Government Printing Office.

Terry, W. C. (1983). Police stress as an individual and administrative problem: Some conceptual and theoretical difficulties. *Journal of Police Science and Administration*, 11(2), 156-165.

The National P.O.L.I.C.E. Suicide Foundation Inc., August, 1999 from http://www.psf.org/media.htm

Thompson, J., & Solomon, M. (1991). Body recovery teams at disasters: Trauma or challenge? *Anxiety Research*, 4, 235-240.

Thompson, G. J. & Walker, G. A. (2007). The verbal judo way of leadership. New York: Looseleaf Law Publications.

Turkewitz, G., & Darlynne, A.S. (1993). *Developmental time and timing*. Hillsdale, NJ: Erlbaum.

Turvey, B. E. (1995). Police officers: Control, hopelessness and suicide. San Leandro, CA: Knowledge Solutions.

Twenge, J. M., & Campbell, W. K. (2009). Living in the age of entitlement: *The narcissism epidemic*. New York, NY: Free Press.

U.S. Public Health Service. (1999). The Surgeon General's call to action to prevent suicide. Washington, DC: U.S. Government Printing Office.

Van Raalte, R. C. (1979). Alcohol as a problem among police officers. *Police Chief*, 44, 38-40.

Violanti, J. M., Vena, J. E., & Marshall, J. R. (1986). Disease risk and mortality among police officers. *Journal of Police Science and Administration*, 14, 17-23.

Violanti, J. M. & Aron, F. (1994). Ranking of police stressors. *Psychological Reports*, 75(2), 825-826.

Violanti, J. M. (1995, February). The mystery from within: Understanding police suicide. *FBI Law Enforcement Bulletin*, 64(2), 19-23.

Violanti, J. M. & Drylie, J. J. (2008). Copicide: Concepts, cases, and controversies of police suicide by cop. Springfield, Illinois: Charles C. Thomas, Publishers.

Violanti, J. M., Vena, J. E., & Marshall J. R. (1996). Suicides, homicides, and accidental death: A comparative risk assessment of police officers and municipal workers. *American Journal of Industrial Medicine*, 30(1), 99-104.

Violanti, J. M. (2003). Police suicide: Tactics for prevention. Springfield, IL: Charles C. Thomas Publishing.

Violanti, J. M. (2007). Police suicide: Epidemic in blue. Springfield, IL: Charles C. Thomas Publishing.

Vogt, W. P. (1999). Dictionary of statistics and methodology. Thousand Oaks, CA: Sage Publications.

White, E. K., & Honig, A. L. (2001). Death by their own hands: Have we failed to protect the protectors? In D.C. Sheehan, & J. I. Warren (Eds.) Suicide and Law Enforcement (pp. 447-464). Department of Justice, Federal Bureau of Investigation. Washington, DC: U.S. Government Printing Office.

Wilson, E. F., Davis, J. H., Bloom, J. D., Battan, P. J., & Kamara, S. G. (1998, January). Homicide or suicide: The killing of suicidal persons by law enforcement persons. *Journal of Forensic Sciences*, 43, 46-52.

Yehuda, R. (2002). Current status of cortisol findings in post-traumatic stress disorder. *They Psychiatric Clinics of North America* 25(2):341-368.

Yehuda, R., Flory, J. D., Southwick, S., & Charney, D. S. (2006). "Developing an agenda for translational studies of resilience and vulnerability following traumatic exposure." *Annals of the New York Academy of Science*, 1071(1): 379-396.

INDEX

Other Titles of Interest from Looseleaf Law Publications, Inc.

by Thomas E. Baker

Positive Police Leadership
Problem-Solving Planning

Test Preparation & Instructional Strategies
Guide for Positive Police Leadership

Effective Police Leadership – *3rd Edition*
Moving Beyond Management

Test Preparation & Seminar Guide for
Effective Police Leadership

Intelligence-Led Policing
Leadership, Strategies & Tactics

Test Preparation & Instructional Strategies Guide for
Intelligence-Led Policing

Improving Motivation and Morale
A Police Leader's Guide
by Jody Kasper

Processing Under *Pressure*
Stress, Memory and Decision-Making in Law Enforcement
by Matthew J. Sharps

METTLE
Mental Toughness Training for Law Enforcement
by Laurence Miller, Ph.D.

Condition to Win
Dynamic Techniques for Performance-Oriented Mental Conditioning
by Wes Doss

Developing the Survival Attitude
by Phil L. Duran

The Path of the Warrior – *2nd Edition*
An Ethical Guide to Personal & Professional Development in the Field of Criminal Justice
by Larry F. Jetmore